PALGRAVE STUDIES IN THEATRE AND PERFORMANCE HISTORY is a series devoted to the best of theatre/performance scholarship currently available, accessible, and free of jargon. It strives to include a wide range of topics, from the more traditional to those performance forms that in recent years have helped broaden the understanding of what theatre as a category might include (from variety forms as diverse as the circus and burlesque to street buskers, stage magic, and musical theatre, among many others). Although historical, critical, or analytical studies are of special interest, more theoretical projects, if not the dominant thrust of a study, but utilized as important underpinning or as a historiographical or analytical method of exploration, are also of interest. Textual studies of drama or other types of less traditional performance texts are also germane to the series if placed in their cultural, historical, social, or political and economic context. There is no geographical focus for this series and works of excellence of a diverse and international nature, including comparative studies, are sought.

The editor of the series is Don B. Wilmeth (Emeritus, Brown University), PhD, University of Illinois, who brings to the series over a dozen years as editor of a book series on American theatre and drama, in addition to his own extensive experience as an editor of books and journals. He is the author of several award-winning books and has received numerous career achievement awards, including one for sustained excellence in editing from the Association for Theatre in Higher Education.

Also in the series:

Undressed for Success by Brenda Foley
Theatre, Performance, and the Historical Avant-garde by Günter Berghaus
Theatre, Politics, and Markets in Fin-de-Siècle Paris by Sally Charnow
Ghosts of Theatre and Cinema in the Brain by Mark Pizzato
Moscow Theatres for Young People: A Cultural History of Ideological Coercion and Artistic Innovation, 1917–2000 by Manon van de Water
Absence and Memory in Colonial American Theatre by Odai Johnson
Vaudeville Wars: How the Keith-Albee and Orpheum Circuits Controlled the Big-Time and Its Performers by Arthur Frank Wertheim
Performance and Femininity in Eighteenth-Century German Women's Writing by Wendy Arons
Operatic China: Staging Chinese Identity across the Pacific by Daphne P. Lei
Transatlantic Stage Stars in Vaudeville and Variety: Celebrity Turns by Leigh Woods
Interrogating America through Theatre and Performance edited by William W. Demastes and Iris Smith Fischer
Plays in American Periodicals, 1890–1918 by Susan Harris Smith
Representation and Identity from Versailles to the Present: The Performing Subject by Alan Sikes
Directors and the New Musical Drama: British and American Musical Theatre in the 1980s and 90s by Miranda Lundskaer-Nielsen
Beyond the Golden Door: Jewish-American Drama and Jewish-American Experience by Julius Novick
American Puppet Modernism: Essays on the Material World in Performance by John Bell
On the Uses of the Fantastic in Modern Theatre: Cocteau, Oedipus, and the Monster by Irene Eynat-Confino

Staging Stigma: A Critical Examination of the American Freak Show
   by Michael M. Chemers, foreword by Jim Ferris
*Performing Magic on the Western Stage: From the Eighteenth-Century to the
   Present* edited by Francesca Coppa, Larry Hass, and James Peck, foreword
   by Eugene Burger
Memory in Play: From Aeschylus to Sam Shepard by Attilio Favorini
Danjūrō's Girls: Women on the Kabuki Stage by Loren Edelson
Mendel's Theatre: Heredity, Eugenics, and Early Twentieth-Century American Drama
   by Tamsen Wolff
Theatre and Religion on Krishna's Stage: Performing in Vrindavan by David V. Mason
Rogue Performances: Staging the Underclasses in Early American Theatre Culture by
   Peter P. Reed
*Broadway and Corporate Capitalism: The Rise of the Professional-Managerial Class,
   1900–1920* by Michael Schwartz
Lady Macbeth in America: From the Stage to the White House by Gay Smith
Performing Bodies in Pain: Medieval and Post-Modern Martyrs, Mystics, and Artists
   by Marla Carlson
*Early-Twentieth-Century Frontier Dramas on Broadway: Situating the Western
   Experience in Performing Arts* by Richard Wattenberg
Staging the People: Community and Identity in the Federal Theatre Project
   by Elizabeth A. Osborne
Russian Culture and Theatrical Performance in America, 1891–1933
   by Valleri J. Hohman
Baggy Pants Comedy: Burlesque and the Oral Tradition by Andrew Davis
Transposing Broadway: Jews, Assimilation, and the American Musical by Stuart J. Hecht
The Drama of Marriage: Gay Playwrights/Straight Unions from Oscar Wilde to the Present
   by John M. Clum
*Mei Lanfang and the Twentieth-Century International Stage: Chinese Theatre Placed and
   Displaced* by Min Tian
Hijikata Tatsumi and Butoh: Dancing in a Pool of Gray Grits by Bruce Baird
Staging Holocaust Resistance by Gene A. Plunka
Acts of Manhood: The Performance of Masculinity on the American Stage, 1828–1865
   by Karl M. Kippola
Loss and Cultural Remains in Performance: The Ghosts of the Franklin Expedition
   by Heather Davis-Fisch
Uncle Tom's Cabin on the American Stage and Screen by John W. Frick
Theatre, Youth, and Culture: A Critical and Historical Exploration
   by Manon van de Water
Stage Designers in Early Twentieth-Century America: Artists, Activists, Cultural Critics
   by Christin Essin
Audrey Wood and the Playwrights by Milly S. Barranger
Performing Hybridity in Colonial-Modern China by Siyuan Liu
A Sustainable Theatre: Jasper Deeter at Hedgerow by Barry B. Witham
The Group Theatre: Passion, Politics, and Performance in the Depression Era
   by Helen Chinoy and edited by Don B. Wilmeth and Milly S. Barranger
*Cultivating National Identity through Performance: American Pleasure Gardens and
   Entertainment* by Naomi J. Stubbs

Cultivating National Identity through Performance

American Pleasure Gardens and Entertainment

Naomi J. Stubbs

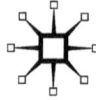

CULTIVATING NATIONAL IDENTITY THROUGH PERFORMANCE
Copyright © Naomi J. Stubbs, 2013.
Softcover reprint of the hardcover 1st edition 2013 978-1-137-32686-7
All rights reserved.

First published in 2013 by
PALGRAVE MACMILLAN®
in the United States—a division of St. Martin's Press LLC,
175 Fifth Avenue, New York, NY 10010.

Where this book is distributed in the UK, Europe and the rest of the world, this is by Palgrave Macmillan, a division of Macmillan Publishers Limited, registered in England, company number 785998, of Houndmills, Basingstoke, Hampshire RG21 6XS.

Palgrave Macmillan is the global academic imprint of the above companies and has companies and representatives throughout the world.

Palgrave® and Macmillan® are registered trademarks in the United States, the United Kingdom, Europe and other countries.

ISBN 978-1-349-46002-1   ISBN 978-1-137-32687-4 (eBook)
DOI 10.1057/9781137326874

Library of Congress Cataloging-in-Publication Data

Stubbs, Naomi J., 1981–
    Cultivating national identity through performance : American pleasure gardens and entertainment / Naomi J. Stubbs.
        pages cm.—(Palgrave studies in theatre and performance history)

    1. Gardens—United States—History. 2. Gardens—United States—Social aspects. 3. Amusements—United States—History. 4. Performance art—United States—History. 5. United States—Social life and customs. I. Title.
SB451.3.S88 2013
635.0973—dc23   2013012386

A catalogue record of the book is available from the British Library.

Design by Newgen Knowledge Works (P) Ltd., Chennai, India.

First edition: September 2013

10 9 8 7 6 5 4 3 2 1

For Grandpa

Contents

List of Images	ix
Acknowledgments	xi
A Note on Sources	xiii
Introduction	1
1. Performing Nation: The Pleasure Garden as a Space for Defining America	21
2. Performing Place: The Rural/Urban Tension	43
3. Performing Class: The Challenge to and Reaffirmation of Class Divisions and Hierarchies	65
4. Performing Race: Native Americans and African Americans Within the Gardens	87
5. Beyond the Pleasure Garden	109
Appendix	131
Notes	135
Selected Bibliography	161
Index	173

Images

Cover: Niblo's Garden. *Gleason's Pictorial* (Boston), 6 March 1852, vol 2, no. 10. Author's collection.

I.1	Vauxhall, Philadelphia. *An Evening in Vauxhall Garden, 1819*	4
I.2	*Gray's Ferry sketch*. Ba 7 G775, Historical Society of Pennsylvania	11
1.1	Vauxhall, London. J. S. Muller after Samuel Wade, *A General Prospect of Vaux Hall Gardens*, engraving, 1751	27
1.2	Vauxhall, New York. *Vauxhall Garden 1803*	27
2.1	Warner & Hanna, *Plan of the City of Baltimore*, 1801	50
2.2	Extract from *Plan of the City of New York, in North America: Surveyed in the Years 1766 and 1767*	52
3.1	*McArans [sic] Garden, 1840*	72
3.2	Vauxhall, Philadelphia. *Vauxhall Garden at Northeast Corner of Broad and Walnut Streets*	72
3.3	Vauxhall, New York. *Vauxhall Garden and Theatre, and Cook's Circus*	73
3.4	Extract from *Map of Boston in the State of Massachusetts: 1814*	74
4.1	"Have you any flesh coloured silk stockings...?" E. W. Clay, *Life in Philadelphia*, 1829	100
4.2	"How do you like de waltz, Mr. Lorenzo?" E. W. Clay, *Life in Philadelphia*, 1829	101
5.1	Steeplechase Park (1897–1906)	122
5.2	Photograph of the "Human Whirlpool" at Steeplechase Park, ca. 1910	122
5.3	Postcard of Columbia Gardens, Butte, Montana	124

Acknowledgments

I stumbled upon American pleasure gardens when reading Mary Henderson's *The City and the Theatre*. In it, she refers to Vauxhall as though it were a landmark within New York yet did not directly address the site. Hailing from England, I immediately tied this name to the British original and was plagued thereafter with a number of questions: What was this site like? Was it a replica of the London site? Was it really a pleasure garden? How popular was it? The more I looked, the more it became clear that there were scores of pleasure gardens in New York—many operating under the name of Vauxhall. As I expanded my search, I learned that there were literally hundreds of these sites across America and they were referenced in poems, plays, novels, and countless newspapers and reference works. However, I could find very little written on the subject of the numerous American pleasure gardens.

In tackling this seemingly never-ending quest to uncover where these sites were found, who went, what they saw, and what function the venues played, I have drawn upon the expertise and support of countless people and institutions. My learning of pleasure gardens came from a reading assigned by Marvin Carlson in a graduate school class, and since that moment, he has been very supportive of my quest and served on my dissertation committee (this book being an offshoot of that same dissertation). Heather S. Nathans provided more references, suggestions, and advice than I knew what to do with! Her boundless energy, support, and enthusiasm for my work spurred me on and gave me a model to aspire to. David Savran reminded me not to overlook the obvious—something I have a tendency to do. The chair of my committee, my mentor, and my role model, Judith Milhous, was always patient, efficient, thorough, honest, and generous in her advice and suggestions, and helped me keep perspective through this sometimes daunting undertaking.

Throughout this process, I have been supported by many of my colleagues at the Graduate Center and by members of the American Theatre and Drama Society. Bethany D. Holmstrom provided much needed encouragement as I agonized over deadlines, research trips, funding issues, and logistics; her friendship and collegiality have made this whole process enjoyable. Peter Zazzali patiently and thoughtfully read early drafts and provided me with helpful and carefully considered feedback and suggestions. I add to this list, Jim Wilson, Mark Cosdon, AnnMarie Saunders, Robert Davis, Amy E. Hughes, Michelle Granshaw, and many others who have listened to and read my work, made suggestions, provided references, and shared advice on how to navigate the process of publication.

Institutional support has been provided by the Martin E. Segal Theatre Center, and the Graduate Center and LaGuardia Community College, CUNY, in addition to numerous archives and libraries. Financial support from the Theatre department of the Graduate Center, CUNY (including chair funds for travel and a Tackel Grant), the Graduate Center (including Sue Zalk Travel Awards, Doctoral Student Research Award, and Gilleece Fellowship), and LaGuardia (an EDIT grant and awards from Academic Affairs) have provided the financial means to complete this project in a timely manner. Archivists and librarians at The Historical Society of New York, the Museum of the City of New York, New York Public Library, the Library Company of Philadelphia, the Historical Society of Pennsylvania (especially Hillary S. Katvia), the Harvard Theatre Collection, South Carolina Historical Society, Library Company (Charleston, SC), Maryland State Archives, Maryland Historical Society, and University of Minnesota (especially Rebecca Moss) have proven to be invaluable. At these primary places of research, I encountered many individuals who helped me search for evidence of these ephemeral sites.

Portions of my work on pleasure gardens have been published in other venues, including the Website, www.americanpleasuregardens.com, *The Pleasure Garden, From Vauxhall to Coney Island* (edited by Jonathan Conlin, Philadelphia: University of Pennsylvania Press, 2012), and the forthcoming *Theatre, Performance, and Analogue Technology* (edited by Kara Reilly, Palgrave, 2013). My thanks to the various editors and publishers for allowing me to reprint these works. My editorial team, especially Robyn Curtis and Kristy Lilas, have provided much needed guidance through the stages of getting this to press.

Lastly, my thanks must go to my family, who supported my decision to leave my home country to live in New York and embark on what they perceive to be a crazy career path. My parents and grandparents, and my sisters, Helen and Rebecca, have shown tremendous understanding—thank you.

A Note on Sources

Sources on pleasure gardens are very limited; many venues were short-lived, and their programs of entertainments have not been systematically preserved or collected. As such, I often construct arguments based on a small number of documents. Throughout this study, I have taken care to read these documents appropriately and to not allow one incident or document to represent the activities of the site for the years on which the archives are silent. However, the limited nature of sources does have several significant implications—particularly the silences and the areas of focus. The records are silent on the design and layout of most gardens, for example, and the (probably African American) laborers who actually planted and maintained the gardens are not recorded. Account books, scripts, and staff records are also absent from archival collections. A more pervasive problem within this study, however, is the fact that there are a greater number of documents available for the pleasure gardens that operated in New York than in any other city. A combination of a large number of newspapers and previous scholarly work in related fields has meant that details of the New York sites are more numerous and easier to locate than the other cities discussed here. One immediate impact of this is that despite the present book attempting to discuss sites in a number of east-coast cities, New York examples often eclipse the others. This is often unavoidable, and where non-New York details are available, they have been given particular attention.

Introduction

Now largely forgotten, pleasure gardens were once popular and pervasive sites in the nineteenth century. Perhaps better known through the British venues of Vauxhall and Ranelagh, these privately owned entertainment venues were also found in nearly every city in nineteenth-century America, providing a mixed clientele with a host of entertainments, ranging from vocal concerts and refreshments, to firework displays, Fourth of July celebrations, and dramatic interludes. The patrons of these venues, the policies enforced by the proprietors, and the various activities occurring within these sites present a wealth of opportunities for exploring the performance of American identities through popular entertainments. Like the theatres, museums, and circuses with which they had close connections, these sites contributed to the discussion of what it meant to be American in the period following the Revolution.[1]

Focusing on the period 1789–1855, this study investigates the performances at the gardens (on and off the stage) and relates these to the ongoing experimentation with identity in America during these years.[2] Exploring the concepts of nation, culture, class, and race, I examine the activities and attendance at the gardens in relation to issues of identity construction. I argue that these gardens were heterotopic sites, in that they signified multiple—often contradictory—aspects of American national identities: They were British venues with British names yet were used to assert American independence; they witnessed the reinforcement of racial and class-based divisions and concurrent assertions of equality; and they allowed identification with both the urban and the rural simultaneously. I argue that the gardens allowed patrons to perform various national identities through participation, observation, and association. Further, I assert that these venues played an important role in American cultural history, as they provided a site for early American vaudeville, sustained fireworks as an important means of celebrating the Fourth of July, and ultimately contributed to the development of American world's fairs and amusement parks.

The term "pleasure garden" has been periodically used to designate a garden grown for ornamental purposes (such as a flower garden), but in the twentieth century it has become the term of choice for a series of outdoor entertainment venues that operated in England and across the globe in the eighteenth and nineteenth centuries. Pleasure gardens were not always called such while in operation, with descriptors such as rural retreats, pleasure grounds, Vauxhalls, and garden theatres being popular contemporary terms for them, yet "pleasure garden" is now the accepted term for such venues.[3] So what is a pleasure garden exactly, then? Within this study, I adopt the definition of pleasure garden put forward by Thomas Garrett: "A privately-owned (as opposed to a governmentally owned) enclosed ornamental ground or piece of land, open to the public as a resort or amusement area, and operated as a business."[4] This definition excludes commons, public parks, and other such free public green spaces found in towns and cities, identifies the venue as being a business open to the public (rather than a country estate with limited access to its grounds), and includes the availability of some form of organized amusement or entertainment.

Pleasure gardens are widely acknowledged as originating in London in the late seventeenth century. Often beginning as the grounds to manor houses or as tavern gardens, the earliest prototypes of these London venues could be found in or near the city, with Spring Gardens and New Spring Gardens being the first such sites. While Warwick Wroth identifies 68 distinct pleasure gardens, including the popular Ranelagh and Marylebone Gardens, it was the rise of Vauxhall that initiated the craze for pleasure gardens in England that was to last into the nineteenth century.

Vauxhall opened on the south bank of London in 1661 under the name of "New Spring Gardens," offering walks and refreshments. Jonathan Tyers took on the lease of Vauxhall in 1729 and added paintings, balls (such as the *ridotto al fresco*), and suppers to the list of attractions. It was the appointment of Christopher H. Simpson as master of ceremonies in 1797 that marked the start of the "golden age" of Vauxhall, with fireworks, balloon ascents, and tightrope walkers (such as Madame Saqui) being introduced.[5] After passing through the hands of a variety of proprietors who offered such additions as American bowling, a hall of mirrors, and a shooting gallery, the doors finally closed (after a number of "final" nights) in 1859.[6] This British site has been the subject of much recent scholarly attention from a variety of disciplines, yet the history of this form extends far beyond the British Isles.[7]

Pleasure gardens in the style of Vauxhall emerged across the globe—from Paris to Istanbul, and from the Netherlands to Dunedin, New

Zealand.[8] Largely neglected to date, America had a rich history of pleasure gardens from coast to coast, yet these gardens have received little scholarly attention to date; only a 1944 article, a 1974 dissertation, and a 1998 book chapter and special issue of *Performing Arts Resources* have taken pleasure gardens as their focus.[9] These sites, however, were fascinating, housing performances by performers and patrons alike, and closer examination reveals that far from simply being British imports, American pleasure gardens were crucial in the experimentation with and creation of American national identities. In order to address these aspects, however, we first need to examine the nature of the performances that occurred within pleasure gardens and how these relate to national identities. These performances took two main forms: those on and off the stage.

The pleasure gardens were home to indoor and outdoor theatres presenting full-length plays and interludes in addition to pyrotechnic displays and exhibits. From Shakespearean plays to comic afterpieces, a host of scripted performances were presented on a variety of stages. In addition, presentations by Native Americans (such as war dances) were offered to paying spectators. These performances are especially relevant in this discussion of identities due to the content of the plays (themes and characters) and the focus on the "authenticity" of performances undertaken by "others." These more traditional, staged performances can be viewed alongside the performances undertaken by patrons—conscious and unconscious performances of self-display guided by various rules and regulations.

British pleasure gardens have been identified as being sites in which to see and be seen, and this can be seen to be the case in the American sites, which were similarly a forum for parade and self-display.[10] As figure I.1 and the cover illustration both show, the American exemplars were perceived as sites in which one would parade in fine clothing while observing fellow patrons. In figure I.1, we observe a couple at the center of the image walking along a path, while two ladies to the right watch; behind the couple to the left of the image, a gentleman stands and looks out over the scene; others behind him are turned to watch an unknown performance. There are various configurations of seeing and being seen depicted here. The arches depicted at the back of the painting would have enhanced this further through visually containing the patrons in their (un)conscious performances as though in an artistic frame.[11] Similarly, the cover image depicts people in the garden watching one another and being watched by those on the balconies. As they engage in games, promenades, and conversations, they are watching, being watched, and thus in turn being cast as performers themselves.

4   Cultivating National Identity through Performance

Figure I.1 Vauxhall, Philadelphia. *An Evening in Vauxhall Garden, 1819.* HSP Photograph collection [V59], box 2, folder 1, Historical Society of Pennsylvania.

But pleasure gardens were more than grounds on which individuals could parade; the gardens framed any performance occurring within their limits in a number of particular ways. In addition to the literal framing by arches, performances by patrons were framed within British cultural heritage and conceptions of the rural. As I assert in chapter 1, the understanding that the pleasure gardens were British venues meant American patriotic performances (such as Fourth of July celebrations) were imbued with additional layers of meaning. And as I argue in chapter 2, it was the context of the performances of patrons against the constructed backdrop of the country that was so important in their role in identity construction. Far from providing an inert backdrop, the pleasure gardens were part and parcel of the performance itself.

The fact that pleasure gardens were indeed gardens is an important consideration when examining the performances of patrons occurring therein. The space of the garden (along with the public park) is seen by Erving Goffman as impacting the individual, in that there is a fluidity in the social rules when compared with other public spaces; Goffman argues that gardens are among the limited number of spaces where the rules governing social interactions are "loosened."[12] While Goffman focuses on free, public outdoor spaces, the similarities with pleasure gardens can be seen, as unlike more controlled spaces, pleasure gardens allowed more social freedom and experimentation. However, it should be remembered that pleasure gardens were not typically free to enter. Indeed, the very fact that they often had an admission charge and/or codes of conduct makes them all the more intriguing—while individuals were not freed from all social rules and expectations, there was more room for exploration of personal performances of class and national identities than in other venues (such as the enclosed playhouse or assembly room).

Further, unlike other forms of entertainment, pleasure gardens allowed visitors to walk around in a manner/direction of their choosing in an outdoor setting and admire structured performances and exhibits of artwork and curiosities, as well as interact with other patrons. In his study of the roles of power in Vauxhall, London, Gregory Nosan identifies the importance of the various patterns of movement around the space of a pleasure garden and the interaction between the artworks, space, and patrons.[13] Nosan argues that the space of Vauxhall, London, allowed individuals to perform national identities by their patterns of movement and engagement with the space. Similar interactions of various magnitudes were occurring in the American pleasure gardens allowing conscious and unconscious performances within the context of the gardens to take on varying meanings and readings.

In using the term "performance" in this study, I am primarily concerned with ideas of performance as role playing. I argue through this discussion that it was in the pleasure gardens that patrons were able to "try on" aspects of American identities, being at times able to play as though of a different social class, participate in national celebrations, and perform against a background of racial others. In this volume, I assert that Americans performed (with varying degrees of consciousness) elements of their national, social, and racial identities within the space of the pleasure gardens through a form of role play. Concurrently, I am also interested in the more overtly constructed performances in the form of presentations, plays, and dances. The performances undertaken by Native Americans (or Native American impersonators) in the pleasure gardens, for example, were billed as entertainments and placed upon a stage before a paying audience, adopting what should therefore be seen as a transparently constructed performance. Performance is thus additionally defined as "the action of performing a play, piece of music, [or] ceremony," presented "in front of an audience," and will be differentiated from my earlier use of the term by designating it "staged" or "theatrical performance."[14]

Having established that a variety of performances were taking place in pleasure gardens, it then needs to be asked what we can learn from these performances. Operating as they did between the Revolution and the Civil War, American pleasure gardens were popular at a time when national consciousness was in its infancy, and as a popular entertainment, pleasure gardens allow us to access these performances of identities.

Of course, the study of performance in relation to national identities is not a new topic, as many studies of theatre and performance have examined this connection. From the pioneering efforts of Francis Hodge to the more recent texts by Rosemarie K. Bank, Heather S. Nathans, and Jeffrey H. Richards, many scholars have acknowledged the particular efficacy of theatre in allowing for the exploration of national and cultural identities.[15] Theatre is especially effective in exploring and communicating such national identities, as the presence of the audience allows for a communal experience and for instantaneous feedback. While these scholars acknowledge identity to be a fluid construct identifiable only by markers or traces, they do note theatre as being a fruitful means of exploring what it meant to be American in the period 1775–1865. Although pleasure gardens have not yet been subjected to this form of investigation, they, too, are cultural forms that demonstrate the ongoing process of renegotiation and redefinition of what it meant to be American through their housing of staged entertainments, and they, too, bear these traces.

As identified above, the performances occurring within pleasure gardens were not only of the staged variety, but also of the performance studies brand, and examination of these, too, reveal markers. Len Travers, David Waldstreicher, and Simon Newman have examined the role of such performances in their studies of street festivals and the development of political celebrations and national consciousness(es).[16] Waldstreicher in particular notes how American political identities were constantly negotiated through public presentations of the self and of political parties, with individuals and groups believing themselves to represent the "true" American political or personal identity. Both Waldstreicher and Travers stress that any discussion of "national consciousness" requires an awareness of the fact that the majority of the population left no record of their thoughts on such a concern—only absences remain.[17] This difficulty in recovering these numerous points of view means that any discussion of American identities must be undertaken with care and with an awareness of multiple interpretations. In pursuing this line of enquiry, I do not argue for a single identity being represented within the space of the pleasure garden; rather I assert the value of the forum as a venue for the constant (re)negotiation of what American identities were and what they were perceived to be. Throughout this study, I pay particular attention to who was accepted or denied entry to the gardens, to celebrations of nationality (especially Fourth of July celebrations), to the activities and entertainments seen within the gardens, and to the language used to publicize the venues as instances of these traces and interpret them appropriately.

It is also important to remember that these plural identities were felt and performed simultaneously. Although Benedict Anderson notes the formation of an "imagined community" through the conception of simultaneous time and space, he does not account for how the variety of notions became unified (if, indeed, they did at all). As Malini Johar Schueller and Edward Watts note in their volume *Messy Beginnings*, there must have been, at least in the early stages, a multitude of different understandings of what it meant to be American in operation concurrently.[18] As such, it is not possible (nor desirable) to seek a singular American identity; of much more value and interest is an exploration of the various ways this concept was approached, developed, and negotiated through the public space of the pleasure garden. I, therefore, refer to American national identities in their plural form.

This plurality in pleasure gardens is best read through Foucault's concept of heterotopias. As he argues in "Of Other Spaces," "we do not live in a homogeneous and empty space," but rather in spaces imbued with multiple meanings and significations.[19] As Foucault articulates it, heterotopias have six elements: they are present in every culture; they may function differently at different times; they contain different, seemingly incompatible spaces; they are linked to moments of time; they are both open and closed; and they function in relation to other, real spaces. As space does not exist in a vacuum, he argues, spaces can only be read in relation to the individuals and things within them and the various significations they bring. Each of these elements opens up pleasure gardens to further analysis of their form and function.

For example, the pleasure gardens had a "system of opening and closing that both isolates them and makes them penetrable," as in order to enter, "one must have a certain permission and make certain gestures."[20] As discussed in chapter 3, the appearance that the gardens were open to all was contrasted by the rules and regulations that were increasingly enforced. The pleasure gardens were presented as an open space yet were simultaneously closed, and this tension was ultimately to erupt in rioting. More crucially, it is the apparently contradictory nature of the pleasure gardens and what they signified that is the heart of what makes them so fascinating—they were rural yet urban; modern yet nostalgic; British yet American; democratic yet class-defined. This ability for the space to juxtapose "in a single real place different spaces and locations that are incompatible with each other," is key to viewing the pleasure gardens as heterotopias, capable of holding all these significations concurrently.[21] With national identities in particular, this ability to support multiple identities was central.

In celebrating the nation, the Fourth of July can be seen to be a crucial touchstone for national identity as it created an "imagined community of the Revolutionary American nation," which allowed for the shared belief in a singular national identity, even when partisan politics and flawed democracy put the very idea of a unitary identity in doubt.[22] Even while these celebrations wore the mask of a single, democratic national identity, there were significant exclusions from these celebrations in particular, and from pleasure gardens more generally, and thus a multiplicity of ideas of American identity could be harbored in one celebration.

In this book, I investigate the ways in which Americans have seen themselves as "American," by looking at what this means on a national and local scale and as seen through the pleasure gardens (in terms of layout, entertainments, clientele, location, and management policies). In order to do this, where and when the American pleasure gardens could be found, and what kinds of performances occurred within them first needs to be uncovered.

In examining the American sites, I have largely confined the scope of this study to a selection of the gardens found in the east-coast cities of New York, Boston, Philadelphia, Baltimore, and Charleston (South Carolina). While pleasure gardens could also be found in New Haven, Richmond, and New Orleans, for example, these selected cities were among the largest cities during the pleasure garden craze, and thus had more venues than other, smaller towns and cities.[23] Within these five cities, I have focused on a select number of venues in order to provide focus within the various chapters. These principal case studies have been selected on the basis of the degree of documentation and their representative nature (in terms of location, size, duration, and/or types of entertainment offered), and are outlined very briefly below.

* * *

New York was home to a large number of pleasure gardens, many of which have been surveyed in Garrett's study. By far, the most popular name for a pleasure garden in New York was Vauxhall, after the London original, and these sites resembled their namesake to varying degrees (as discussed in chapter 1). The first of these sites is recorded as appearing in 1750, when, according to D. T. Valentine, the "Bowling Green Garden, [which] was for many years one of the chief places of resort for pleasure-hunters from the city" changed its name to Vauxhall.[24] "On the shore of the North river, about the present junction of Warren and Greenwich Streets," the site operated as a business under the management of Samuel Francis, offering balls, exhibits of wax figures, vocal and instrumental concerts, fireworks, and refreshments until 1774.[25] Mr. Miller opened a later Vauxhall (Vauxhall Rural Felicity) on Great George Street in June 1793, and Peter Thorn established yet another named "New Vauxhall" at 5 Pearl Street in 1797, but both of these were short-lived.[26]

An additonal three Vauxhalls were operated by a French confectioner named Joseph Delacroix—one at 112 Broadway, another at the Bayard estate (which approximates to today's Grand, Broome, Crosby, and Lafayette Streets),[27] and a third and final one located between Broadway and the Bowery, "between Great Jones and Eighth streets," to the north of the earlier sites.[28] It was this last site run by Delacroix that was to be the most successful and enduring of the various Vauxhalls in New York.

Operating from 1805, this final Vauxhall showcased recitals, fireworks, vocal and instrumental concerts, exhibits of statues and busts, and Fourth of July celebrations.[29] Employing actors from the theatres in Philadelphia and New York, the theatre within these gardens presented such pieces as Elizabeth Inchbald's *Animal Magnetism*, David Garrick's *The Lying Valet*, and Isaac Bickerstaffe's *The Padlock*. Delacroix's ambitious programs continued for two years, with an increasing number of plays being offered each season and improvements being made to the theatre structure (such as the addition of a covering to the "theatre" in 1808).[30] However, a fire in August 1808 destroyed the distillery, store house, part of the theatre, and, it would appear, Delacroix's passion for his work; he reopened the gardens in May 1809, but his announcements and programs betray a weary disposition and were accompanied by a series of advertisements offering the remainder of his lease for sale.[31]

From 1821, Vauxhall Garden was managed by Timothy Madden, who introduced several balloon ascents, nitrous oxide demonstrations, wire-walking, tumbling, and marksmanship. In 1828, the gardens began to be broken up, with the first intrusion being the construction of Lafayette Place straight through Madden's gardens. This division was the first of several encroachments with the gardens being parceled up in increasingly small lots run by such managers as Samuel Rockenberg and P. T. Barnum, though the site ultimately eroded away entirely by 1855.[32]

As Vauxhall Garden slowly diminished in size, a substantial portion of Vauxhall's clientele began patronizing a new pleasure garden from as early as 1830, when, according to Edwin Burrows and Mike Wallace, "the upper classes deserted the déclassé Vauxhall and turned to William Niblo's new concern, established in 1828 at the northeast corner of Broadway and Prince."[33] Niblo had operated the Bank Coffee House from 1814 at Pine and William Streets where he generated a loyal customer base of "prominent merchants." Initially operating under the name of "Sans Souci," the gardens quickly became known simply as "Niblo's Garden," offering concerts and illuminations.[34] Over the years, the venue was described as a "romantic retreat" offering "exquisite music" and attended by "the *bon ton*."[35] Burlettas, farces, and firework displays were presented, and from 1838, the Ravel family performed their acrobatic acts, making Niblo's Garden "the most prominent and popular place of amusement in the city." In addition, "on popular occasions," the performer Antonio Blitz noted, "a number of side entertainments were given in convenient locations, erected for this special purpose."[36]

In 1848, William Niblo turned his attentions to the Astor Place Opera House, the site of repeated attempts to establish opera in the city. As a man of "tact, honor, and talent," it was hoped that Niblo would revive this theatre and successfully stage opera for the city's elite.[37] During Niblo's transfer to the Astor Place Opera House (known later in the season simply as "Niblo's Opera House"), construction was underway at his old site, resulting in a theatre, ballroom, gardens, hotel, ice cream saloon, and promenade opening the following season.[38] Although Niblo retained a portion of the garden (a strip of land 257 feet long running between the hotel and theatre), the focus thereafter was on events within the numerous buildings, and he removed fireworks, outdoor concerts, and garden acrobatics from his programs of events. At this point, Niblo's ceased to be a pleasure garden, although it retained the name "Niblo's Garden." The theatre at Niblo's original site began producing Italian and English opera, and is perhaps best known for producing *The Black Crook* in 1866. Niblo's Garden finally closed its doors in 1895.[39]

Although Vauxhall and Niblo's Garden were the chief pleasure gardens within New York City, they were not the only gardens to be found within the city, with at least 50 such sites operating at some point.[40] New York's gardens were numerous and diverse, and no study can hope to capture the sheer range of gardens located within the city limits. As two of the most long-lived and well-known gardens, however, Vauxhall and Niblo's Garden stand out as primary sites of interest.

Philadelphia similarly boasted a substantial number of pleasure gardens during the post-Revolutionary and antebellum periods, including Gray's Ferry (1789–1792), Harrowgate (1789–1791, 1810), Vauxhall (1813–1825), and McArann's Garden (1839–1842).[41] Although none was especially long-lived, these venues offered a variety of entertainments and were perceived as worthwhile endeavors by their proprietors, who often invested substantial sums of money into their creation and operation. Several of these gardens began as part of other business ventures, including a way station (Gray's Ferry), a mineral spa (Harrowgate), and a botanical garden (McArann's).

Starting in 1747, George and Robert Gray operated Gray's Ferry (also known as "Lower Ferry") and the adjacent 12-acre gardens located about four miles out of the city. By 1787, the gardens at Gray's Ferry boasted artificial mounds, nongeometric plantings, ruins, Chinese bridges, a hermitage, cascades, grottoes, meandering paths, and views built into the design, some of which can be seen in figure I.2.[42] These gardens were eventually opened to the public in the form of a pleasure garden in May 1789. The Grays offered free concerts weekly at 4 p.m., refreshments were available (with fresh fish being particularly noted), and patrons could hire the house and gardens for private dinner parties, dances, and/or club meetings.[43] Visitors travelled to the site by a wagon (operating twice daily) and by a ferry operating from Middle Ferry (a bridge closer to the city).

The Gray brothers were especially notable for their Fourth of July events. In 1790, for example, they presented "Odes, Songs and Musick," the

Figure I.2   *Gray's Ferry sketch*. Ba 7 G775, Historical Society of Pennsylvania.

"Bridge dressed with Shrubbery and Colours for each State in the Union," the ship *Union* "dressed with the Colours of all Nations in Alliance with the United States," "an artificial Island, with a Farm-House, Garden," "a transparent Painting of the illustrious President of the United States," "a beautiful display of Fire-works," and the exhibit of "a Vault, composed of 12 Stones, with the Key at Top, represent[ing] the Completion of the Federal Union by the Accession of Rhode Island."[44] In 1791, a "disturbance" occurred on the Fourth of July, when several people gained admission without paying by scaling the walls and fences and then, upon being ejected, threw stones at the door keepers and pulled down some fences, inciting a riot.[45] Early the following year, the Grays sold the gardens and all its contents, and Gray's Ferry ceased to be a pleasure garden, returning to its former function as a tavern or way station.

A spring located four miles outside of Philadelphia on the Frankford road operated as a pleasure garden for a limited time under the names of "Harrowgate" and "Vauxhall."[46] First advertised in 1786, George Esterly offered his mineral spring, land, and buildings for rent on the condition that the tenant construct suitable buildings to make best use of the waters. Esterly opened the baths and springs to the public himself later the same year (suggesting that no suitable tenant came forward). The health-giving qualities of the springs were frequently advertised alongside notices for alcoholic beverages available at the gardens, leading Thomas Scharf and Thompson Westcott to comment sarcastically that "brandy and rum did not destroy the virtues of the Harrowgate mineral waters."[47] This site operated as a pleasure garden between 1789 and 1792, offering vocal and musical concerts, plays, illuminations, transparencies, various acrobatic displays by John Durang, and exhibits of paintings, in addition to the dining facilities, baths, a circular fishpond "running around a small island on which stood a Chinese temple," groves, gravel walks, fruit trees, and flowerbeds.[48] But, "as all such places have their zenith and decline, so had Harrowgate," which, according to F. H. Shelton, closed in 1817 due to "the creation of newer and nearer resorts and amusement centers."[49]

A more central Philadelphia Vauxhall was found on Broad Street between Walnut and Chestnut Streets, on land owned by John Dunlap Jr. (inherited from his father, Colonel John Dunlap), operating between 1813 and 1825.[50] The site was opened by John Scotti, who is listed in the city directory as an Italian perfumer and hair dresser.[51] After opening his Vauxhall toward the end of the 1813 summer season, Scotti began his full seasons of entertainments in 1814 with grand balls and galas, until Charles

Magner took on the site in 1818.⁵² Much like his predecessor, Magner offered concerts, balls, and refreshments, and he also exhibited curiosities (such as the "velocipede," essentially an early form of bicycle, in 1819) and produced a variety of performances (such as the "Lecture on Heads," a satirical monologue based on various character "types" using busts as props).⁵³ While Magner continued as proprietor, others tried their hand at managing the venue over the years, including orchestra leader James Hewitt, who presented farces and light comedies using a troupe of actors he called the Vaudeville Company.⁵⁴ These performances took place in the Pavilion Theatre located within the grounds, on the northeast corner of Walnut and Broad Streets.⁵⁵ In 1819 and 1820, Monsieur Guille made several balloon ascents, one of which was delayed in 1819 due to bad weather, resulting in a riot that led to the destruction of the grounds.⁵⁶ After closing in 1825, the gardens became an outdoor restaurant until the site was sold in 1838, at which time the Broad Street front was purchased by James Dundas who built a residence there.⁵⁷

McArann's Garden—"a spacious and popular resort, capable of containing many thousand people"—began life as a botanical garden run by John McArann, opening around 1823.⁵⁸ Operating on Filbert Street between Schuylkill Fifth and Sixth streets, the gardens first opened to the public as a venue for entertainments with a "series of concerts of vocal and instrumental music" beginning in June 1839.⁵⁹ The initial success of these concerts led to an expanded bill by August 1839, when the proprietors added the Ravel family, a magician, fireworks, and illuminations to the bill. The season of 1839 convinced McArann of the economic viability of such a venue, and he expanded his offerings again the following year, constructing the "Vesuvius amphitheatre," capable of accommodating 3,000–4,000 spectators.⁶⁰ The amphitheatre was the home to a thrice-weekly exhibit of the eruption of Mount Vesuvius, and this 50-cent exhibit (complete with fireworks, concerts, and refreshments) was advertised until 9 June 1839. The following year, the events were scaled back drastically and the few advertisements available for 1840 boast only of "rural charms," fireworks, and refreshments. Clearly, the entertainments were not the money-maker McArann had hoped for, as he filed for bankruptcy in April 1842 and offered the contents of the gardens for sale in April and May of 1843.⁶¹ Indeed, even though McArann's Garden continued to operate into 1842 (after the filing), advertisements made note of the gardens' unprofitable nature (citing the weather as the chief reason for the failure). This was to be the end of McArann's Garden—after just three years of operation, the gardens closed to the public.

Despite their varied origins, different operating practices, and rather short life span, each of these sites was a success in some way, demonstrating their eagerness and ability to adapt to changing public taste. Gray's Ferry, Harrowgate, Vauxhall, and McArann's were just four of numerous such venues to be found in Philadelphia, yet the four case studies highlighted here provide a good cross-section of the types of gardens and activities to be found in Philadelphia. Other cities did not have such varied examples of pleasure gardens, and, by way of contrast, Boston's pleasure garden history is very limited. Boston witnessed the establishment of only one pleasure garden (Washington Gardens), but there were attempts to open others.[62]

In February 1798, advertisements in the *Columbian Centinel* and *Federal Gazette* announced the intent of "a number of gentlemen" to open a Vauxhall in Boston "in the course of the ensuing summer." Further details appeared in March of the same year, when Snelling Powell (an actor at the Haymarket Theatre and brother of C. S. Powell) and J. B. Barker (or Baker, manager of the Haymarket Hotel) placed advertisements in several Bostonian newspapers for their proposed Vauxhall Garden.[63] They sought 200 subscribers paying $50 each in order to establish the gardens at a site in the Boston area, in "the rural groves at the western end of West-Boston Bridge."[64] However, these gardens never opened, and no mention of them surfaces in any of the four major newspapers of Boston after 26 March 1798.

These gardens did not open for a variety of reasons, including the haste with which the plans were put together. Snelling Powell had been an actor at the Federal Theatre when it burned down on 3 February 1798, and like the other actors employed by the theatre, Powell found himself suddenly without an income. The first outlines of the plan for Powell's Vauxhall appeared in the newspaper on 10 February 1798, just one week after the fire. Powell's unemployment, combined with the speed with which the first advertisement appeared after the fire, suggests that rather than a carefully considered proposal for an entertainment venue suitable for the population at hand, this project may have been a hasty response to an unfortunate situation.

A more successful Bostonian venture came in the form of the Washington Gardens, which opened on 22 June 1814, on Common Street, and was renamed Vauxhall, Washington Gardens in 1815.[65] The house and grounds were owned by James Swan, who leased it to John H. Schaffer (initially on a short-term lease, but later on a ten-year lease at a rent of $1,500 per year in 1818), with the right to construct buildings on the site. While operating under the name of Vauxhall, the site offered vocal concerts, illuminations, transparencies, and fireworks under the direction of James Hewitt until 1818 (later manager of Vauxhall, Philadelphia, described above). In 1819, having reverted to its former name, the Washington Gardens Amphitheatre opened on the site, offering plays, magic shows, slack rope acts, equestrian displays, and ventriloquist acts, with the gardens being occasionally used for firework displays and a balloon ascent. In its final years as a site of entertainment, the land was used for stables, the house for boarding and dining, and the amphitheatre for exhibits and amateur dramatics. The gardens closed after the ten-year lease expired in 1828, and after Schaffer was sued by the city for failing to pay for a theatre license.[66] Unlike its fellow urban centers in the North, Boston was home to only one relatively short-lived pleasure garden.

Baltimore hosted a variety of pleasure gardens both within and outside of the city, including Jalland's Gardens, Gray's, Toon's, Spring Gardens, and the Columbia Gardens. Each of these offered something slightly different from its competitors.[67] Gray's/Chatsworth, and Easton's/Columbia Gardens were among the most popular and well-documented of the various sites, and they provide a good cross-section of the varieties of pleasure gardens found in Baltimore.

Chatsworth Gardens was a large estate just to the northwest of Baltimore. Part of the land operated as a pleasure garden from 1794 to 1805 (with a one-night revival in 1808) under the names Gray's Gardens (while it was under the management of John Gray), and then Chatsworth Gardens (under John J. Mang). This "partial retreat from the noise of the town" was situated about half a mile from the city and offered illuminations, fireworks, refreshments, and subscription dinners.[68] In 1800, John J. Mang assumed management of the gardens, changed the name to refer to the name of the estate on which the gardens were initially constructed (Chatsworth), and offered Fourth of July celebrations, illuminations, concerts, and fireworks. The operation of this site as a pleasure garden was short-lived, with events between 1800 and 1808 being intermittent (boarding and citrus fruits became the focus of advertisements). Gradually the grounds were sold off in parcels, with notices of sale appearing from 1809.[69] George Busch is listed in the 1810 city directory first as being the "keeper" of public gardens, and then as the "inn-keeper, Gray's Gardens" in 1812, suggesting he continued the site as an inn. However, this was apparently not a successful investment, as the site was offered for sale again in 1812 and 1814.[70]

A more long-lived venture was found in Baltimore starting in 1789 and operating under a variety of names. In 1789, Margaret Myers opened her house and gardens to the public. Calling the gardens "Rural Retreat," she offered patrons "recreation and refreshment" and "Boxes...for the Accommodation of Parties in the Summer Season."[71] Situated on the corner of Bond Street and Dulany Road, this site closed in 1791, when Myers offered the house and gardens for rent (though she remained in residence).[72] In 1801, Nicholas W. Easton reopened the "Rural Retreat" offering waters, shaded walks, fireworks, ice cream, music, and liquors, renaming it "Easton's Garden." Easton's management continued through 1803, but by 1804, Thomas Leaman was advertised as proprietor, listing the site under the names of both "Rural Felicity" and "The Seige of York," with music and dancing among the offerings.[73] According to his memoirs and contemporary advertisements, John Durang and his son, Christopher, were engaged by Leaman for three seasons (1804–1806), presenting the paying public with acrobatic acts on the slack rope, songs, dances, and skits. In 1804, Durang "constructed a stage with a cover and dressing rooms underneath, an orchestra in the front, a curtain with the decorations of scenery." Durang further notes that a "circus ring was formed" to which he "introduced horsemanship."[74] Under Mr. Leaman, variety shows were presented twice a week throughout the season (June through September), with dialogues, songs, vocal and instrumental concerts, transparencies, dances, mechanical exhibits, slackrope acts, and acrobatic displays on the bills of performance. The name of the gardens was changed by Leaman to "Columbia Gardens" (not to be confused with the Columbian Inn on the same street), and the venue was to operate under this name for the remainder of its existence.

Leaman continued as proprietor of the gardens until at least 1808 and the site then passed through a variety of hands, including Mr. Peters and Mr. Ravali, who displayed their "Grecian and Roman exercises," sword swallowing, slack rope acts, and fireworks, in May 1833, and Mr. Scott and Mr. Dick provided fireworks for 25 cents in the same year, advertising them as being instructional and not injurious to morals.[75] After becoming a tavern and then hotel, the site continued to operate through to 1847.

Despite its subtropical climate and cosmopolitan nature, Charleston, South Carolina, was home to a very small number of pleasure gardens, and again it was a Vauxhall that was the principal site, first opening in 1795.[76] A lease held by the South Carolina Historical Society reveals that Harriot Horry (of the Pinckney family) rented a plot of land bounded by Queen, Broad, and Friend (now Legare) Streets to two performers, Joseph Bulet (or Bulit) and Antoine Lavalette, to establish "a public but decent and reputable place of entertainment in the city of Charleston under the denomination of

Vauxhall or Garden of recreation" for a term of three years.[77] In the same year, Citizen Cornet advertised that a "Vaux-hall" would be opening at 44 Broad Street, offering concerts of French music, balls, and dinners.[78] This appeared to be a year-round operation and so must have been located within a building and not out in the gardens. Starting in June of 1799, Alexander Placide, manager of the Charleston Theatre, offered a variety of entertainments of a familiar variety: fireworks, illuminations, transparencies, ice cream and other refreshments, puppet shows, musical and vocal concerts, and dramatic interludes. The fact that several of the performers and pieces performed overlapped with the Charleston Theatre suggests that Placide used the gardens as the summer residence for his theatre company. Charles Dibden's *The Waterman*, John Hodgkinson's *The Purse; or, American Tar*, and Inchbald's *Animal Magnetism* were among the plays performed at both the theatre and the gardens.[79]

After Placide's death in 1812, the garden passed through the hands of a variety of managers, none of whom met with any great success. In 1817, a French visitor, the Baron de Montlezun, described the choice of name as being "pompous," referring as it did to "an enclosure of half an acre which comprises a café, baths and several square fathoms of grass plots" and little more.[80] As addressed in chapter 1, this relationship between American sites and European counterparts was central to the way the gardens were perceived by many. After being sold in 1816, 1817, and again in 1821, the gardens closed their doors to entertainment and became a school for young boys.

In a 1944 magazine, two American historians argued that "the history of one [pleasure garden], so far as general character is concerned, is virtually the history of all"; yet the gardens described here show a number of differences.[81] They offered many of the same amusements (several even hosted the same performers), but they operated for very different periods of time (ranging from 3 to 50 years), were located in different areas of their respective cities, were run by persons of different national origins (chiefly American and French), began as a variety of sites (from tavern, to botanical garden, to spa, to private estate), and were repurposed as very different sites after closing as formal gardens. These various gardens thus provide a good cross-section of the gardens operating in the United States during this time period.

In this study, I use these various examples, to explore the role of the pleasure gardens in the display of and experimentation with American identities in the east-coast cities of the new Republic. I examine the main forms of entertainment and question how they may have contributed to or allowed for performances of national identities by focusing on the language used in their descriptions. The importance of class and nation is teased out, and the position of the Native American and African American within these venues is addressed. Breaking my study into chapters based on aspects of American identities, I explore nation, agrarianism, class, and race in relation to the pleasure gardens of America, focusing on the period 1789–1855, and on the gardens found in New York, Philadelphia, Boston, Baltimore, and Charleston, identifying patterns, contrasts, and trends among the various sites.

In chapter 1, "Performing Nation," I explore the ways in which understandings of the American nation were performed by both proprietors and patrons. The American gardens are first examined in relation to their invocation (explicit or otherwise) of the English gardens, allowing for an investigation into American national/cultural identities as being formed in opposition to England (following Eric Hobsbawm and others).[82] I challenge the oft-repeated statement that American pleasure gardens were simply direct imitations of English venues, and instead examine the simultaneous alignment with *and* distancing from English culture.[83] I argue that attempts to create and define American national identities were seen within the pleasure gardens through asserting them to be distinct from and superior to British exemplars, while simultaneously borrowing elements from these same sites in order to create the "heritage" required for national identities.

I then employ a second model of national identities to examine the performance of nation through participation in celebrations and commemoration, without opposition to other national identities being explicitly invoked. Fourth of July celebrations were particularly important in terms of this exploration, and as the gardens often played a central role in the festivities, the events held there will be studied in terms of their facilitation of the performance of nation at a local level. Drawing on David Waldstreicher, Len Travers, and Simon Newman, I explore the role of celebration and commemoration in creating and sustaining national identities.

In "Performing Place," I focus on the very nature of pleasure gardens; unlike other entertainment venues, pleasure gardens were *gardens*, and it is this that makes them unique in terms of what they contribute to the conversation regarding performance and identities. Tapping into broader conversations about the rural–urban tension in the American consciousness at this tumultuous time, I argue that these sites allowed for the modern and nostalgic, technological innovation and rural simplicity to coexist at a time when a psychological and physical transition was being seen from the rural to the urban. Although the opposition of rural versus urban and industrialization versus agrarianism are commonly assumed to be binaries, I argue here that pleasure gardens and the later forms of these sites provided a bridge between the two, allowing citizens to embrace cities and technology as an intrinsic part of American identity, without dismissing the importance of agrarianism and self-sufficiency. The very nature of the venues coupled with the gradual introduction of increasingly sophisticated technologies allowed citizens to embrace both aspects of American identities without apparent contradiction. At the heart of this duality was the location of the various pleasure gardens respective to the country and city, combined with the activities and exhibits within them.

In "Performing Class," I hone in on one aspect of American identities—class. Pleasure gardens in England were touted as spaces of social equality, and so it may not seem surprising that Americans adopted this "democratic" form of entertainment; if America was indeed fostering a society in which all classes could mingle without distinction or prejudice, the pleasure garden ought to be the ideal space in which to see it realized. However, far from being sites of peaceful union between social classes in the "blooming lap of maternal nature," pleasure gardens became the focus of class tensions and disputes.[84] Initially presented as genteel spaces open to all, proprietors granted access to almost everyone while concurrently asserting ideas of exclusivity. As this social experiment began to show signs of failure, managers instilled increasingly strict rules and codes of conduct in an attempt to secure an elite audience and to exclude those not performing as they "should." In turn, this led to unrest, discontent, and ultimately violence and rioting at several of the pleasure gardens. I argue that while the pleasure gardens appeared to present a classless space to which all were welcome, they in fact provided a venue in which patrons were encouraged to "perform" class. While some proprietors fostered these performances, believing "equality" could be realized within their sites, most ultimately introduced measures that led to class divisions and tensions, reaffirming hierarchies of class in doing so. In addition, these performances should ultimately be deemed failed performances as they were read by observers as unpersuasive constructions. Class, it will be seen, was an ever-present feature of American identities during this period, which played out within the pleasure gardens in distinct ways through the behavior of proprietors and patrons alike.

In chapter 4, I examine how race was performed within the gardens, focusing upon Native Americans and African Americans who were largely excluded as patrons yet had a significant presence within the gardens.

Native Americans were presented in the context of anthropological exhibits, being simultaneously embraced as part of American heritage and distanced as a race to be pitied. The choice of dances and ceremonies enacted within the gardens and the selection of plays performed (including both *Pocahontas* and the burlesque *Po-Ca-Hon-Tas*) are examined in terms of their possible reception, focusing on conceptions of authenticity and place within American identities.

African Americans were likewise excluded as patrons, despite their role in the construction and maintenance of the gardens. Permitted entry as waiters, and presented on stage in the constructed form of minstrelsy, African Americans were provided with distinctly inferior roles to play within the American venues. Uncovering previously undiscovered instances of African Americans opening their own pleasure gardens, this chapter also questions the roles of fear, class, and prejudice in relation to race within the operations of these gardens. In exploring the roles of these races within constructions of American identities, performances of redface, whiteface, and blackface, on and off stage are considered in conjunction with the performances of the white patrons and spectators.

In addition to drawing out the main arguments of this book, the conclusion questions what became of the pleasure gardens, arguing that they were the predecessors of a variety of entertainment forms, including vaudeville (indeed, the first recorded American usage of this word was at a pleasure garden), rooftop gardens, world's fairs, and amusement parks. An exploration of the significance of pleasure gardens in relation to the wider picture of American cultural forms concludes this study, positioning this fascinating entertainment venue within its historical cultural context.

1. Performing Nation: The Pleasure Garden as a Space for Defining America

> Ye Belles and Beaux, who take delight,
> In pastimes gay to spend the night,
> To *Vaux-Hall Garden* each repair,
> Where music soft and debonnaire,
> With pleasing raptures fires the mind,
> And dying murmers to the wind;
> Where the *jet d'eau* delights the eye,
> Throwing water to the sky;

Describing a typical evening at a pleasure garden, the first part of this 1799 poem describes a scene that could easily be set in Vauxhall of London; the simple amusements, choice of language, and even the name of the garden itself all conjure up an evening spent at Vauxhall in London. Yet the closing couplet places us firmly outside of England:

> While *Hail Columbia!* from the band,
> Proclaims a free and happy land.[1]

The evocation of a distinctly English entertainment venue followed by a proclamation of freedom from the same country presents a revealing juxtaposition. This poem, printed in a Charleston newspaper, was one of several such descriptions of the numerous pleasure gardens found throughout the United States of America in the late eighteenth and early nineteenth centuries that was suggestive of the London site while also asserting independence. Despite appearing to be the same as the British exemplars "in heritage, in plan, in ambience, in entertainments offered, in refreshments offered, and even in admission procedures," the American pleasure gardens were also decidedly distinct, and assertions of similarities were frequently accompanied by declarations of difference.[2] In this manner, the pleasure gardens were popular sites in which the complex operations of nation building and identity creation functioned on a local level in various experimental, contradictory, and ever-fluid ways.

"Nation" and "national identity" are loaded and elusive terms, yet are crucial to any discussion of how the gardens operated at this complex point in American history. There are various schools of thought on these terms, and as some definitions exclude antebellum America from considerations of nation (with some scholars even arguing the United States was not, in fact, a nation prior to the Civil War), it should not be taken for granted that theories of nationalism apply to all periods equally.[3] The modernist school is the most applicable to this discussion, as it positions "nation" as a modern construct, and not the product of a continuous ethnic and cultural history, thus allowing for modern nations such as the United States of America to be given due consideration. The definition of a nation proposed by Anthony D. Smith draws from this school and is a helpful one: "A named human population occupying a historic territory and sharing common myths and memories, a public culture, and common laws and customs for all members."[4] It is this definition that I find to be a good touchstone and so will build upon it here.

Yet applying this definition to a discussion of the United States presents certain immediate questions—what were the common myths and memories in this new nation? Was the Revolution the only shared memory? What were the customs and public culture to be, and how were they to be different from those of England? The often unconscious attempts to answer these questions led to much redefining of what the American nation was and how it functioned, with history and memory being actively constructed. In doing this, national identities were constructed.

National identities need to be fostered and actively pursued in order for a nation to be perceived as such by citizens. Drawing from Smith a second time, national identity is "the maintenance and continual reinterpretation of the patterns of values, symbols, memories, myths, and traditions that form the distinctive heritage of the nation, and the identification of individuals with that heritage and its pattern."[5] The "continual" aspect is an important consideration here, as identities are constantly in flux at the best of times, but at this especially dynamic and uncertain period, much was at stake in identifying and maintaining these "patterns." Such "patterns" were addressed in American pleasure gardens in two distinct ways: the questioning of the relationship of America with the former imperial power (and related reassessments of relationships with other established nations) and the repeated attempts at legitimizing the new nation through public celebrations and commemorations. In both instances, the gardens provided a physical space in which citizens could align themselves with the expressions of national identity presented through entertainments, policies, advertisements, and music (among other aspects), and patrons were able to participate in—and thus identify with—the patterns and heritage presented.

In this chapter, I investigate the manner in which both proprietors and patrons used the gardens to explore and create national identity. The American gardens are first examined in relation to invocations of the English gardens, allowing for an investigation into American national/cultural identities as being formed in opposition to England.[6] As the pleasure gardens of America flourished after the Revolution, the changing relationship between America and England was complex and constantly in flux. I challenge the commonly accepted idea that American pleasure gardens were simply direct imitations of English venues, instead examining the simultaneous alignment with *and* distancing from English culture.[7] The relationship between the American gardens and those of France also warrant attention, as celebrations of French political figures and holidays reveal ideological affiliations. I argue that attempts to create and define American national identities were seen within the operations of the pleasure gardens in the attempts to position them as distinct from the British exemplars through drawing contrast between them. Simultaneously, however, these same American gardens borrowed elements from the British sites both consciously and unconsciously in order to assert the "heritage" required for national identities. In doing this the gardens operated as effective heterotopias, allowing for multiple (often contradictory) meanings and functions to operate concurrently.

A second model of national identities allows for a study of the use of pleasure gardens in the performance of nation through celebrations and commemoration, without opposition to other nations being explicitly invoked. Fourth of July celebrations were particularly important in terms of this exploration, and as the gardens often played a central role in the festivities, the events held there are examined here in terms of their facilitation of the performance of nation at a local level. Drawing on David Waldstreicher, Len Travers, and Simon Newman, I explore the role of celebration and commemoration in creating and sustaining national identities. In doing this, I do not aim to present one narrative for the manner in which these gardens witnessed the development of national identities, but rather to explore how these gardens allow us to gain insight into multiple manners of creating and understanding American identities.

AMERICA AND ENGLAND

America and England share a past fraught with intimate connections and passionate conflicts. This history need not be recounted here, but it is nonetheless obvious that any attempt to forge American national identities inevitably involved renegotiating the links to England. Examinations of the cultural relationship between the two countries have often set up a binary with American cultural and national identities being formed in direct opposition to British cultural identity.[8] Various scholars have argued Americans sought to define themselves as a nation committed to the ideas of equality, democracy, and self-reliance, and in opposition to the monarchical country of England with its strict hierarchical class structure determined by birth. Discussions of this binary can be seen in David Gerstner's exploration of how British and American art were gendered as female and male opposites, for example, and in Kim Sturgess' assertion that all American culture has been constructed in direct opposition to British culture, with the single exception of Shakespeare.[9]

An alternative approach has been to consider early American culture to be the same as British—a mere replica. Noting the British origins of many of the early settlers, it has been suggested that the colonists simply brought their culture to America with them. The theatre of the period under discussion here in particular has been characterized as a wholesale import, from the design of the theatres to the plays and the actors that toured them. In his book on identity in American theatre, for example, Jeffrey Richards notes that the stage "types" seen on the American stage in American-authored plays were essentially the same as the British prototypes.[10] Similarly, in his study of American theatre during the Revolution, Jared Brown argues that the "theatre in America was predominantly British Theatre."[11]

Yet, American culture in its entirety was neither the same as nor opposite to that of England. When looking at early American dramatic literature, attempts to distinguish works from their British counterparts were seen in writings such as Royall Tyler's *The Contrast* in which he proclaimed that American "native themes" could be depicted in literature with a "refinement [which] may be found at home" in "homespun arts."[12] Yet even within this attempt to present a "native" and "homespun" play, its structure and form reflected that of English drama; Tyler set out to distance his play from English drama, yet at the same time, embraced it.

The problem of defining a new American culture while simultaneously drawing on that of England (whether seeking to emulate it or using it unconsciously) was a problem tackled within the pleasure gardens of America. On the one hand, Americans were embracing the form of the British pleasure garden complete with the design, entertainments, and exhibits, even stressing the similarities as a means of establishing their own cultural value, and on the other, they were actively seeking to create a new national and cultural identity by distancing their entertainment forms and social conventions from the English. Proprietors of gardens argued for the value and significance of American cultural forms by citing England's version as a source of legitimacy, while concurrently dismissing the English venue as inferior and immoral. The establishment of pleasure gardens in America spoke to the aims of asserting a culture of national value and worth by both drawing on England for legitimacy, and dismissing the English model as corrupt and/or inferior.

Recent scholarship by Schueller and Watts and Michael Warner proposes a variety of ways to view the relationship between England and America. Rather than advocating for a simplistic view of Americans having merely adopted British culture as their own, these scholars, working within a postcolonial framework, identify a more complex use of British culture by Americans. Warner identifies a shift in which "white Creoles in British America learned to think of themselves as colonized rather than as colonizers," while Schueller and Watts advocate for an awareness of the "messiness" of the founding of the American nations, noting that "the struggle between imperial and local claims to cultural authority," the establishment of and resistance to "Anglophone colonial power," and the "entanglements" that result are the main areas demanding focus.[13] These approaches allow for a more nuanced reading of the relationship between England and America, working within a dialectical relationship between nations. In terms of the American pleasure gardens, the proprietors of these various sites pursued conflicting impulses of adopting the culture of their heritage and defining themselves in opposition to it.

Before pleasure gardens became popular in America, they were well known as a British form, with Vauxhall having especial popularity. Views of Vauxhall, London, were advertised for sale as early as 1754, and sheet music for the songs performed there was sold from 1768.[14] The theatres of

Charleston and Philadelphia presented performances of the Vauxhall Echo (a popular song in the London venue) in 1794 and 1799, respectively.[15] In Boston, the Vauxhall of London was depicted in act two of William White's *The Poor Lodger*, and advertisements for this play highlighted this specific scene.[16] Conversations overheard at Vauxhall were reprinted in Philadelphian newspapers along with the lyrics for popular songs.[17] When pleasure gardens finally opened in the major American cities, it was the London venue that they looked to as a model, and despite several of the proprietors being of French descent, "their standard for excellence as explained in their advertisements, was not a Parisian garden but the London Vauxhall."[18]

The very fact that the name "Vauxhall" was selected for several of the main pleasure gardens in America suggests an attempt to recreate or at least reference the London garden. The reference to London is made more apparent when it is noted that the highlighting of features shared by both Vauxhall, London, and the American venue was a common tactic in advertising. For example, when the opening of Washington Gardens, Boston, was announced, newspapers proclaimed that the gardens were planned "on the scale of Raneleigh [sic] and Vauxhall Gardens in the vicinity of London," and that the elegant design was comparable with "the celebrated Gardens of that name near London."[19] Similarly, Delacroix advertised his first Vauxhall in New York as resembling Vauxhall, London ("as near as the situation of the place wou'd admit").[20] Other London gardens were also invoked, as seen in advertisements for Harrowgate, which was compared to "those [gardens] in the vicinity of London" and Gray's Ferry, which was described as being "like Bagnigge Wells," though Vauxhall was the most commonly cited model.[21] These descriptive references to Vauxhall are further reinforced by a consideration of the layout of the gardens, which reveals direct and indirect references.

The layout of Vauxhall, London, is well known (see figure 1.1), and its rectangular divisions and straight paths were echoed in the Charleston garden's "several square fathoms of grass plots,"[22] as well as in the last Vauxhall in New York's "seven irregularly sized [rectangular] seed beds separated by wide grass-filled avenues, bordered with hedge, and filled with low, bushy plants" (as seen in figure 1.2).[23] Detailed images for most American sites do not survive, so we cannot fully understand their layout, but generally a trend can be seen in which the gardens were laid out much along the lines of Vauxhall, London. The physical similarities are clear, suggesting the pleasure gardens in America imitated the layout of the London site.

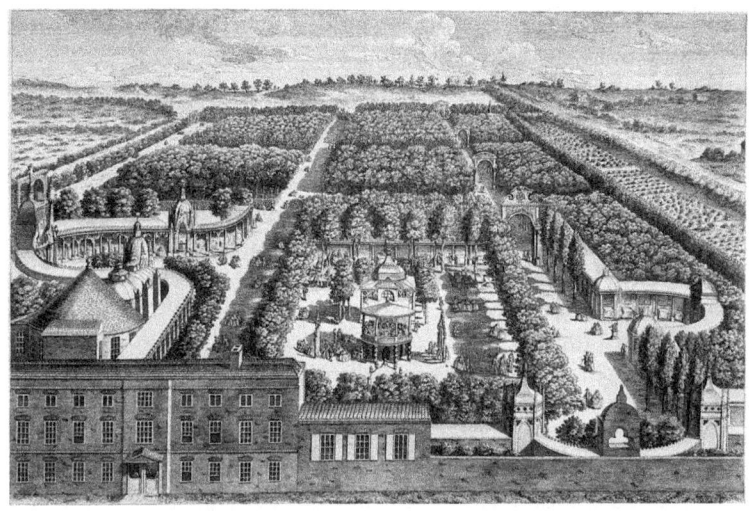

Figure 1.1 Vauxhall, London. J. S. Muller after Samuel Wade, *A General Prospect of Vaux Hall Gardens*, engraving, 1751. Private collection, David Coke.

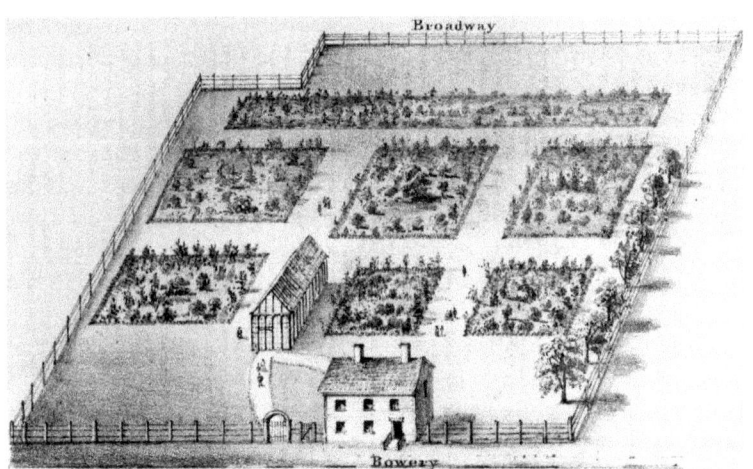

Figure 1.2 Vauxhall, New York. *Vauxhall Garden 1803*. Lithograph by G. Hayward, NY. Illustration from *Manual of the Corporation of the City of New York* (New York: D.T. Valentine, 1856. Prints & Photographs Division, Library of Congress, LC-USZ62–115483).

It should be noted, however, that the design of Vauxhall, London, was not typical of early-nineteenth-century English garden design; the use of straight lines and symmetry was more indicative of French garden design than of the landscape garden for which the English were becoming known. Far from being "natural," the English landscape school led by the practices of such figures as Humphrey Repton and "Capability" Brown required great feats of engineering and construction. Moving away from the use of straight lines and symmetry, this school sought to combine fluid lines, surprises, and "imitations of nature." The Vauxhall model was, in fact, the direct opposite of what could be termed "English garden design" at this time, demonstrating that what was "English," was not at all simple to define. In the instances where grid-like layouts were adopted, they appeared to reference the London site, and not British design sensibilities more broadly.

Other gardens demonstrated an interest in embracing English garden design more specifically. Gray's Ferry provides an example of an American pleasure garden composed in the emerging English landscape style. The partial illustration of the gardens shown in figure I.2 can be supplemented by the description of the site in the journals of Reverend Manasseh Cutler of 1787, in which a walk through the gardens is described in great detail.[24] The gardens are described as consisting of "a number of detached areas, all different in size and form," containing "three very high arched bridges... in the Chinese style," "a hermitage," a view of "one of the finest cascades in America," "grottoes wrought out of the side of ledges in the rocks," and "a curious labyrinth," traversed by alleys, which "were none of them straight, nor were any two alike." The whole is described as both a "work of art" and "the bounty of nature without the aid of human care," and it was this paradox (natural yet artificial) that lay at the heart of the English landscape style.[25] Indeed, it is also revealed in this passage that the design of the gardens was created by an English designer. Gray's Ferry was thus laid out in a recognizably English manner.

Adopting both English garden design and the specific design of Vauxhall, London (reflecting a French design concept), the various proprietors of the pleasure gardens of America drew (inconsistently) from English culture when implementing their designs. While fundamentally opposed to one another in terms of style, these very different models were both adopted as being English, and contributed to the "messiness" of what was being emulated.

The various pleasure gardens offered entertainments much like those found at the London venue, and concerts, fireworks, and variety performances graced the programs of most of the English and American venues. Some rather explicitly identified such similarities: Delacroix described his Vauxhalls as displaying colored lights "in the style of London Vauxhall," hosting a gala in the "style of London Vauxhall," and offering Vaudevilles "upon the same plan as the Royal Garden of Vauxhall, in London."[26] There were also specific references to performers and songs as being *of* Vauxhall, London. For example, the "Pandean Music Band" of London's Vauxhall was to appear at Vauxhall, New York, every Thursday through most of the 1811 season.[27] Further, some of the songs performed within the various gardens had been performed at the London venue, and where plays were performed, they were most frequently English plays. Although there were a small number of American creations staged within the gardens, these were typically fireworks exhibits themed around an idea or basic story, or a marginally adapted version of an English play.

It might appear to an outside observer that America had desired and ultimately created replicas of the London form. It was no longer necessary to envy the entertainment venue of London, as various American cities had created their own copies; "No more shall we sigh for the charms of [London's] Vauxhall," one observer proclaimed.[28] However, this was not mere imitation with the aim of having a comparable venue. Rather, what began as claims of comparability (highlighting similarities with the London site) became declarations of superiority. Niblo's Garden was described in 1849 as being vastly superior to any other such venue (particularly, Vauxhall and Cremorne), for example. This attitude could also be seen in references to a specific feature of London's Vauxhall being surpassed in American sites. Although not initially created for Vauxhall, the small mechanized "tin cascade" was widely acknowledged as an important part of anyone's visit to the London site.[29] In what seems to be a reference to this feature, Delacroix advertised the "Falls of Niagara," which were to be on a larger scale than the London automaton.[30] Not only was this model larger, but it was also based on a specific American natural wonder that a commentator describes as the "roaring, thundering, deafning [*sic*], cataracts of Niagara, in the savage wilds of America," which clearly surpassed the "little, curious, gently-murmuring, glittering *tin* cascade" of Vauxhall, London;[31] the American gardens and their American models of natural American wonders were positioned as superior to anything the London site could offer.

The quality of entertainments of the London site also came under attack, with one description reading, "noise, plenty of noise, is all they care for in music; and their Vauxhall is so tedious, that one leaves it for home with the gravity of a monk on quitting his chapel for his cell."[32] Even the layout of the American gardens began to be noted as being superior, with Vauxhall, Philadelphia, being described in 1819 as being more tastefully arranged than Vauxhall, London.[33] Dismissals and derogatory comments were increasingly used to assert the superiority of the American sites.

It is also clear from a number of comments printed in newspapers that the American gardens were positioned as vastly superior to the Vauxhall of London in terms of morality.[34] A 1785 newspaper printed a mock list of taxes that suggested that "white necks, red cheeks, and lily hands" could be found at London's Vauxhall, while another implied that London's Vauxhall had become little more than a common marriage market as early as 1765.[35] At the same time, a commentator on Gray's Ferry in 1790 remarked that the pleasure gardens in America were intrinsically moral in this "polished nation."[36] The American venues, while initially citing Vauxhall, London, as a model venue, later positioned themselves as aesthetically and morally superior to the London site.

The relationship with England was especially important in defining national identity in the northern cities, and the prominent and dynamic relationship between England and America was played out within the gardens. Often contradictory in nature, the discourse at times drew on the history and culture of England for cultural legitimacy, and at other moments spurned it as being inferior. This is the "messiness" that Schueller and Watts cite in their study of American literature and customs, with the "the struggle between imperial and local claims to cultural authority" being played out through the establishment and development of the form of the pleasure garden in America. The resistance to "Anglophone colonial power" combined with the desire to seek legitimation from this same power created "entanglements" that formed neither a wholesale adoption nor rejection of English cultural authority.[37] This dynamic not only changed with time, but was also often contradictory at any given time—both embracing and rejecting the mother country. It was in alignment with and opposition to England that the proprietors often positioned their gardens. By attending such gardens and by participating in the activities offered therein, patrons were participating in a discussion that used English culture both as a "useful foil" and as a source for the construction of American national identities.[38]

It is important not to oversimplify either the emulation or distancing seen, or to conclude that American gardens conversed with London's Vauxhall exclusively. The references to "Vauxhall," for example, should be read with care, as the use of this name did not always indicate the London site. The pleasure garden phenomenon was not merely seen in England and America, but rather was seen across the globe, throughout Europe and as far away as New Zealand, where Dunedin hosted its own Vauxhall.[39] As Garrett argues, the word "Vauxhall" took on a generic meaning in Europe and was simply a word used to refer to "all such pleasure resorts," and not to indicate the specific London venue.[40] Indeed, this can be seen to be explicitly the case in certain advertisements and accounts in America, such as in Durang's description of how Mr. Esterly "established a Vauxhall" in Philadelphia.[41] The term "Vauxhall" can thus be seen to be a problematic one; often referring to the specific London venue, this term was also used in a generic way without a specific referent.

A further complication arises when proprietors made it clear that they were invoking another specific site by using the term Vauxhall. Certain managers referred to a general "European Vauxhall," and specifically to the Parisian Vauxhall (also spelled "Wauxhall") in the advertisements for their gardens.[42] The explicit references to the French site were frequently accompanied by mentions of French customs, persons, and celebrations, with various entertainments and exhibits being billed as being from France. In Vauxhall, New York, for example, advertisements were placed for Monsieur Guille's balloon ascent, with his French origin being clearly stated.[43] The foregrounding of the French origin of several performers implies that England was not the sole source for legitimacy when seeking cultural imports or authority. Indeed, associations with France added more than "cultural legitimacy" to the sites—they bolstered certain American ideals, namely freedom and equality.

AMERICA AND FRANCE

The political alliance of France and America against England during the American Revolution and the unfolding of the ideologically affiliated French Revolution gave rise to the perception of close connections between the two countries. The reality of the bonds of ideology and politics between these two countries is debatable and has been questioned by several scholars, yet the fact remains that there was, at least, the perception of affinity and fraternity.[44] The elusive yet powerful relationship could be seen in events within the grounds of several gardens, where the legitimacy of the American nation was bolstered by emphasizing links with the established nation of France.

In 1795, for example, Gray's Gardens, Baltimore, hosted an event specifically for Bastille Day, advertising illuminations and a subscription dinner, and the nearby Jalland's Garden also celebrated this anniversary, offering a musical concert and fireworks in honor of the occasion.[45] The observation of the French anniversary was linked to the perceived close affinity many Americans saw between them and the aims and ideals of the emerging French Republic. At Gray's Ferry in 1790, the Fourth of July was celebrated with an exhibit created especially for the occasion, including "the arms of America and France entwined by LIBERTY."[46] In this event, the Gray brothers used the gardens as a space to foreground the close alliance with the French, integrating the two nations within a common ideal.

Yet the relationship between the American and French nations was occasionally upset, and the XYZ Affair provides an example of a period of time in which relations turned sour.[47] When the attempts at bribery by three French agents were made public in 1798, the public attitude toward the French swiftly changed to be one of outrage. There was little by way of protest or demonstration against the French seen within the gardens, but it is worth noting that the Vauxhall site in Charleston was closed from 1797 to 1799. Run by the Frenchmen Lavalette and Bulet and then Bulet's widow, this venue faded away for the few years during which the XYZ Affair was at fever pitch. It was only in July 1799, when tempers cooled, that Placide reopened the site.

The direct references to France and comparisons with the French Vauxhall could also be seen in northern gardens such as an advertisement in New York in 1797, when a recreation of the illuminations of Vauxhall, Paris, was displayed with fireworks at Rickett's Circus (the same site as Vauxhall Garden).[48] A further reference could be seen in the small number of advertisements for Bush Hill in Philadelphia in which it was compared to both the London and Paris Vauxhalls.[49] However, the explicit invocation of the Parisian venue was limited in northern cities. Indeed, despite the fact that the manager of one of the longest-running pleasure gardens in America was a Frenchman (Joseph Delacroix of Vauxhall, New York), he more frequently invoked the London site than the French.

Unsurprisingly, it was in the southern cities that French culture was drawn upon more frequently when seeking to legitimize the gardens. From its opening, Citizen Cornet of Charleston highlighted the similarities of his Vauxhall with French sites, offering French music while the nearby theatre presented *French Vauxhall Gardens; or, the Amusements of the Day*.[50] When Alexander Placide (himself a Frenchman) took on the site, he announced his *jet d'eau* and included *Feu de joy* [sic] in his program of events.[51] Probably reflecting the prevalence of the French language within the city, the use of such French terms and emphasis on French music was more prevalent in Charleston's garden than in those of the northern cities.

In both the north and the south, while the degree varied, a very positive relationship with the French was seen within the gardens. Instances of French performers in the American gardens and of visiting French dignitaries became more frequent in the 1820s, and many French balloonists displayed their talents in the gardens, their arrivals surrounded by descriptions highlighting their French origin. In addition, several French dignitaries paid visits to the gardens, and post-1820, perhaps the most significant demonstration of the attitude of Americans toward the French could be seen in their respect for General Lafayette.

General Lafayette was a figure for whom many Americans held a special affinity; serving as an emblem of both the Revolutionary ideal (fighting for the American cause without seeking financial reward) and of the American "mission" (returning to France with those ideals and being a key player in the French Revolution), Lafayette held an important place in the popular American imagination. As Anne Loveland argues, the reality of Lafayette's actions, ambitions, and motivations was overshadowed by a wide admiration of positive aspects of his character.[52] Serving as a symbol of Republican values and as a hero, Lafayette inspired a degree of hero worship that allowed Americans to focus on the American ideals he had come to represent. When Lafayette visited America in 1824 and 1825, proprietors of various pleasure gardens responded enthusiastically to his tour of the States. Washington Gardens in Boston, for example, held a fireworks exhibit in August in honor of his visit, and New York's Castle Garden held a ball for him.[53] As will be discussed below, Lafayette was only one of several figures of national importance who were celebrated within the pleasure gardens. However, this French individual serves as a clear example of the fraternal bond many Americans felt they had with the French, and celebrations of him were rather celebrations of the ideas he had come to represent, which were seen as American identity personified—revolution and liberty.

The relationship between America and France was an important and mostly positive one, but it was not as pronounced or as violent in its swings as that with England. This relationship was seen within the gardens through celebrations of French anniversaries and persons, and through comparisons being made between the French and American sites. While the degree of French influence was generally muted in most cities, the close alignment with French culture in Charleston is reflected in the pleasure gardens in various ways. In the sites of New York, Philadelphia, and Boston, however,

French influences were not as central to the construction of the identities of the gardens (or rather, of the people within them), yet such affiliations did become more visible at all these sites at moments of particular interest (such as Bastille Day celebrations and the impact of the XYZ Affair). The changing attitude of the American people toward the French in terms of national self-definition was thus demonstrated within the various gardens, thus adding to the messiness of this heterotopic space.

Other nations were also invoked within the gardens (either through comparisons or exhibits). For example, among the busts of English authors discussed above were Classical figures, including Cicero, Ajax, Apollo, and Demosthenes, suggesting that authority and legitimation also came from a general association with the cultures of antiquity.[54] Italian- and Chinese-style illuminations and entertainments were presented at many of the venues, including those in Philadelphia and New York, and Spanish dancers (and those of other European nationalities) were presented at Niblo's Garden.[55] Yet the references to these nations were not as pronounced or as central to the pleasure gardens and the creation of American identities.

But what do these largely superficial affiliations and recognitions have to do with national identity as created and experienced by patrons and citizens? This question can be answered both in relation to how the gardens were positioned by proprietors and how they were experienced by patrons. People choose to be seen in certain places, engaging in certain activities, and associating with certain people; decisions made about day-to-day activities can have political, social, and economic impacts that all speak to an individual's desire to be perceived (by others and themselves) in a particular way. As Simon Newman and Len Travers argue, participation in certain activities and attendance at certain venues allowed for a sense of shared national identity to be created and sustained. Just as drawing upon the UK venues provided cultural legitimacy, the fact that the pleasure gardens were imbued with associations with French ideologies and affiliations allowed for patrons to share in these components of identity as part of those identities through their sheer presence, in that they performed their leisure activities within French frames.

However, much of the continual redefinition of what American national identity meant took place not in relation to other, established, nations, but within the country itself. In terms of the entertainments offered, for example, although many gardens did present or reference English and French entertainments, several also offered performances that could only be deemed American in nature. For example, Vauxhall, New York, presented "singing, dancing, Yankee Stories" and "Grand Trials at

Negro Dancing" in 1841, and various minstrel performances throughout the 1840s.[56] Indeed, certain exhibits and entertainments were ultimately exported to England where they were seen in the London Vauxhall; the American Bowling Saloon (offering patrons "real" American drinks made by "real" Americans) opened in 1848, being expanded the following year as the American Grand Saloon.[57] However, in terms of creating and defining national identities, acts of commemoration and celebration had a more profound impact.

It was the use of public festivals and ceremonies that allowed Americans to perform the "values, symbols, memories, myths, and traditions" necessary to legitimize a nation and to perform various national identities, creating opportunities for individual members of the nation to participate in its creation.[58] I will now turn to investigate the various ways in which the pleasure gardens allowed for the exploration of American identities through cultivating patriotism, celebrating anniversaries and victories, and commemorating battles and significant dates, and how participation in these events allowed patrons to create and perform such identities.

PATRIOTISM, COMMEMORATION, AND CELEBRATION

As discussed above, national identities require distinctive "values, symbols, memories, myths, and traditions," and in this section I explore how celebration and commemoration coupled with the adoption of focal figures and calls for patriotic activities allowed these elements to be rehearsed within the gardens.[59] The gardens were presented as being patriotic venues in which patriotic endeavors could be pursued. Commemorations and celebrations of national victories were likewise seen in the gardens, along with Fourth of July spectacles. Drawing from the myriad of events in and commentaries on the gardens, I investigate how the gardens operated as sites in which myths, symbols, and memories were performed.

In the years following the Revolution, the patriotic nature of pleasure gardens was remarked upon by several commentators. In 1789, for example, an article signed "A Votary of the Patriotic Muses" identified three principal reasons why Americans should patronize the gardens: they promote American industry (above European "toys") and are linked to the valuable practice of agriculture; they allow for people to mix regardless of class; and they "elevate the human mind" due to the "genius of the place" nature affords.[60] While the accuracy of the second reason is highly debatable (and will be discussed in chapter 3), the idea that the gardens were patriotic endeavors was made clear through the observations of this correspondent in that the venues supported American trade, built upon the patriotic concept of agrarianism, allowed for equality, and bettered individual citizens. In a similar piece published a year later, the presence of gardening in all "polished nations," the necessity of such entertainment venues in avoiding immoral behavior, and the influence music has upon national character are all foregrounded with a view to present pleasure gardens as patriotic venues suited to the furtherance of the American ideal character. The elegance of the Gray's Ferry site was also credited with improving the "taste of their country," with being "truly patriotic," and with providing evidence of industry and wealth within the nation.[61]

These multiple and often abstract ways in which the gardens were touted as patriotic were seen in many cities, and the patriotic nature of various industries was frequently highlighted within the gardens. In Washington Gardens, for example, a display of "Mechanic Arts" (such as casks and ship blocks) was advertised as being "intimately connected with the real *Independence* of our country" due to the possibilities such industries presented for America to be independent from Europe in terms of trade.[62] Similarly, Niblo's Garden hosted numerous American Institute exhibits from 1834, which included silk, fruits, flowers, agricultural products, and mechanical apparatus;[63] offering prizes for various categories of exhibits, these events were described in very patriotic tones. In an address at the closing of the 1843 exhibit, it was observed that excessive importing of goods leads to a dependence upon other countries (primarily England), thus the encouragement of agricultural and mechanical innovations was for the good of the country. Indeed, in the same address, it was observed that America was achieving this goal to a degree, noting that "Europe, which has been conspicuous for her machinery, certainly the last century, has scarcely sent us a specimen, which has not soon been returned, amended and improved by American Ingenuity."[64] In advertisements in the run up to such exhibits, citizens were explicitly encouraged to consider contributing to the show, thus becoming a part of the patriotic display.[65] These exhibits, which showcased the industrial achievements of the nation, were surrounded by praise for the innovations of Americans, and were accompanied by firework displays and other celebratory events. These kinds of exhibits were seen on a smaller scale in other pleasure gardens (such as Washington Gardens), and demonstrate instances of the sites being used as a forum for demonstrating patriotic industry. In attending or contributing to these events, individual citizens were provided with a means to celebrate the achievements of the nation within a patriotic framework.

While advancements in industry were an important element in the development and recognition of national independence and values, battles and military accomplishments figured more highly within the pleasure gardens as a means of asserting national legitimacy. In both the act of fighting for one's country and in commemorating battles and military victories, individual citizens were presented with a way to actively participate in the creation of national identities on the global stage—asserting ideas of a nation worth fighting for and of its superiority over other nations.

As the pleasure gardens were a place of entertainment and a leisure resort, it is not surprising that commemorations of soldiers who died fighting for their country were given little attention within the gardens. However, in Harrowgate Gardens, a "Grand MONUMENT of the HEROES who have fallen in the glorious cause of Liberty" was unveiled in 1792.[66] In 1835, retired officers of the ninth regiment were honored at Niblo's Garden with the presentation of a silver vase and pitcher.[67] A military presence was also seen in the gardens with various events and processions, such as the "Grand military and civic celebration" at Columbia Gardens, Baltimore, in 1846.[68] The performance of songs such as "Columbia Land of Liberty" by James N. Barker and the display of "naval battles and presidents" further enhanced this idea.[69] Commemorations of specific battles could be seen in Vauxhall, New York, where there was a depiction of the "Nautical Exploits of the American Squadron in the Mediterranean" in 1805, and a mechanical representation of the Battle of New Orleans in 1815.[70] By observing and celebrating such military achievements, proprietors were highlighting national achievements and strength, while patrons were given the opportunity to view artistic depictions of monumental battles in America's history, and witness the events on a larger scale than previously allowed for while participating in a commemoration of the battle through their attendance. While the realities of war were rarely acknowledged (the memorial at Harrowgate being the closest to lamenting the impacts of war), the ideas of national strength, pride, and victory were present and tangible in a number of sites furthering the idea of America as a powerful and legitimate nation on the global stage in a public space.

Within the gardens, individual figures were likewise celebrated in order to help establish national myths and values. For example, various presidents were given specific attention within the gardens, ranging from exhibits and transparencies to events celebrating the visits of presidents. Various proprietors paid homage to George Washington in their gardens:

the naming of Washington Gardens, Boston; the exhibit of a transparency of Washington in Gray's Gardens, Baltimore, in 1808 and Vauxhall, Charleston, in 1809; and the celebration of his birthday in the Boston gardens in 1819, for example.[71] President James Monroe's visits to New York and Boston were marked with special programs of events in 1817 in pleasure gardens.[72] Past and present presidents (along with Lafayette, discussed above) were adopted as "hero-symbols," which, as Anne Loveland argues, served an important function in nation-building; the primary function of such figures was "to symbolize and perpetuate collective values, particularly in periods of rapid change and social reorientation." These individuals, she continues, are "an important part of any national ideology [and] served in America as substitutes for the symbols, heraldry, inherited titles, and traditions to which older cultures looked for values and continuity."[73] Loveland identifies the value of nationally recognized figures appearing to represent common values and (albeit recent) traditions. While individuals may have held differing opinions of these various figures, presidents and other public officials created a focal point of commonality. Within the gardens, the celebration of such figures created a locus for national identity formation, presenting opportunities for maintaining and reinterpreting "shared values, symbols, memories, myths, and traditions"—the acts necessary for national identity to be formed and developed.

By far the most widespread public celebration of the American nation within the gardens was, however, the Fourth of July, and each of the sites under discussion here hosted special events to mark the occasion, thus allowing for the public celebration of (and thus performance of) the American nation. Many of the pleasure gardens served as the focus for one or more elements of the day's festivities, with orations and fireworks being among the many events taking place there. Newspapers record a great number of Independence Day celebrations connected with the pleasure gardens, with toasts, dinners, special concerts, fireworks, and transparencies being exhibited specifically in honor of the founding of the country.

Of all the events staged at the various gardens on the Fourth of July, fireworks were perhaps the most important and widespread. In 1820, Joseph Delacroix argued that far from being incidental to the day, "the productions of the Pyrotechnic Art are now considered the most elegant and appropriate" for the Fourth of July celebrations.[74] Indeed, fireworks are still considered indispensible to Fourth of July celebrations throughout America, and their display has become emblematic of American Independence. As Michael Lynn has argued, the history of fireworks (both in terms of their past exclusivity and use in depictions of battles) has made them very effective as a "republican tool for promoting nationalism" in both France and America.[75] Although the first use of fireworks to mark independence in America was not within a pleasure garden, subsequent years saw pleasure gardens emerge as the primary site for such exhibits.[76] Indeed, when newspapers printed commentary on the previous day's entertainments and celebrations of the Fourth, it was only the gardens that were noted for illuminations and fireworks—the fireworks were a chief celebratory act of the Fourth, and the gardens were the primary venues for viewing these displays.[77]

The gardens touted other events as an appropriate way for Americans to unite and to celebrate the birth of the nation. The "Glorious Anniversary" was marked with combinations of transparencies, concerts, performances, orations, and (of course) fireworks being presented to the public.[78] Joseph Delacroix was particularly notable for the extravagance of his Fourth of July celebrations, and his detailed programs allow us to get a more comprehensive view of what exactly a patron could expect to encounter at Vauxhall on the Fourth. For example, on the Fourth of July, 1817, Delacroix presented a "Grand Concert" (opening with "Monroe's March"), an address, 29 firework exhibits (all itemized, including the "Star of Freedom, 12 feet in diameter" and "The United States, represented by 19 suns revolving around a center"), and the "Eruption of Mount Etna," all set in his Vauxhall, with "transparent paintings" commemorating the peace of 1783 and 1813 and "several thousand lights."[79]

Transparencies and panoramas were also employed to present the "shared history" of the nation, and they were typically unveiled for Fourth of July celebrations, furthering the establishment of an historical nation with a shared past and thus anniversary. A prime example can be found described in detail in a newspaper from 1798, describing a multisided transparency in Vauxhall, New York. The transparency was 16 feet high and having four fronts, depicting the following scenes:

1. The arrival of C. Columbus in America, where the Indians are seen descending from all parts of the woods and mountains, and a Gent holding the following words, "Very welcome, let us be friends," the three vessels of Columbus seen, and the landing from the boat.
2. On returning to the right, twelve columns are seen; on the thirteenth is placed AMERICA, accompanied by "Justice, Fortitude and Wisdom," with this inscription, "never shall this monument be broken." And round this work erected July 4, 1776.
3. Represents the evacuation of New York by the English as seen in Broadway, Nov. 25 1783, the entry of Gen. Washington through

Broadway with his troops. In the river is discovered a number of transports and frigates full of English troops, also the American flag is seen flying in the place where the English formerly stood; on the top of the above piece an Eagle holds "Liberty in one claw and Minerva in the other" with this inscription, "E Pluribus Unum."
4. Represents jupiter darting lightning upon ENVY, and on the side of a column is fixed a brook in which these words, "constitution, bill of rights," the American military dance round the column. There is seen several Old soldiers wishing to participate in the rewards, which a Geni in the air promises in these words, "Those who deserve will receive."

Lastly is seen upon each column, Washington, Adams, the Sun and Moon with their accompanyments [sic].[80]

The patriotic elements of this particular display are made especially clear, with such symbols as the Eagle, the Constitution, and the first two presidents being portrayed along with significant (albeit romanticized) moments from American history. Dividing the item into various scenes allows for the viewer to perceive stages to the history of the nation, beginning with the discovery of the land. Within the pleasure gardens, citizens were thus able to witness and identify with the commemoration, celebration, and narration of their shared history, traditions, and memories.

The importance of such public festivals and events in relation to the exploration of national identities has been discussed at length by David Waldstreicher, Simon Newman, and Len Travers, and they variously argue for the manner in which parades, festivals, and feasts allowed individuals to contribute to, and experiment with, national identities.[81] Newman argues that it was "in their rich array of parades, festivals, civic feasts, badges, and songs that most Americans experienced national politics," while Waldstreicher notes that such "celebrations enabled ordinary citizens to practice national politics."[82] The Fourth of July was a particularly important festival in the Early American calendar, as it was central to the "formation and communication of national identity and national consciousness in the early republic," as Travers argues, allowing for "a mythos of national identity and national interests that transcended local and regional concerns."[83] Martial music, grand fireworks, and galas were among the ways in which the gardens allowed individuals who lacked an official role in the festivities (such as military persons participating in a militia muster, or political figures who could deliver orations or attend dinners) to participate in the celebration of the nation. By attending a concert of military music, marveling at a "transparency of America," or simply consuming the popular turtle soup at the public venues, an individual could actively participate in the celebration of (and thus construction of) ideas of national identities.[84]

National identities were created, explored, and performed within the gardens in a variety of manners. Ranging from variable associations with the English and French gardens allowing for identification with or disassociation from the respective nations, to methods of celebration and commemoration, the gardens hosted multiple ways in which patrons could explore what it meant to be American. Through the performance of individuals in a variously coded space, the gardens were able to cultivate a variety of national identities through a variety of means, creating and reiterating "symbols, memories, myths, and traditions," drawing on English "heritage" as well as creating an "American" mythos.[85]

The pleasure gardens allowed for these processes in a host of manners; the actions of proprietors and decisions they made with regards to entertainments and advertisements, the declarations and testaments printed in the press by various "commentators," and (crucially) the attendance of patrons of the nation at these sites all allowed for the alignment of individuals with broader ideas of national identity. Through participation in events and attendance at sites associated with various national ideas and ideals, patrons interacted with other citizens and with shared ideas and concepts.

Within the construction of American identities, there were a variety of other issues at play, with negotiations taking place over the role of ideologies and demographic groups in American identities. Asserting American patriotism was not just about defining the nation, but about defining the beliefs, values, and customs unique to the nation. In exploring these ideas, several factors became especially visible, including the importance of the rural ideal. In chapter 2, I turn to the still-prevalent idea of America as a rural idyll, and the tension between America as a pastoral paradise and an industrial powerhouse; nostalgic yet modern; agrarian yet industrialized; the heartland simultaneously the metropolis. This tension, although still apparent, was especially volatile in the nineteenth century. Concerns over vice, corruption, and greed were intrinsically tied to the rapid urbanization being witnessed and this was in contradiction to one of the most prevalent mythologies tied to the idea of America—that of the rural idyll and the idea of America as an untamed wilderness. Pleasure gardens did much to address this anxiety by providing a rural idyll in the heart of the city, and by introducing new scientific advancements and technologies within this "safe" forum.

2. Performing Place: The Rural/Urban Tension

The United States as a country attempting to define itself on the world stage through growth in the fields of technology and engineering has been repeatedly reasserted in recent years. From President Obama's 2011 State of the Union address when "maintaining our leadership in research and technology" was cited as being "crucial to America's success," to the various initiatives to recruit students to Science, Technology, Engineering, and Mathematics (STEM) programs, science and technology have been presented as being crucial to America's international strength.[1] This focus on technology is central to America's current identity as a world leader in the twentieth and twenty-first centuries, but is a far cry from the ideas upon which American political thought was founded, when self-sufficiency and working the land were paramount. The transition from untamed Eden to our "Sputnik moment" was aided by the concomitant development of pleasure gardens. Combining both the city and the country in one site, the pleasure gardens were unique among entertainment venues in that they confronted the rural and urban tension and the related issues of agrarianism and industrialization. Through their locations, the exhibits and entertainments they housed, and the language used in naming and advertising them, pleasure gardens allowed city-dwelling citizens to adapt to rapid industrial change through bridging the past and future, and the rural and urban, in a manner that allowed both nostalgia and progress to be experienced concurrently. Pleasure gardens thus provided a forum in which Americans were able to navigate the gradual slippage in the centrality of agrarianism in American identities.

Conceptions of the untamed virgin wilderness and the romantic rural idyll were central to American identities; from Franklin to Jefferson, early American leaders couched proclamations of the unique nature of the new nation in terms of the rural. Yet with the rapid growth of cities in the nineteenth century, east-coast Americans were confronted with an ideological shift as the promise of progress was accompanied by a fear of vice, immorality, and loss of sense of self, which the rural had formerly shielded Americans from. This subject has received much attention; from Leo Marx's *The Machine in the Garden* to discussions of plays by W. H. Smith, Royall Tyler, and William Dunlap, individual morality and national identity in relation to the growth of cities has been a central talking point.[2] What I assert in this chapter is that pleasure gardens served an important function in the role of the rural and urban within the construction of American identities; they allowed citizens to experience the country within the city, thus reducing anxieties over rapid change, and also provided them with a forum in which to assess technological advances (and concurrent urbanization and mechanization) in harmony with (rather than opposition to) the rural ideal. As the role of the rural ideal in American identities adapted to changing realities, pleasure gardens provided a heterotopic space within which to navigate the transition.

Although the oppositions of rural versus urban, and agrarianism versus industrialization are commonly assumed to be binaries, I argue here that pleasure gardens provided a bridge between the two, allowing citizens to embrace cities and technology as an intrinsic part of American identities, without dismissing the importance of agrarianism and self-sufficiency. The very nature of the venues coupled with the gradual introduction of increasingly sophisticated technologies allowed citizens to embrace both aspects of American identities without apparent contradiction. At the heart of this duality was the location of the various pleasure gardens respective to the country and city, and the activities and exhibits occurring within them.

The importance of the rural ideal in Early American consciousness has been identified by a number of historians and theorists. Noting the tensions between the rural and the urban and their competing claims to American consciousness, Thomas Bender describes agrarianism as "a political philosophy and a definition of a social ideal" that figures such as Benjamin Franklin, Thomas Jefferson, and Alexander Hamilton saw as central to an American way of life; "simplicity, farming, virtue, and Republicanism" he goes on to argue, "were fused into a national ideology."[3] Leo Marx similarly observes that "the pastoral ideal has been used to define the meaning of America ever since the age of discovery."[4] As a national ideology, this mode of thought saw Americans as being defined by their closeness to nature, their self-sufficiency (and lack of dependence on such corrupt countries as those of Europe), and their lack of vice.

This ideal was realized in a myriad of forms—from political speeches, to leisure activities, to literary and artistic works. It saw simple natural scenes and agrarian lifestyles as being moral, chaste, pure, and noble with the realities of hard labor and poverty carefully excised. This chaste ideal was intrinsically tied to the concepts of patriotism and independence, as living off the land prevented reliance upon others (especially foreign powers) which in turn implied a complete freedom. As an element of American identities, the rural ideal has been a pervasive and resilient feature. Despite agriculture being a commercial venture from early in the nation's history, the concept of the independent yeoman farmer, living a life of self-sufficiency, has been a popular one. This "agrarian myth," as Richard Hofstadter terms it, built on the flawed understanding that the "yeoman farmer" was admirable for "his honest industry, his independence, [and] his frank spirit of equality."[5] The purity, innocence, and morality of this myth was a crucial part of its appeal.

The yeoman working the virgin land quickly became part of the political rhetoric of both political parties. As Richard Hofstadter observes, "the family farm and American democracy became indissolubly connected in Jeffersonian thought," while the Whigs appealed to the common man "and elected a President in good part on the strength of the fiction that he lived in a log cabin."[6] Political success depended in part on presenting an image of a rural, small-town individual. The belief in the ideal that all great men rise from humble beginnings was central to the persuasiveness of this idea, and meant that agrarianism and the rural idyll were part and parcel of American democracy and patriotism. Similarly, the writings of Benjamin Franklin and Thomas Jefferson identify the "honourable" [sic] and "virtuous" associations of agricultural pursuits.[7] These agricultural impulses were tied with Jeffersonian democracy, which held that responsible use of land to support natural industry was a patriotic endeavor.

Yet, despite its political power, this concept was a mere fiction, and one that was clung to tightly. Indeed, "the more commercial [nineteenth-century American] society became, the more reason it found to cling in imagination to the non-commercial agrarian values," despite its obvious falsehood. This rural ideal was just that—an ideal, an illusion, a creation—yet it was a powerful one that was perceived to shield innocence and purity. In part it provided a counterpoint to the perceived vice and moral pollution posed by cities, as the country was considered to have a wholesomeness that the "depraved populations of cities" lacked.[8] The popularity of this element of national identities (however fictional) draws upon what Leo Marx calls the "sentimental" concept of pastorialism, seen in the "inchoate longing for a more 'natural' environment" among city-dwellers.[9] Pleasure gardens presented sentimental pastorialism in their reliance upon nostalgic visions, innocent amusements, and focus on the natural features, but these were artful constructions devoid of reality, as the rural ideal in all its various forms did not, and could not, exist.

The only people who could have possessed anything like this nostalgic vision in the nineteenth century were those who were wealthy enough to own a country estate. As Tamara Thornton notes in *Cultivating Gentleman*, having some understanding of agriculture and possessing land outside of urban developments was an important element of being a true "gentleman" in America.[10] Associations with the country not through manual work, but through founding agricultural societies and owning a country estate were important elements of being a gentleman in eighteenth- and nineteenth-century America. In addition, the rest, repose, and tranquility of mind that comes with the concept of the rural idyll was best viewed in the nineteenth century from a position of wealth; those who owned country estates and hired people to contend with the manual labor were able to indulge in the idea of being self-sufficient, at one with nature, and born of the land, while not breaking a sweat. Because of this, the understanding of agrarianism as a democratic ideal was fundamentally flawed (a fiction dealt with in more length in chapter 3).

Despite the double-fictionality of the rural idyll (neither a physical reality nor a truly democratic idea), it was a pervasive philosophy. As Hofstadter argues, the agrarian myth "had become a mass creed, a part of the country's political folklore and its nationalist ideology" by the early nineteenth century, created through "a kind of homage that Americans have paid to the fictional innocence of their origins."[11] Intrinsically tied to this philosophy were ideas of democracy, patriotism, innocence, and purity. This simple way of life was presented as the embodiment of true freedom, and thus weilded great political power. Even today, politicians point to their humble origins and small-town upbringing in order to communicate characteristics of honesty and patriotism to their voting audience. In the nineteenth century, anxieties regarding industrialization and the fears of the vices that cities brought with them presented a challenge to this ideal, which in turn lent it more power; the fear of its destruction rendered it more powerful and thus was clung to more tightly. Naturally, not all citizens of the newly formed nation adopted the "pastoral ideal" as central to their self-conception as an American, and few city-dwellers practiced farming or self-sufficiency, yet a national consciousness emerged, which saw rural simplicity and virtue as central to American identities.[12]

In the period between 1780 and 1830, pleasure gardens were an ideal entertainment venue for the newly formed nation as its citizens struggled to identify what American identities were, due to their ability to position the rural in harmony with the urban through location, access, and content. As rural retreats increasingly situated within the city limits, these venues allowed city dwellers to escape from the chaos of the city while not venturing too far from their city landscape, allowing the ideals of the rural to be seen adjacent to the city. The idea of rural simplicity and its relationship to the founding ideals of America were allowed to be sustained even in the heart of a city as the country was quite literally brought into the city, allowing residents of nearly every income bracket to enjoy the benefits and identify with the ideals of the country without having to face the realities of this illusion or sacrifice the conveniences of the city. Pleasure gardens (with their gardens and festivals of regional agriculture) offered urban Americans the opportunity to participate (albeit to a small degree) in America's resilient passion for rural culture, and they promised a product to their patrons, whether through patriotic participation in Fourth of July events, gleaning new knowledge from strolling among the Mechanic Fairs, or presenting home-grown flowers at the displays of the New York Horticultural Society.

(RE)CONSTRUCTING THE RURAL IDYLL

Pleasure gardens sustained the fiction of the rural idyll as central and then allowed for a gradual transition to a more modern present (using nostalgia in tandem with technological advances) through a number of strategies. The focus of advertisements for entertainments within the gardens was squarely on the innocent, simple, moral, chaste, and patriotic nature of gardens, while they simultaneously housed increasingly advanced technologies. Through the language of the advertisements and the content of the displays, the otherwise modern (and potentially "threatening") technologies introduced within increasingly large and densely packed cities were rendered more palatable and thus more able to become intrinsic to ever-evolving American identities. Initially positioned as sites in which one could escape the city and indulge in a nostalgic vision of the past, these venues increasingly provided a space for the inclusion and showcasing of technology and urbanization. This transition from a rural retreat to a haven of modernity followed a gradual but steady progression, and while the exact dates over which this transition occurred varied from location to location, the general pattern can be seen to occur in each of the sites that operated for more than a couple of seasons. The locations of the sites was a large part of how this was managed, and both the "rural" settings and scenes of rural life were carefully cultivated to support this fiction of the rural idyll.

Many of the earlier pleasure gardens were found outside of the city, and although they were somewhat sanitized and idealized rural settings, they were, indeed, in semi-rural locations. As outlined in the introduction, gardens such as Gray's Ferry (1789–1792) and Harrowgate (1789–1791, 1810) could be found several miles outside of the city and provided a physical escape from the city. Gray's Ferry's 12-acre garden boasted artificial mounds, nongeometric plantings, ruins, Chinese bridges, a hermitage, cascades, grottoes, and meandering paths.[13] Similarly, "Harrowgate" (also operating under the name of "Vauxhall") operated as a pleasure garden between 1789 and 1792, offering vocal and musical concerts, plays, illuminations, transparencies, various acrobatic displays by John Durang, and exhibits of paintings, in addition to the dining facilities, baths, a circular fishpond "running around a small island on which stood a Chinese temple," groves, gravel walks, fruit trees, and flowerbeds.[14]

Gardens such as these allowed individuals to participate in rural culture by literally retreating to it. After just a short journey, individuals could gain entry to a large garden equipped with refreshments and basic amenities, allowing them to escape the trappings of city life to indulge in scenes and activities of a nostalgic past. This gave the experience a sense of excursion or holiday for some and allowed individuals to escape to a "retreat" from the noise and chaos of the city. Yet, the gardens patrons retreated to were far from the realities of agrarian life due to the artifice of the gardens themselves.

The highly constructed nature of these gardens allowed them to appear as visions of an agrarian ideal, yet they were full of artifice. From the constructed ruins, to the designs of walks, and other British landscaping elements, these sites were anything but a window onto the realities of country life, and instead capitalized on what Hofstadter terms the "agrarian myth," appealing to the sense for nostalgia held by many.[15] As discussed in chapter 1, the British landscape school of design (which was central to the design of many of the American pleasure gardens) appeared to be a mere pruning of natural landscapes but was, in fact, a mammoth undertaking of reconfiguring landscapes and adding features such as hills, lakes, and ruins in order that they might look like a particular version of a "natural" landscape. As such, the pleasure gardens with their "artificial mounds," constructed islands, "meandering paths," and hermitages allowed a rural ideal to be presented, with idyllic, unspoiled nature being the front for what was actually a labor-intensive and highly artificial creation. The gardens as innocent, rural, and idyllic sites was in fact a deliberate construct, making the pleasure gardens' depiction of "true" nature actually a deliberate and carefully articulated statement about the rural landscape. In designing sites outside of cities in this deliberate way, proprietors were constructing a stage on which they might present patrons with a performance of the rural ideal, against which patrons might also perform. The location (outside of city limits) coupled with the scenery (a constructed version of the rural) set the stage for performances of the rural illusion.

Such out-of-city gardens were not long-lived, however. Despite allowing for literal retreat from the city and a supposed immersion into rural culture, the inconveniences of these sites were soon to be their downfall. Chief among these problems was the fact that transportation was required and these gardens thus required additional time and expense to visit. The shift from the outskirts of the city to the heart of the city suggests not only a repurposing of the site to meet increased urban pressures on the land, but also a change in popular taste. Citizens who might once have valued the garden as a rural refuge now required the amenities of a hotel and tavern (either to support their leisure hours or to conduct their business).[16]

Similarly, some of the "nuisances" of rural life were to infringe upon some sites. In Boston, for example, a pleasure garden was supposed to open in Boston in 1798 under the name of Vauxhall, but ultimately did not.[17] In part, this was because of concerns regarding the location: an advertisement in the *Federal Gazette* on 8 March warned potential subscribers and patrons, noting the "frequent objections [which] have been started on the score of *Musquitoes* [*sic*]."[18] A "correspondent who has been some time in the West-Indies" published a "sovereign remedy" for this nuisance in the *Federal Gazette* which, if not indicative of a real problem with the site, certainly suggested to potential subscribers that there would be an issue with these pests. The combination of these factors made the gardens located outside of cities decidedly less appealing due to the intrusion of the unpleasant realities of the countryside.

Some proprietors attempted to establish their venues on the periphery of the city; at once rural and urban, outside the city but only just, these sites attempted to literally straddle the border between country and city, by positioning themselves on the extreme edges of a city. In Baltimore, as figure 2.1 illustrates, pleasure gardens were constructed on the very edge of the city limits, straddling the town and country simultaneously. Chatsworth Gardens (labeled Gray's Gardens, the name under which it was operating at the time) is represented by eight squares at the top left of

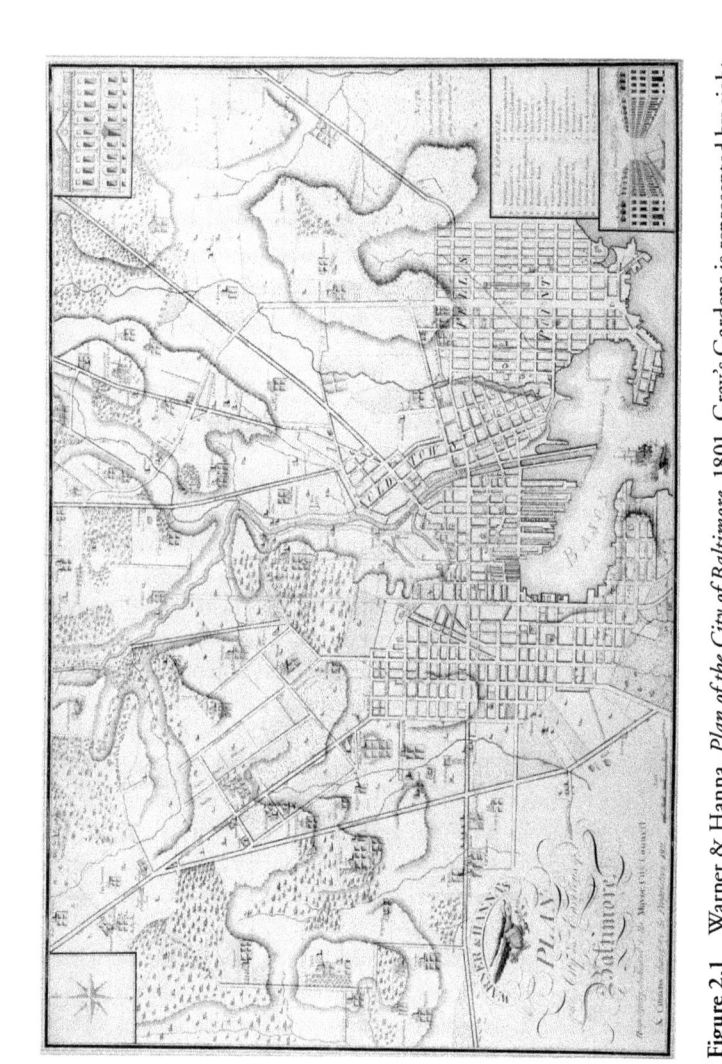

Figure 2.1 Warner & Hanna, *Plan of the City of Baltimore*, 1801. Gray's Gardens is represented by eight squares at the top left of the city; Rural Retreat is above the "F" and "E" of "Fell's Point." Maryland Map Collection, BC 016, Special Collections, University of Maryland.

the city, while Rural Retreat is positioned above the "F" and "E" of "Fell's Point." Both of these gardens were located (at least initially) on the very edge of the city, allowing them to inhabit a somewhat liminal space—both the country and the city, while actually neither.

However, city growth made this difficult to maintain. As the map in figure 2.2 illustrates, several pleasure gardens were established on the very edges of the ever-expanding city of New York. This map of 1767 shows a garden operating under the name of Vauxhall on the west of Manhattan, bounded by Chambers, Warren, and Chapel Streets. Just to the north of that site, Ranelagh Gardens is clearly labeled. Both of these sites existed on the very outer limits of the city. Just a short time later, however, as the city expanded north, these gardens closed and new establishments opened further north (again, just at the edge of the larger city). In 1798, for example, Delacroix opened another garden under the name of Vauxhall at the site labeled "Ns Bayard" in figure 2.2. While financial reasons are likely to have been at the heart of these decisions (land within the city would have commanded a higher price, presumably, as the city grew around them), the gardens moved just far enough to be outside of the city, but not so far that they were too removed from the bustle and convenience of the urban landscape either. Eight years later, Delacroix closed the Bayard site and opened a new venue just south of today's Astor Place in an attempt to again stay one step ahead of the rapid growth. In doing this, these pleasure gardens attempted to straddle the urban and the rural simultaneously by occupying the liminal space of the not-quite-urban, not-quite-rural city limits.

However, the peripheral nature of the three Vauxhalls initially established outside of the city was not long-sustained in any of the locations, despite Delacroix's best efforts; contemporary comments such as "its walks skirted with trees flowers and shrubs [is] beside so much city confusion" reveal that the gardens were soon to be found within New York City itself.[19] The juxtaposition of rural and urban within sites that attempted to be rural (despite being in an urban locale) was difficult to sustain due to rapid development and the economic value of the land, and the various pleasure gardens were quickly enveloped within the city, despite attempts to straddle both.

It became increasingly common to find a pleasure garden within the heart of the city. Gardens could be found in the center of such cities as New York, Boston, Philadelphia, Baltimore, and Charleston, South Carolina, in the early nineteenth century, as contemporary maps and written records illustrate. In being positioned in this way, pleasure gardens were able to bring all of the positive associations of the countryside into

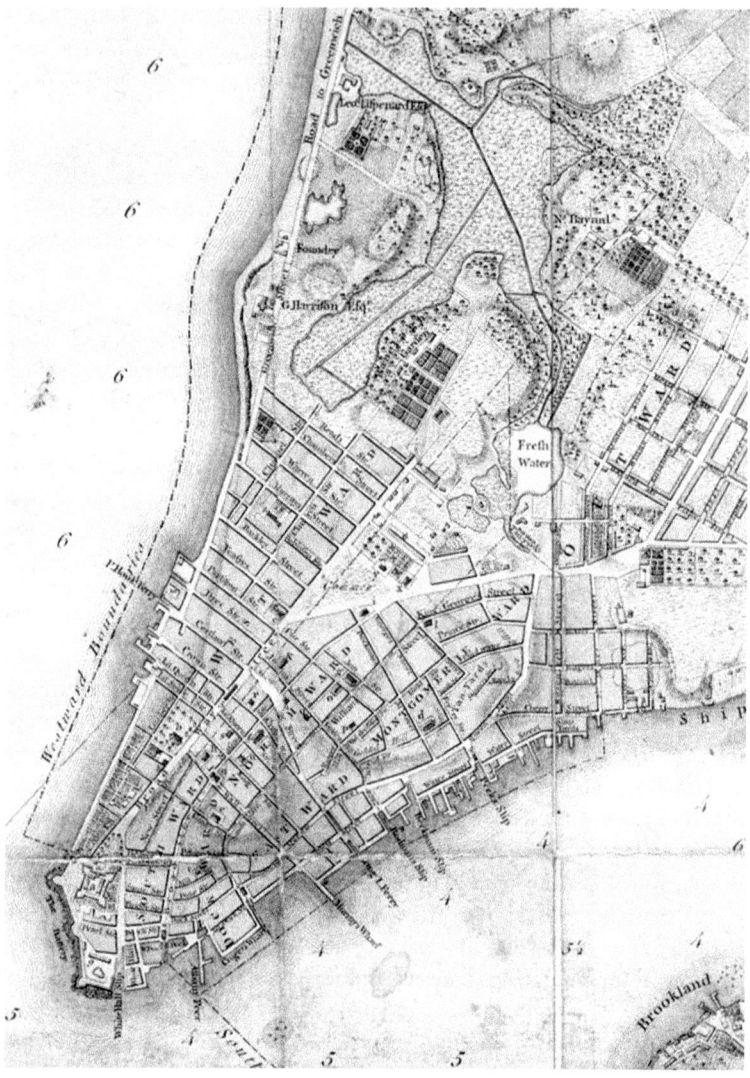

Figure 2.2 Extract from *Plan of the City of New York, in North America: Surveyed in the Years 1766 and 1767*. Vauxhall is represented by the four shaded squares on the western edge of Manhattan; Ranelagh to the west of "Fresh Water"; a future Vauxhall further North at the Bayard estate. I. N. Phelps Stokes Collection, Miriam and Ira D. Wallach Division of Art, Prints and Photographs, The New York Public Library, Astor, Lenox, and Tilden Foundations.

the heart of many cities in a way that allowed access to citizens who would not have necessarily owned a garden or country estate of their own. Sites such as these provided an escape from the increasingly large, industrial, and densely packed cities that housed them, yet they were framed and contained by the urban landscape. Often, their position in the heart of a city was pitched as being both convenient and providing an escape from the city.

Niblo's Garden, for example, could be found in the heart of New York between 1828 and 1848 (continuing to 1895 as a theatre). Opening first under the name of Sans Souci, this site presented a clear investment in the rural and agricultural illusions: the display of exotic flowers, the showcasing the gardens through the use of illuminations, and the housing of the New York Horticultural Society's balls.[20] Despite being located very centrally, Niblo attempted to provide a rural escape for city dwellers. As time passed and the city continued to grow, however, this focus was to shift slightly, with an increasing number of enclosed constructions being erected in order to accommodate such performers as the Ravels and Antonio Blitz.[21] Despite the increasing frequency of indoor exhibits and plays presented on the covered stage, one reporter declared that he still found Niblo's Garden's "legitimate attractions so great that the idea of wasting an hour amid the crowd and heat of the little theatre appears intolerable"—he preferred the fountains, music, ice cream, plants, and people-watching. Another writer called the venue a *"rus in urbe"* (or "an illusion of the countryside in the city") in 1841, suggesting that despite the gradual shift in focus from the simple rural creation to the more contained and structured venue did little to remove the perception that the venue provided patrons with an escape from the city.[22] Indeed, despite being in the heart of the town, the "rural" element was still important to Niblo, and he went to great lengths to accentuate the garden aspects of this *rus in urbe*.[23] The flowers and shrubs of the gardens were particularly noted in advertisements, and there were strong links between Niblo's Garden and the Horticultural Society.[24] Although Garrett notes, "the trend at New York's pleasure gardens was to de-emphasize the garden aspects—the trees, shrubs, flowers, lawns, gravel walks, and fountains—and to emphasize the entertainments, in particular those of a more popular nature," Niblo worked hard to retain the garden elements in the early years of operation.[25] Natural components were central to their success and had to be preserved if the venue was to continue. However, in the heart of the city, the fiction of the rural idyll was hard to sustain with the hustle and bustle of town so close at hand, so proprietors selected names and descriptors to emphasize their rural features.

As pleasure gardens became increasingly prevalent, central locations became increasingly popular. In each of these centrally located gardens, attempts to highlight the rural aspects of the venue through name choices were perceptible. Despite being in the heart of built-up urban areas, these venues suggested to patrons they might gain all of the physical and mental benefits of being in the country without having to abandon the convenient yet immoral city. Gardens with names such as "Rural Retreat" (Baltimore) and "Vauxhall Rural Felicity" (New York) provided citizens with a "partial retreat from the noise of the town" allowing them to escape "the heat and fatigues of the day" and to "enjoy rural life."[26] Similarly-centrally located gardens could also be found in Charleston (Vauxhall), New York (Vauxhall, Chatham Garden, and Castle Garden) and Philadelphia (Vauxhall and McArann's Garden). Operating on Filbert Street between Schuylkill Fifth and Sixth streets, McArann's Garden was described variously as a "pleasant place of retreat and amusement," "rural and picturesque," and a place to enjoy "rural charms" and "rural life," while being only a "short promenade" from the center of the city, though next to a busy street.[27]

Patrons were able to hold on to the idea that the countryside was part of their realities, and provided sanctuary from the chaos of the city. Yet, whether in the city or straddling its outer limits, pleasure gardens were designed to appear as rural despite being in urban locations. The fiction of their rural nature was further bolstered by careful name choices and descriptors, presenting patrons with carefully constructed rural "stages" upon which to perform. These were stages on which oneness with nature might be performed, however artificial and carefully crafted such performances might be.

These "stages" were further cultivated through the use of performers and props designed to highlight and frame the rural nature of these sites. Advertisements for various gardens reveal how proprietors would actively seek to associate the activities and philosophies of the country with the city gardens. By highlighting those features of their sites most clearly conforming to the rural idyll, proprietors capitalized on ideas of rural innocence and its relationship to patriotism through the language choices in advertisements and entertainments offered.

Such gardens were supplemented with such constructed scenes as "Thirteen young Ladies and the same number of gentlemen dressed as Shepherds and Shepherdesses" in order to build upon the illusion of an idyllic vision.[28] In dressing the gardens with actors and sets of overtly agrarian scenes, the Gray brothers emphasized both the rural nature of the location, and the innocence and simplicity of the associated ideas and persons. The "natural" garden in a barely rural location was able to sustain this illusion through the wording of advertisements and the entertainments offered. The fiction of this untenable rural idyll was thus sustained through these sites.

Early American pleasure gardens typically presented patrons with concerts, dances, and refreshments described in relation to the garden elements of the site and highlighting the simplicity and innocence of the offerings. Natural elements such as the grounds, plantings, and bodies of water were among the advertised draws. The Gray brothers, for example, chose to focus their early advertisements for Gray's Ferry on the "groves, arbours, and a great collection of shrubs, trees and flowers," and the "summer houses, alcoves and seats."[29] Other advertisers focused on simple fountains and water features, including Chatham Garden's grand hydraulic display and fountain described as "novel, innocent, and amusing," and Vauxhall, Charleston's "jet d'eau."[30] Common forms of performances included concerts, songs, and dances, such as Harrowgate's weekly concerts, and the pastoral garland dance and comic ballet advertised for the Columbia Gardens, Baltimore, in 1805.[31] Such simple (and low-tech) amusements were presented as being "novel" and "amusing," but, more crucially, as "innocent."[32] Having the venue take the form of a garden was an important aspect of embracing rural identities, but having such sites house simple and "innocent" entertainments added to the sense of safety in this nostalgic vision, creating a start contrast with the cities in which they were set.

The pleasure gardens thus provided patrons with a forum in which to embrace the rural as part of their routine lives—not simply as an inert backdrop to routine interactions, however, but rather as the stage on which individuals could enact an aspect of their identity. By choosing to enter the space of a pleasure garden, patrons were electing to step out of the city framework and enter into a nostalgic realization of rural ideals. Walking on graveled paths, surrounded by trees and plants, and encountering simple and innocent amusements, patrons were thus electing to participate in otherwise routine interactions with fellow citizens in a decidedly different environment from their daily realities. The performance of patrons within the space was informed in part by the context of the performance, and choosing to engage in such a locale expressed a desire to engage with the nostalgic vision of this aspect of American identities and the innocent attributes in the face of the ever-expanding city and accompanying vices. The pleasure gardens thus provided a buffer for citizens to interact with a pure and "safe" ideal while simultaneously inhabiting an urban space.

The power of the agrarian ideal did not stem from ideals of innocence and morality alone, however, but also from the patriotic nature of this philosophy, and the pleasure gardens capitalized on this as well. Nationalistic sentiments were made explicit in advertising and commentary, and one article of 1789 describes Gray's Ferry as being patriotic for several reasons, noting:

> the expence [sic] is very moderate, and promotes domestic circulation, great part of it consisting in the consumption of our native delicacies...An agricultural people, as we are, should be fond of gardening and ornamental planting, [and pleasure gardens] awaken a taste so natural and noble, and by displaying the charms of our country, will make us love it the more. [In addition] those rural entertainments are congenial with republican manners, and have a salutary influence on public liberty.[33]

For many reasons, this commentator was in no doubt that pleasure gardens (in this case, Gray's Ferry) were patriotic venues due to their very nature. Other arguments could be made for the gardens being patriotic for their use as site for Fourth of July celebrations (as discussed in chapter 1). Linking patriotism with conveniently located rural settings, the advertising for the gardens allowed the agrarian ideal of Early America to be sustained in the popular imagination even in the heart of major cities. As cities did, inevitably, develop, and increasingly sophisticated technologies became important to the American economy, this attention to the patriotic nature was to become more pronounced in the pleasure gardens, as the daily realities of an increasing percentage of citizens became city-dwelling and technology-dependant. However, rather than instigating a fundamental shift in American identities in the early nineteenth century, citizens attempted to seek out a middle ground; rather than abandoning their identification with rural simplicity, "Americans were seeking ways of having both nature and civilization"—the two were not seen as mutually exclusive.[34]

INTRODUCING TECHNOLOGY

Pleasure gardens, by their very nature, allowed patrons to enjoy elements of the countryside even while in the heart of the city, and initially at least, the virtuous, simple, and honest associations of the countryside were embraced as part of the marketing for pleasure gardens, as seen in the entertainments offered. As the nineteenth century dawned, advances in technology were drawn into the gardens and presented in a way that allowed them to be embraced as part of the innocent and patriotic identity, and allowed technology to be embraced concurrently with (and not in place of) the simplicity and safety of the rural idyll.

The earliest technologies to be introduced to the gardens were very simple. Illuminations and colored lamps began to be introduced to enhance the natural beauties of the sites. Ranging from simple oils lamps to colored lamps, various proprietors would boast of the sheer number of lamps provided. Part security, part adornment, these lamps served to keep the garden well lit during the evening hours (thus assuring patrons of the respectability of the site), while delighting patrons with hundreds of colored lights. It was common for additional lights to be advertised for Fourth of July celebrations, such as Mr. Mang's advertisement for Chatsworth Gardens, Baltimore, in 1800.[35] Vauxhall, New York, boasted as many as 4,000 colored lamps for one Fourth of July celebration, while Washington Gardens in Boston presented patrons with "700 transparent and variegated lamps... tastefully disposed throughout the gardens."[36] These simple oil lamps were updated in several of the later sites to include gas lighting—a new technology in the early nineteenth century.[37]

The introduction of gas as a source of illumination was first studied in England in the eighteenth century, but its commercial and residential applications were not seriously explored until the turn of the century, and pleasure gardens were one of the first venues to utilize gas lighting for public spaces. Along with theatres and other public buildings, American citizens were able to encounter the marvels of gas lighting in pleasure gardens in the early nineteenth century, including Washington Gardens in Boston, which displayed gas illuminations in honor of a presidential visit in 1817.[38] As a relatively cheap site to gain admittance to, pleasure gardens were the venue within which many Americans were introduced to such technological developments, and they were introduced in a manner that accentuated (by making visible) features of the gardens in the evening hours. Against the backdrop of the gardens, patrons were thus able to experience simple technologies through being present within the space. Simple technologies were introduced in a manner that tied very closely to the rural idyll and to associations of innocence and simplicity.

Techniques of lighting were also used to entertain patrons with other forms of simple entertainment that drew on ideas of innocence and nostalgia, including shadow puppets and transparencies. Shadow puppets presented patrons with novel yet simple entertainment at several gardens, including Harrowgate in Philadelphia. This low-tech display appeared on programs as "Les Petites Ombres Chinoises" and later "Les Grandes Chinoise."[39] For the most part, such technologies were family-friendly and could be seen as being innocent while novel. More common among the gardens, however, were panoramas and transparencies presenting grand scenes.

Large-scale paintings and transparencies were increasingly regular exhibits found at a variety of pleasure gardens; from the "Battle on the Frontier of Paris" panorama exhibited at Washington Gardens, Boston, to the "Transparency of Tripoli" seen at Columbia Gardens in Baltimore, such large-scale images became common objects of fascination found at pleasure gardens (along with other venues). Far from being simple images, such exhibits reveal much about interactions within pleasure gardens through their size, format, and content. Unlike standard paintings, panoramas introduced a new technology of painting that allowed viewers to see a "pictorial representation of a panoramic view," or literally "a view of the whole."[40] First introduced in England in the late eighteenth century by Robert Barker, early panoramas often presented spectators with a 180-degree view of a city or battle, leading patrons to stand and observe the painting, not seeing everything at once, but rather moving or turning their heads to "read" the full content of the image.

Despite the static nature of these paintings, they encouraged a sense of action and of storytelling, with the patron being made both observer and performer, as the active movement of eyes and heads allowed the narrative of the battle to unfold. The "Battle of New-Orleans," for example, is described in an advertisement as though a series of scenes in a play, beginning with "The British troops are discovered, advancing silently to the attack," followed by "The alarm gun is heard in the American Camp, and immediately after the firing commences," and "The enemy is driven back in confusion," along with ten other such scenes, concluding with "The English fleet is seen in the distance under a press of sail."[41] In moving from image to image (or scene to scene, as the case may be), patrons were able to interact with this patriotic material and participate in its unfolding.

In presenting such scenes, artistic and mechanical advances were presented to the public not as idle amusements, but as intrinsic to the celebration and commemoration of the nation. Despite the fact that such technologies were British in origin, the manner in which they were used in the American pleasure gardens allowed patrons to embrace such technologies without them being tied to the decadence and frivolity of other English arts and technologies. By adopting American nationalistic content for the form, panoramas and transparencies were able to gain much wider acceptance. And while pleasure gardens were not the only space in which such arts were displayed, they were most commonly viewed within the gardens, where they were displayed on days when attendance would have been at its peak.[42] Although the centrality of the rural was becoming increasingly diminished in the ever-evolving American consciousness, it remained tied to ideas of American-ness, and by presenting patriotic scenes and celebrations in these rural-yet-urban spaces, proprietors were combining technology, patriotism, rural, and urban associations and ideals in one space.

The earlier conception of patriotism as being intrinsically tied to the rural idyll, simplicity, and innocence was thus being gradually supplanted by increasingly urban and modern ideas. Starting with simple low-tech displays tied to the agricultural nature of the sites, pleasure gardens subtly manipulated what this identity meant in an increasingly modern and urban country. By closely tying the former to the latter, pleasure gardens provided a space within which modernity and nostalgia could be reconciled; increasingly sophisticated technologies could be presented and interacted with in a "safe" space, thus enabling their acceptance.

Several of these exhibits were augmented by displays of fireworks and increasingly elaborate mechanics. A depiction of the Battle of New Orleans in transparent paintings at Vauxhall in New York, for example, was supplemented by fireworks, as were the naval battles seen at Washington Gardens in Boston.[43] Whether designed to accompany battle depictions, accompanying live music, or as a stand-alone entertainment, fireworks were a common feature of many gardens even from their earliest years, and became increasingly elaborate and frequent as years passed. Although little is known about the specifics of firework technology developments in the early nineteenth century (indeed, Simon Werrett notes that "the history of fireworks [of the nineteenth century] seems to have gone up in smoke"), it is possible to ascertain a few details.[44]

Fireworks of the late eighteenth and early nineteenth centuries were not the same as what we have come to understand as fireworks today. The colors of fireworks, for example, were very limited before the 1830s, but as advances were made, different colors began to be introduced. Additionally, fireworks did not always refer to sparks fired into the air, but could also indicate the use of *macchine*, employing static fireworks at ground level. Popular in both Europe and America, Italian *macchine* were "elaborate temporary edifices for fireworks" introduced in the eighteenth century.[45] Although these were sometimes simple recreations of known buildings or sites, others were "fantastic imaginary structures, full-scale temples in three dimensions, constructed with wood and iron frames, and hung with trompe l'oeil painted cloth and papier-mâché and stucco decorations prepared by a small army of carpenters, turners, painters, and sculptors."[46] Several exhibits in New York gardens appear to be such displays, including the "Facination [sic] of the Rattle Snake," "Druid's Grove," and "Enchanted Garden."[47] While other displays did not have the same pastoral overtones (such as the interlude centered around pyrotechnic displays of serpents, fires, and a devil entitled *Tit for Tat; or, The Fire-Worker's Pleasure Day*), most firework displays promoted the rural elements of the gardens, through recreating and exhibiting groves and gardens within the space of the gardens.[48] The innocent, pastoral, and simple content combined with the location of such displays continued to emphasize rural aspects of the garden while the technologies became increasingly modern and advanced.

Fireworks were also used to allow volcano eruptions to be depicted, including McArann's Garden in Philadelphia, which hosted such displays from 1840. His display was described as being:

> A correct, beautiful and stupendous **Panoramic View**, (erected by Mr Ward at an expense of several thousand dollars) presenting the City and Bay of Naples, and town of Portici, with Mount Vesuvius and its grand and Terrible eruptions. A lake of real water; a vast Amphitheatre, villages around Naples, beautiful vineyards, castles, cathedrals, illuminated palaces, temples in ruins, deserted mountain towers, tents, shipping in port, entrance into Port of American and other vessels, band of music on the water, songs, duets, and glees in Naples, Portici, and on the bay, the mountains on fire, escape of Porticians from Portici.[49]

In the midst of this scene, patrons could witness the "eruption of the mountain," described as "exhibiting an appalling effect of sublime conflagration and stupendous destruction."

This display was accompanied by patriotic tunes, including Star Spangled Banner and Hail Columbia, keeping the focus on American nationalism, even while the scene depicted was Italian. This "Magnificent Spectacle of Mount Vesuvius, with its Terrific Eruption" was comparable to many others presented across the United States, including the "grand, electrical" Mount Etna presented at Vauxhall in New York with its "mountains and vollies of fire," and the "Splendid Fete" at Vauxhall in Boston including a depiction of Mount Etna.[50]

Even as advances were being made in the science of fireworks technology, efforts were made on the part of the proprietors to assure patrons that such displays were not frivolous or deviating from the simple and innocent ideals the gardens initially embodied. An advertisement for

Columbia Gardens in Baltimore stated clearly that fireworks should be considered "instructional" and so should be "encouraged in a country like this," as they "excite a thirst for scientific knowledge" while not "injuring the morals of youth."[51] Even as the exhibits and entertainments became more technologically sophisticated, assurances that they remained educational, moral, and appropriate for the rural setting continued to be posted. In doing so, the proprietors of the gardens were able to introduce such technologies while maintaining the illusion of simplicity and morality associated with the rural ideal and the pleasure gardens more generally.

This balance between simplicity and technology, and between nostalgia and innovation, continued through the advertising of the various gardens, and increasingly novel entertainments began to be added to the program. Periodically, the gardens would be selected to exhibit and demonstrate such inventions as the "velocipede" (an early bicycle), "grand automaton Lilliputian figures," and an automated "Falls of Niagara," and attempts were continually made to frame such exhibits as being productive and morally sound.[52] Balloons and parachutes were one of the more commonly exhibited inventions, appearing at many gardens along the east coast, from Boston to Charleston, South Carolina.

In some cases, simply the inflation of the balloon was a spectacle to many, with patrons arriving in droves to witness the marvel (and riots emerged from such displays at Philadelphia and New York in part due to the sheer number of people there, discussed in chapter 3). People such as Michel Guille, Mr. Guerin, and Mr. Humbert advertised such ascents at Vauxhall (New York), Washington Gardens (Boston), Columbia Gardens (Baltimore), and Vauxhall (Philadelphia), while other venues even offered patrons the opportunity to go up in the balloon themselves (for a fee, of course).[53] Pitched as "experiments," advertisements emphasized the scientific nature of such exploits, and Mr. Humbert's experiment was advertised with such specifics as "36 feet in circumference" and "inflated on Montgolfier system." Additional details such as "the balloons will be divided in the colors of our country, and in its ascent will wave the flags, eagle and stripes," and transparencies of various generals being hung from the second balloon allowed these "experiments" to have strong nationalistic overtones.[54] Rides in balloons were pitched as providing "restoration of health" and views of "landscapes" and "views" (again allowing their benefits and ties to nature being emphasized, rather than novelty, technology, or thrills). In allowing patrons to witness balloon ascents, view the balloon close up, and, potentially, go up in a balloon themselves, displays such as these allowed patrons to get close to such technological innovations and embrace a personal connection to such features within the setting of a garden—these balloons were not yet another noisy, smog-causing, labor-eliminating symptom of industrial progress, but rather a marvel to be enjoyed in a pastoral setting with no hint of immorality or corruption.

While balloon ascensions were a popular feature of many pleasure gardens across the globe (and not just in the United States), I hold that these displays of a new technology served a different function in the American gardens, as the sites were not just a convenient location for such displays and rides (though they certainly were selected in part as a matter of convenience given that they were among the often limited open spaces within many cities), but they helped to allow such marvels be enveloped within the idea of rural simplicity, allaying fears of corruption, vice, and progress for progress' sake. Simultaneously, they encouraged citizens to embrace technological developments as part of American identity. An explicit introduction of inventions and technological advances were introduced to the gardens through the American Institute Fairs, which were held at various pleasure gardens in New York, and these fairs mark the years in which levels of technology in the gardens (for entertainment and practical use) reached their peak, and also marked the beginning of the decline of the popularity of these gardens, as world's fairs, expositions, amusement parks, and public parks replaced the various functions of the pleasure gardens.[55]

Pleasure gardens served an important function: providing an urban population with the rural setting so crucial to evolving American identities. These gardens provided a pseudo-rural forum in which new technology could be introduced in a manner that maintained the centrality of the pastoral and assured citizens of the morality of such developments, by allowing the two to interact in a rural-yet-urban space, all the while assuring patrons of both the innocent and progressive nature of such exhibits. It was the reassurance of patrons that such exhibits were in keeping with the rural ideal at the heart of Early American patriotism through asserting both patriotic sentiments and rural simplicity that led to pleasure gardens serving such an important role by allowing patrons to interact with technology.

The pleasure gardens did more than provide an inert space in which patrons might interact with technological developments—the stage provided by pleasure gardens was one that allowed for performances of innocent and chaste amusement to take place against a rural and serene backdrop. The proprietors of the various gardens carefully constructed rural settings in urban locations and used name choices and descriptive terms to support this construction. Despite the inherent fiction of these pseudo-rural spaces, they did present patrons with "safe" spaces in which to identify with rural ideals. It was in these spaces that technological advancements were slowly introduced. This interaction allowed multiple (superficially contradictory) identities to be performed and embraced concurrently by patrons.

At the turn of the century, America was transforming from an agricultural nation that imported many of its manufactured goods to an independent nation encouraging the growth of American industry. As John Frick notes in his article on the Palace Gardens of New York, the country was making "the inexorable transition from a rural, agrarian, pre-modern society to an urban, industrial, modern one," and the pleasure gardens are an interesting participant in this development, as they often existed quite literally on the cusp between the two—the rural setting immediately adjacent to the commercial center.[56] The physical location of these gardens betrayed issues of conflicting national identities in terms of economic and social change.

Yet the tension between the country and the city was just one conversation taking place within the (often unconscious) discussion regarding what it meant to be American; in chapter 3, I turn my attention to changing understandings of class relations that were undergoing a similarly seismic shift.

3. Performing Class: The Challenge to and Reaffirmation of Class Divisions and Hierarchies

> People of all conditions mix in friendly, pleasing society, walk under the same magnificent arch of Heaven, and sit down in the blooming lap of maternal Nature: the rich and the poor meet in the same tranquil shade, like the oaks and willows: and the lovely free-born daughters of America, whether in silk or homespun, croud [sic] the gay parterre, like the tulips and the lilies of the valley.[1]

On the Fourth of July 1817, playwright and politician James Nelson Barker delivered a speech in Vauxhall, Philadelphia, addressing the role of class in American society. He argued that America is not and should not be defined politically by a class structure, and refuted the need for a hierarchy in which people foist themselves to a position of superiority at the expense of those below. He knew class to be an inescapable element of American society, arguing that any civil society "will naturally divide itself into classes," but what makes America particularly enviable, in his view, was not its lack of class divisions ("which our enemies have falsely imputed to us") but America's lack of a hierarchical class structure (especially on a political level).[2] It was clear to Barker that democracy and the ideals important to the new nation did not mean absolute equality, but rather political equality, and that this could be gained even in a society divided into classes with different (often competing) goals. However, class conflicts and tensions were present, and they were to erupt in violence and bloodshed at the very site of Barker's oration in Vauxhall, Philadelphia, just two years later, with a riot resulting from social exclusion leading to the destruction of the grounds. Class divisions and perceptions were not as stable or inert as Barker (and others) believed or hoped, and the site in which he stood was one of many pleasure gardens in which the limits of equality and class were tested.

The Vauxhall of London has often been characterized as a place accessible to all levels of society, with the gardens allowing for social mixing between the various personages there—from the Prince of Wales to prostitutes, and everyone between. Although the degree of this social mixing may not have been as extensive as once thought, the possibility of social inclusion was much admired within England and has been repeatedly cited.[3] Given this popular understanding of the English gardens, it may not seem surprising that Americans adopted this "democratic" form of entertainment; if America was indeed fostering a society in which all classes could mingle without distinction or prejudice, the pleasure garden ought to be the ideal space in which to see it realized. The opening epigraph confirms that the idea of social equality was perceived within the American venues in their infancy.

However, pleasure gardens in America fell far short of this egalitarian ideal. Despite the suggestion in the above epigraph that people of all classes were able to socialize in "friendly, pleasing society," American pleasure gardens were infused with clear class distinctions that reaffirmed hierarchies of class. Further, far from being sites of peaceful union between social classes in the "blooming lap of maternal nature," pleasure gardens became the focus of class tensions and disputes. Initially presented as genteel spaces for the middling sorts, proprietors granted almost everyone access while also asserting ideas of exclusivity. As this social experiment began to show signs of failure, managers instilled increasingly strict rules and codes of conduct in an attempt to secure an elite audience and to exclude those not performing as they "should." In turn, this led to unrest, discontent, and ultimately violence and rioting at several of the pleasure gardens. In this chapter, I argue that while the pleasure gardens appeared to present a classless space to which all were welcome, they in fact presented a venue in which patrons were encouraged to "perform" class through displays of gentility. While some proprietors fostered these performances, believing "equality" could be realized within their sites, most ultimately introduced measures that led to class divisions and tensions, reaffirming hierarchies of class in doing so. In addition, these performances should ultimately be deemed failed performances as they were read by observers as unpersuasive constructions. Class, it will be seen, was an ever-present feature of American identities during this period that played out within the pleasure gardens in distinct ways through the behavior of proprietors and patrons alike.

Democracy and equality, and the relation of these ideas to class structure have been and continue to be important and persistent topics of debate in discussions of post-revolutionary America. The myth of an American society without class divisions has been an enduring one. The early-nineteenth-century Scottish travel writer James Flint identified America as not being "divided or formed into classes by the distinctions of title and rank;"[4] the scholar Garrett described antebellum New York as lacking "a rigid social structure," instead presenting "a classless society" in which "all but the extremes of the two ends mixed freely;"[5] and the historian Joyce Appleby describes "a social homogeneity in which Americans began to take pride" after the Revolution.[6] The concept of a "classless society" with a "social homogeneity" was a popular idea that continues to be associated with the founding of the United States, despite its obvious falsehood. As Barker observed, class structures exist in all societies, and antebellum America was no exception. The "equality" that is often cited in relation to class in antebellum America refers not so much to equality of class status, but variously to the idea of perceived political equality, and, more importantly, to the idea of equality of *access* to class status.

Class divisions existed, but they were not seen as fixed, inevitable, or determined by birth. Instead, class was an active process in this new society, which embraced social mobility and sought to further social advancement by distinction through industry, behavior, and self-presentation. An awareness of how one dressed and behaved, and where one was seen could potentially determine social status, as these markers of class could be adopted. As ideas of gentility became demystified, it became possible to behave appropriately and adopt the appearance of persons of a higher class and thus "perform" as though of a different status through dress, manners, taste, etc., with the implication being that the performance was sufficient—class was concerned with behavior and wealth, and not birth. Citizens of the new nation were able to test the limits of class status and their position within American society through such behavior, and the pleasure gardens were a public space that actively encouraged and supported such performances.

Richard Bushman calls this phenomenon a "vernacular gentility," and identifies it as emerging in the late eighteenth and early nineteenth centuries, with outward markers of respectability being adopted by "middling people."[7] A heightened self-awareness was part of this development, which saw people who were not previously identified as being "genteel" turning their attentions to their appearance and actions with the aim of capitalizing on the possibilities of social mobility. Bushman argues that class was not fixed at this time for the middle section of society, and that concerns of class and perceived status were constantly being renegotiated by such individuals. He suggests that an awareness of one's class through behavior, dress, and other manifestations of taste was at the forefront in defining one's identity in America in this period. This concept of class as performance was clearly seen within pleasure gardens. In order to embrace the ideal of social mobility, proprietors presented the "middling sorts" with a space in which they could perform as though of a higher class status. Through a combination of the cost of admission, entertainments offered, and advertising strategies, owners and managers targeted mechanics, artisans, petty merchants, shopkeepers, and tradesmen (a mix of skilled manual and nonmanual tradesmen), and offered them access to a forum for class performance.[8]

Pleasure gardens were neither the cheapest nor the most expensive form of entertainment available to city dwellers during the summer months. The average price for entry to a pleasure garden was about 50 cents, allowing all but the lowest earners to patronize the gardens with relative frequency.[9] It was through considering admission rates carefully that proprietors were able to position their venues as both exclusive and affordable. In most cities, pleasure gardens were only one of a number of popular entertainments available during the summer months. In the summer of 1820, potential patrons would have been able to select from a wide range of amusements in Boston, for example. One could see an exhibit of wax figures, a demonstration of a "pondrometer" (an extravagant scale for weighing people), or hear music (each being 25 cents), see transparencies, paintings, and a panorama (also 25 cents), go swimming in seawater at Canal Bridge (25 cents for warm water, 12.5 cents for cold), or marvel at "Hindoos perform[ing] deceptions, optical delusions, etc, & wonderful feats of Strength and Activity" at the exhibition hall (also 25 cents).[10] On the opposite end of the spectrum, "select oratorios" could be heard at Boylston hall for $1.[11] That same summer, Boston's Washington Gardens was charging the national average of 50 cents and thus was more expensive than most popular entertainments, but less expensive than the most exclusive and costly events available in the summer.[12] Pleasure gardens thus occupied a middle ground, catering to neither the lowest nor the highest classes but rather for the portion of the expanding middle with an interest in social mobility and advancement.[13] The gardens were presented as a space elevated above more plebian entertainment venues but were still within the economic reach of much of the middling sorts.

In order for the space of the pleasure gardens to appeal to the "middling sorts" who sought social advancement through performance, marginally higher admission prices were not sufficient—the space had to be presented as genteel and appropriate as a site for the performance of gentility. Proprietors achieved this goal through printing advertisements that assured patrons the gardens were genteel, tapping into associations with the rural ideal in an urban setting (as discussed in chapter 2) through activities in the gardens, inviting women and families to attend in order to present the site as respectable, and enforcing rules and codes of conduct. This genteel space appealed to the "middling sorts" and their aspirations of social advancement and, in turn, encouraged an emulation of elite "behavior and cultural predilections."[14]

Much advertising for the pleasure gardens consisted of declarations and assertions of the genteel nature of the gardens, including reassurances that the gardens were "respectable and fit places of resort for the best classes of society," attended only by those seeking a "rational, elegant, and instructive species of entertainment."[15] The advertisements betray a concern with appealing to a genteel audience through specific descriptions (stated as directly as "no ungenteel people") and through affirmations of the fashionable nature of the sites (with Niblo's Garden being described as being the "resort of the *bon ton*").[16] Of course, claims of being genteel should not be taken at face value, but they do suggest an attempt to present the gardens as refined and respectable venues, suited to those of taste.

The association of the various sites with the rural idyll was an element seen in the activities at and portrayals of many of the gardens. As discussed in chapter 2, the gardens literally brought the country into the city and embodied the tension between rural and urban. Descriptions of the gardens as possessing "rural beauties" (Harrowgate) or providing "a partial retreat from the noise of the town" (Gray's/Chatsworth) were common descriptors;[17] the "rural and picturesque" McArann's Garden boasted "rural charms" and provided patrons the opportunity to "enjoy rural life," while Easton's of Baltimore provided a retreat "from the heat and fatigues of the day."[18] The idea of the countryside as being an honest and pure space of leisure was frequently drawn upon and directly related to the gardens. Commentators on Gray's Ferry in Philadelphia emphasized the moral and respectable nature of such spaces by noting that a "love of beautiful Nature softens, refines, and elevates the human mind" and that "even rude minds are harmonized by the genius of the place."[19] Respectability was repeatedly assured through persistent reminders of the rural nature of the venues and of the benefits this might provide patrons through association.

Entertainment venues could also position themselves as respectable through having a positive impact on society, whether that be through the nature of the presentations, the conduct enforced there, or more tangible charitable outcomes. The various gardens adopted a number of tactics to appear as such, ranging from benefit events (such as Washington Gardens hosting a benefit following a fire at Petersburgh in 1815) to descriptions in advertisements (such as Niblo's claim that a performance was "chaste").[20] Other commentators also saw fit to highlight the moral nature of these spaces in a variety of newspaper columns, describing the gardens as instrumental in "avoiding immoral behavior," for example.[21] In order to distance Columbia Gardens from accusations of frivolity, a lengthy advertisement was placed that noted how fireworks are not injurious to morals in the slightest and should rather be considered to be instructional.[22]

The advertised presence of women in the gardens was another method employed by the proprietors, and direct appeals were made to women through advertisements, descriptions, and events. With the exception of the very early years of Columbia Gardens, Baltimore, and Vauxhall, Charleston, and the late years of Vauxhall, New York, men were the managers and owners of the gardens, yet the association of the gardens with the "fairer sex" was important to their success. The Vauxhall in Charleston specified having a designated area for women, while Washington Gardens announced in 1815 that they could accommodate "both sexes," and opened a "Ladies SODA Room" in 1819.[23] Vauxhall, New York, presented a fireworks exhibit aimed specifically at women; the "Temple of Love" of 1801 was described as an event suitable for "the Ladies of this city," with tickets (six shillings) admitting one gentleman and "as many women as he thinks proper."[24] Niblo's also encouraged active participation by women in its early years; the exhibit of 1839 was prefaced with invitations for women to submit flowers to be displayed.[25]

However, even in these overt instances of inviting women to the gardens, or highlighting their presence, advertisements made it explicit that women could not be admitted to the gardens if not accompanied by at least one man.[26] Much like the London Vauxhall, prostitution appears to have been a constant threat to the reputation of various pleasure gardens in America, and most proprietors took steps to exclude such women. The refusal to admit "unescorted women" and the employment of surveillance were common to many of the gardens, including the Vauxhall of Philadelphia, various New York Vauxhalls, and Washington Gardens, Boston, and these efforts apparently met with moderate success. Delacroix and Niblo, in particular, were "consistently praised for their ability to exclude 'women of pleasure' from their gardens."²⁷ While women were encouraged to attend the space in order to present the activities there as being genteel, "women of pleasure" were not, for the same reason.

It was not merely women accompanied by a partner who were actively invited to the gardens, but whole families. By offering half price admission to children, many of the gardens expressed a desire to welcome the family unit to their sites in order to promote an image of respectability. Rural Felicity/Easton's openly invited families in 1801 and 1802, while Washington Gardens (Boston), McArann's Garden (Philadelphia), and Columbia Gardens (Baltimore) advertised half-price tickets for children.²⁸ Some gardens, such as Niblo's Garden, Vauxhall (New York), and Vauxhall (Charleston) extended a similar admission policy for children in tandem with events designed specifically for families and/or children, hosting the "Chinese Lady," a balloon ascent, and a "Theatre Picturesque and Mechanique," respectively.²⁹ Unaccompanied children, however, were prohibited by many of the sites, with Washington Gardens and Vauxhall, Charleston, being very explicit about such a policy.³⁰ It was the complete family unit that was sought in order to present an appearance of respectability and gentility.

These various policies designed to actively encourage families were part of the goal of creating the impression of a respectable space, elevated above the plebian entertainments found at taverns and similar resorts. The proprietors of the various gardens appeared to be catering to a demand for respectable entertainment, untroubled by concerns of "prostitutes, drunkards, noisy spectators, and occasional riots, as well as risqué spectacles."³¹ At the turn of the century, pleasure gardens were addressing a then-emergent desire of the "middling sorts" for "chaste entertainment," which "exclude[ed] prostitutes and liquor and encourage[ed] family attendance" in a manner that preempted the "minor revolution" which Bruce McConachie identifies as extending to the theatres in many American cities after 1845.³² The "genteel" space created by the gardens was utilized in this manner as a way of performing gentility.

The ability to enter this space of gentility was made all the more distinct through the delineation of the grounds. The pleasure gardens were not typically marked by hedges or low borders, but rather with high wooden fences designed to prevent outside spectators from looking in. As can be seen in figures 3.1 and 3.2, McArann's Garden and Vauxhall (both in Philadelphia) were surrounded by tall wooden fences designed to prevent onlookers. Similarly, Vauxhall in New York was depicted from the outside showing restricted views and tree tops (figure 3.3). The solitary Boston

Figure 3.1 McArans [sic] Garden, 1840. David J. Kennedy watercolors [V61], K: 3–22a, Historical Society of Pennsylvania.

Figure 3.2 Vauxhall, Philadelphia. *Vauxhall Garden at Northeast Corner of Broad and Walnut Streets.* David J. Kennedy watercolors [V61], K: 7–33, Historical Society of Pennsylvania.

pleasure garden also displays a concern with defined space and carefully delineated borders. As the map in figure 3.4 illustrates, Washington Gardens were immediately adjacent to Boston Common; due to the topography, visitors to the Common would have overlooked patrons of the pleasure garden thus making the distinction between the paying patrons of the gardens and the visitors to the public, free commons apparent. By having a

Figure 3.3 Vauxhall, New York. *Vauxhall Garden and Theatre, and Cook's Circus*. Prints (visual works) of New York City Theatres (TCS 54). Harvard Theatre Collection, Houghton Library, Harvard University.

distinct, clearly marked space, it was clear if one gained entry or not—one was in or out; one was genteel or not.

Initially, these spaces encouraged an inclusiveness that allowed anyone who could pay the admission charge and was prepared to ape gentility to gain entry and to perform within the space. These sites appealed to a very broad conception of the "middle," even allowing those who could not afford to pay to gain admission on specific days; in some of the gardens, there were days when there was no admission charge, which speaks to an encouragement of an inclusive gentility embracing a wider segment of the population than the already large "middle." For example, Harrowgate and Vauxhall, New York, opened for free on Sundays.[33] For a time, Delacroix even permitted free entry every day of the week on which scheduled entertainments were not to take place (that is, music might be offered, but not a formal concert or fireworks). Perhaps subscribing to the promotion of a "homogeneous" society, Delacroix wanted his gardens to be open to all. In this example, there was an active pursuit of the concept of social mobility in Delacroix's policies and a demonstration of an understanding that people of all backgrounds and income levels could socialize in the same space.

However, as these "performances" in public spaces attempted to blur and cross class divisions though physical displays, they simultaneously led to the reinforcement of class divisions. Far from being venues that

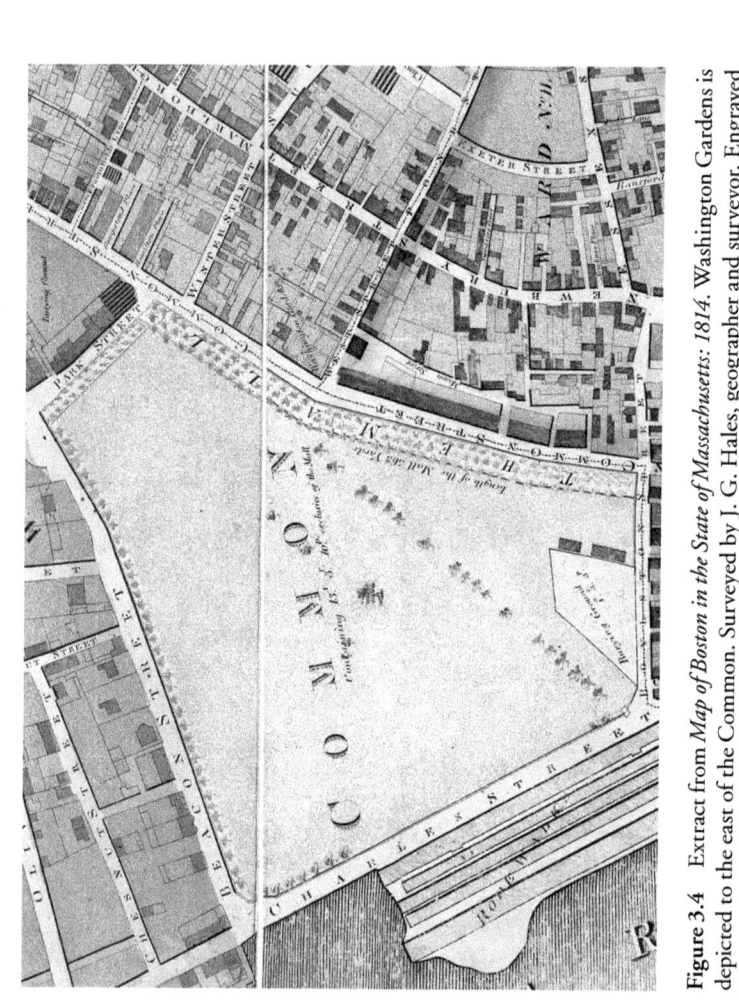

Figure 3.4 Extract from *Map of Boston in the State of Massachusetts: 1814*. Washington Gardens is depicted to the east of the Common. Surveyed by J. G. Hales, geographer and surveyor. Engraved by T. Wightman Jr. Library of Congress, Geography and Map Division.

allowed for the erasure of class distinctions, the pleasure gardens played a role in the renegotiation and ultimate reaffirmation of class lines. When Delacroix waived an admission fee, he permitted entry to "the public in general," but only if "decently dressed."[34] By requiring certain standards of dress, proprietors such as Delacroix (Vauxhall) and Esterly (Harrowgate) were apparently open to promoting or experimenting with a society in which almost all were welcome to socialize in the same space (even if not on the same days), but only with the caveat that all at least aspire to a "vernacular gentility" and to perform appropriate class when in attendance.[35]

This process of cultural stratification and the use of cultural forms to back up class divisions is addressed by Lawrence Levine in his *Highbrow/Lowbrow*. Levine identifies three methods the elite employed in attempting to elevate and define themselves as the superior and distinct class: "retreat[ing] into their own private spaces...transform[ing] public spaces by rules, systems of taste, and canons of behavior...[and] convert[ing] the strangers so that their own modes of behavior and cultural predilections emulated those of the elites."[36] These various tactics allowed for the implementation of cultural elitism and the clarification of class divisions through cultural forms. Levine identifies these tactics as leading to a cultural bifurcation which took place from the 1830s, with divisions being seen between the categories of "highbrow" and "lowbrow." The former was seen as exclusive cultural forms reserved for the elite, and the latter as the popular forms open to and created by the masses.

Indeed, while apparently believing in the philosophy that all could be socially ascendant and attempting to include all segments of the population, proprietors also required patrons to submit to the understanding that genteel behavior was inherently superior. Merely through encouraging and providing the space for the performance of genteel behavior and manners, proprietors were deploying an unconscious tactic of the elite—by desiring to perform as though elite, the "middling sorts" were reaffirming the superiority of the elite. Some of the methods of defining and elevating elite status identified by Levine were seen here in the encouragement to copy elite "modes of behavior and cultural predilections," which were enforced through the continued implementation of "canons of behavior."[37] While it appears that making the site inclusive was a benevolent act imbued with ideals of social equality, the desire of visitors to be in the space and to be able to perform according to the dictates of genteel conduct paradoxically reasserted values associated with class divisions and demonstrated the operations of hegemony.

In view of the apparent inclusiveness of the gardens (and the consequent lack of true elite status being gained due to this openness), segments of the middling sorts who were in the gardens sought new ways to assert their superiority over others. In many of the gardens, the performance of class was not merely to be seen in attending the gardens (or not), but also in the use of the space within the gardens and the performance of class relative to others. Initially, all the pleasure gardens offered simple entertainments with few (or no) restricted areas or places requiring additional charges or requirements to enter. Once patrons had paid the fixed admission price, all were free to circulate in the same areas (at least, in theory). However, with the introduction of theatres and saloons to several of the gardens, admission prices began to vary depending on the position of seating, with Washington Gardens and Vauxhall, New York, for example, advertising more than one rate of admission in local newspapers.[38] In 1820, the theatre at Washington Gardens had tiered admission costs, ranging from 25 cents to $1. Patrons were placed in a position relative to others who had paid more or less than them. This tiered entry cost reflected the practices of theatre in relating seating position to the price paid and thus allowed for a visible arrangement of relative wealth or status within the auditorium. With the introduction of a charge above the standard 50 cents garden entry fee, the gardens allowed for a performance of class not only through individuals entering a genteel space, but also through the physical positioning of patrons relative to one another.

This inclusivity which allowed almost anyone to perform above their station, having led to stratification of the performance of class, then morphed into an attempt at exclusivity—a feature described by Burrows and Wallace as the "key to success" for the gardens.[39] In order to present the venue as more "exclusive," further changes had to be made. In New York, Delacroix modified his admission policies in 1803 when he introduced a "refreshment ticket" that required all patrons to spend two shillings to enter the gardens on days without entertainments (having been formerly able to enter for free), then allowing them to redeem the ticket for refreshments to that value inside the gardens.[40] While Delacroix notes that part of his motivation to introduce such a ticket was to ensure a return on his investment in the site by requiring patrons to purchase refreshments, the majority of his announcement is concerned with the "genteel" nature of some (but not all) of the patrons he had been hosting. Delacroix veers away from the idea that class could be performed through outward shows when he realizes that many who were "genteely dressed... were not genteel in character, [and] therefore not suited to the chief part of the company who frequented his gardens."[41] Delacroix concludes that an outward show of gentility through dress was not sufficient to allow a person to pass as being genteel, deviating from his earlier position. In order to assert a degree of exclusivity, he reintroduces the dividing line of price, enforcing a "refreshment ticket" on most days. How could his garden be perceived as being genteel if "every person has an indistinct right of entrance," he protested.

As admission requirements increased, Delacroix sought to make his Vauxhall a more exclusive venue, and while this pattern of gradual transition toward increased exclusivity was the norm among American pleasure gardens, other gardens aimed to provide an exclusive alternative from their very inception, including one of Vauxhall's main competitors—Niblo's Garden. As Burrows and Wallace note, "after 1830 the upper classes deserted the déclassé Vauxhall and turned to William Niblo's new concern," which was noted as surpassing "all others in elegance and respectability, its status sustained by high entrance fees, expensive food, and urbane entertainments."[42]

Paul Gilje asks how affluent theatre patrons of the early nineteenth century were to "enjoy their moments of high culture without being exposed to the low humor of the poorer classes? The answer," he continues, "was the establishment of different theatres catering to different classes," which became apparent in the 1820s and 1830s.[43] This process was also seen in the gardens of New York, with the establishment of Niblo's Garden drawing the upper classes from Vauxhall to a new location. An instance of the elite "retreat[ing] into their own private spaces," Niblo's presented a space for those trying to define and establish themselves as being elite and distinct from the "middling sorts," allowing them to engage with one another in a space perceived as being genteel, but apart from the masses.[44] In his attempt to distinguish his gardens from the others (including Vauxhall), Niblo incorporated a cultural form that had been adopted as a sign of a high-class status—opera. As McConachie argues in relation to this cultural form, the "rituals of operagoing that assisted in preserving and perpetuating the power of their class" allowed the elite to determine "membership in the fashionable elite" through appropriate behavior at designated sites.[45] For Niblo, however, the mere introduction of opera was not sufficient to gain a more exclusive or upper middle class clientele, and in his attempt to maintain this target audience, he found it necessary to remove most of the traces of the pleasure garden by eliminating much of the garden and its outdoor elements when he renovated the site in 1849 (while presenting his operas at Astor Place).

These class divisions were not only reflected in the entertainments, but also in the geography, which further enforced this physical "retreat to...private spaces." As the novelist and journalist Maria Child noted, "being in the Bowery, [Vauxhall] is out of the walk of fashionables, who probably ignore its existence, as they do most places for the entertainment of the people at large,"[46] and her contemporary, Asa Greene, similarly identified the separation, noting that it "is so vulgar...to be seen walking in the same grounds with mechanics, house servants, and laboring people."[47] Niblo's Garden boasted a more fashionable location distinctly distanced from other venues. The attitudes betrayed in these sources (along with newspaper commentaries and contemporary histories) reveal that there was a physical as well as cultural "retreat" from the more accessible gardens frequented by the large "middle." Yet Niblo's was unable to retain its upper middle or elite status as a pleasure garden, and the outdoor elements were quickly removed, becoming primarily a theatre and hotel.

Levine identifies a cultural bifurcation taking place from the 1830s that saw culture being divided along class lines. The pleasure gardens seemed poised to become a highbrow venue open only to the upper middle classes or even the elite, with Niblo's demonstrating this potential most clearly. However, despite some attempts to restrict access, raise admission costs, and change entertainments, the pleasure gardens were not able to achieve the highbrow status of, for example, opera. Although many of the gardens did display concerns with gentility and made attempts to be exclusive, their increasingly restrictive admission policies and attempts to regulate behavior according to genteel codes ultimately failed, leading in turn to resentment and even violence, and this prevented them from becoming highbrow venues.

These attempts to become exclusive—as seen particularly in New York—were not especially successful, and the pleasure gardens came to be viewed as places "for the entertainment of the people at large."[48] The higher end of the "middling sorts" found their genteel space compromised by inappropriate behavior, while the lower end resented the restrictions presented by the imposition of codes of conduct. These class tensions over the status and accessibility of the space were to erupt at numerous sites in the form of violent riots, which led to the destruction of the grounds of at least four venues. Despite being primed to become highbrow venues through their focus on gentility, the pleasure gardens ultimately became lowbrow sites.

After just a few years, many proprietors had problems with vandalism, theft, and "boisterous" behavior, which made it difficult for them to maintain a genteel space. In Baltimore, for example, the destruction and theft of the lamps at Gray's was reported in 1794, along with several "disturbances" of the peace in 1794 and 1795. Perhaps a more common problem at many of the sites was pickpocketting, with numerous newspaper announcements requesting the return of items stolen from persons at the gardens in Philadelphia and New York, among others.

Attempts were made to regulate this behavior or to exclude the persons responsible through a variety of policies. The introduction of "officers" or constables was the most frequent practice, with Gray's Gardens of Baltimore posting notices of such supervision from 1796, Vauxhall of New York from 1799, Washington Gardens of Boston from 1814, and Columbia Gardens of Baltimore from 1832.[49] Alexandre Placide (manager of the Vauxhall in Charleston) prohibited unaccompanied children from 1809, as he apparently considered them to be the chief culprits of vandalism, and he also implored patrons not to touch the plants.[50] Few copies of the official rules and regulations of each of the gardens are extant (where they even existed), but the principal Vauxhall of New York maintained such a document that was posted in the gardens and was noted in a newspaper in 1826.[51] Within these rules, fines for picking flowers (four shillings), procedures for ejecting unruly persons from the gardens, and the charges for breaking or damaging glasses or ornaments are listed, suggesting that such problems did emerge. Policies were also introduced that reassured patrons that employees would behave appropriately, and Gray's Gardens of Baltimore introduced identification numbers for the waiters in 1796 after some had apparently failed to return with change for purchases.[52]

In these various manners, proprietors attempted to regulate behavior within the space of the gardens in order to maintain order and respectability (mostly excluding those who could not or would not conform), transforming their space through rules. However, even the most successful gardens failed to sustain a genteel space free from the "undesirable element," and attempts to exclude persons through cost led to individuals causing or participating in riots over exclusion. The utopian ideal of all mixing in one space being replaced with attempts at exclusivity backfired at many points in the various careers of the gardens, but for many gardens, it was a riot caused by the exclusion of those perceived to be of the lower middle classes who had previously been granted the right of admission that marked the peak of this problem.

Riots erupted in the gardens in Philadelphia (Gray's and Vauxhall), New York (Vauxhall), and Baltimore (Columbia Gardens), and where the cause is known, the exclusion of certain persons through erecting barriers or increasing admission fee is the most prevalent reason. In Philadelphia, for example, the two documented riots transpired due to people desiring to gain entry without paying. At Gray's Ferry in 1791, a "disturbance" occurred when several people gained admission without paying the required admission fee and were met with opposition from those who had paid.

According to a report in a local newspaper, several people entered the gardens on the Fourth of July, 1791, in order to join the Independence Day celebrations without paying. After being ejected from the gardens by the constables, they "communicated their vindictive sentiments, on account of this treatment, to a number without the garden, who made a forcible attack with stones and clubs upon the door-keepers, and pulled down several fences and palings." Those inside the gardens are then described as "fighting for the right which their quarter of a dollar had purchased" by helping to force the offenders out of the gardens and returning the volley of stones and missiles. The fight (described as a "contest") ended without loss of life, but with "hard knocks on both sides, and much injury to the house and gardens."[53]

The riot at the Vauxhall of Philadelphia arose from a similar instance of exclusion of individuals from a popular event. On 8 September 1819, Monsieur Michel was scheduled to make a balloon ascent and parachute jump, and ticket prices were raised to one dollar. Although many people paid the admission charge, an even larger number (estimated at 30 thousand) assembled in the "vacant lots and fields all around the resort."[54] Those who were watching from outside the gardens were not able to see everything as "a high board fence enclosed Vauxhall Garden." When a young boy climbed up on the fence to get a better view, reports held that he was "struck by an attendant of the garden" and was rumored to have been killed. The response was initially muted: the balloon was damaged with stones, but the event continued on. The inflation of the balloon took much longer than anticipated (due to the damage inflicted by a stone), and tempers continued to rise as three or more hours passed. Eventually "the unruly mass went forward in a determined manner, tearing down the fence, ripping the balloon to shreds, sacking the wines and liquors in the garden"; they "threw stones, broke and tore everything with the balloon to pieces" and "complet[ed] the ruin by setting fire to the pavilion or theatre."[55]

The focus of rioters on removing fences in order to gain access has ties to other instances of fence and hedge destruction. As Gilje identifies, as the city of New York (the focus of his study) expanded north, lands that had once been used by anyone without charge began to be sold and fenced off, and the once-free lands became private property. This led to resentment, which culminated in the destruction of fences and hedges on numerous occasions.[56] The reaction to exclusion of persons from enclosed lands for the use by the wealthy can be seen in the riots described above, where predominantly green space was fenced off and required payment and codes of conduct and dress to enter—the exclusion was no less real in the pleasure gardens than in the fencing off of common lands. Having been first invited into the gardens, the crowds resented the various policies of exclusion and, in some cases, took action and protested by tearing down fences.

Not only did the gardens initially encourage individuals of lower social classes to participate in a cultural form that presented itself as genteel, but the political scene was one that encouraged the belief in social equality. By retracting this superficial equality, the gardens became the focus for riot, and this reaction against exclusivity ultimately led to the decline of the fashionable nature and highbrow aspirations of the gardens, as the lower classes claimed the gardens for themselves. After such tensions, the gardens and the form they took (in terms of entertainments offered and the types of acceptable behaviors) switched from focusing on exclusivity and highbrow claims to a decidedly more popular and lowbrow appeal. Embracing this change (or, perhaps, forced to for economic reasons), proprietors introduced changes to the offerings of their gardens, presenting minstrelsy, variety acts, magicians, etc.

In 1802, for example, Columbia Gardens (then called Easton's Garden) offered fireworks, ice cream, and suppers. By 1805, mechanical representations of battles, songs (including one titled "the Learned Pig"), a ballet dance, a pageant, a hornpipe, and a "concert on the clarinet" were offered on one night.[57] McArann's Garden in Philadelphia opened with a focus on the plantings and the occasional concert, but by 1840 was offering an enactment of the eruption of Mount Vesuvius, fireworks, minstrel performances, illuminations, and a concert on one night.[58] Delacroix's early Vauxhalls offered evenings with simple concerts, fireworks, and refreshments, but by 1845, the gardens hosted minstrel performers, "the wonderful tattooed man," dancers, singers, and other variety acts, which were described as having "caught the attention of the Bowery people, who attend...in great numbers."[59] In tandem with the switch from simple entertainments of music, fireworks, and refreshments to increasingly diverse and popular acts, the admission price of several venues fell from 50 cents to just 25 cents. Niblo's Garden, McArann's Garden, Columbia Gardens, and Vauxhall, New York, all illustrated a drop in admission price that coincided with the change in entertainment types.

This change from highbrow to lowbrow entertainment and the corresponding change in audience has been described by most commentators in a decidedly negative manner. Eberlein and Hubbard note how "Harrowgate gradually sunk into a state of rowdyism," while Garrett notes Vauxhall as being a victim "of a decline in the quality of patronage" with "the most sensational entertainments...attracting the lowest riffraff or clientele."[60] This use of terms such as "decline" and "sunk" reflects the hierarchy that was (and is) in place that sees popular forms as being decidedly lowbrow and of the lower classes as being inherently less worthy. In actuality, the proprietors of the gardens were not "victims" of "decline," but rather, were embracing their new market. While there was a decline in admission cost (and thus revenue from admission on a per head basis), a degree of success was ensured due to the broad appeal and high rates of attendance (thus maintaining a sizeable income all told).

A shift can be seen toward increasingly eclectic acts with less concert music and opera, and more popular performances (including magic shows, acrobatics, ventriloquism, and impersonations). Although the timing and duration of the shift can be seen to vary, the change to being a lowbrow form was a universally demonstrated pattern. It is in this form that the gardens are most frequently depicted in literature, and these sources suggest that while the gardens were indeed seen as being lowbrow, they simultaneously showed traces of their past as a place where social elevation could be performed. The idea of class as performance, however, is seen as ineffective and is openly mocked.

Chapter 29 of Cornelius Matthews's *The Career of Puffer Hopkins* is set in Vauxhall, New York, where the title character attends a ball organized by the "Round-Rimmers." This fictional society is described as a "fraternity of gentlemen" who are seen as "classical gentry" and have exclusive "haunts of their own," yet occasionally "condescend to join the common world in certain of their observances."[61] In this chapter, they decide to host their complimentary ball at Vauxhall with Puffer Hopkins (described as "an eloquent...and popular politician") being one of two "attractions" in the form of distinguished guests. The (comically) elite men select Vauxhall as a suitable venue to engage with the "commoners," while making it clear that both the site and the persons they are inviting are beneath them.

The guests who attend the ball are described in a manner communicating their ineptitude at performing as though belonging to a higher class. Of their appearances, Hopkins notes that the young ladies are either "red-nosed and flat-breasted" or "of a rounded form," while the men stand "with their arms a-kimbo on their hips." When observing the dancing, he notes how the couples are "throwing out limbs," with gentlemen "thumping the floor with their heels at every descent," and ladies occasionally "losing balance" and dashing "headlong into the ruffles of one of the stationary young gentlemen." Even the speech of the guests (which is described as being "in a dialect which was in a great measure intelligible") is not above ridicule.[62] The overt mockery of the lower classes attempting to perform above their station is implicit in Hopkins' biting words. While being a place where class can be performed, the performances are transparent and thus failures, to be mocked and disdained by the elite.

The gardens as a place of the lower classes aping higher classes and also of romance can be seen in two other literary sources that focus on the antics of Mose and Lize. Mose the Bowery b'hoy and his "gal" Eliza or "Lize" are central figures in both Benjamin Baker's play *A Glance at New York* and Francis A. Durivage's poem "Love in the Bowery."[63] Bowery boys (or "b'hoys") were typically American-born apprentices (often to butchers) and were a New York phenomenon in the 1840s and 1850s.[64] Mose was the stage form of this "type" and was depicted as being a volunteer firefighter, famous for his brawling, loyalty, and his courting of his g'hal, Lize.

The final scene of *A Glance at New York* takes place in Vauxhall, with "arches of variegated lamps" and dancing forming the setting. The scene is short but finds time to gently mock the characters in this supposedly refined space. Lize's attempts to follow proscribed behavior are ridiculed, for example, when she requests "a cup of coffee, and nine doughnuts" for herself, instead of the typical restrained and modest refreshments expected to be consumed.[65] However, despite the light mockery, the gardens are presented as being a relatively refined space where the men behave courteously to women, and at the very end, when Mose is summoned to a fight, the violence is kept outside the gardens. While unable to pass as being of a high-class status, the space is seen to have a refining influence upon the characters—correcting and modifying their behavior to conform to different codes of conduct.

Much like Baker's play, the seven-stanza poem by Durivage identifies Vauxhall as a suitable space for the courting of a Bowery b'hoy and g'hal, while simultaneously finding the time to mock their behavior. After falling in love at first sight with a "gal" while "running" with his fire crew, the narrator of the poem seeks to find her again. His first port of call is "Wauxhall" as the natural place to find a "beautiful" and "lovely" lady. There he spends a "happy, happy evenin'" with his love (apparently so happy, he repeats the line twice), and he gives her "cords of peanuts and a [*sic*] apple."[66] The element of romance and the obligatory consumption of food is noted in both this poem and the play *Glance at New York*, and in both, these romantic performances are mocked. In "Love in the Bowery," the dialect of the narrator coupled with the ending to the tale serve to ridicule the characters of lovers. The narrator misspells words such as "Wauxhall" and pronounces words like "shut" and "recollect" incorrectly ("shet" and "recollex"), and the simplicity of the male character is highlighted throughout. At the end of the poem, the b'hoy learns that she is wedded to another, and he simply "cuss[es] a few" and moves on to another g'hal.

In this play and poem, Vauxhall is portrayed as the backdrop against which central characters court; while Mose is known for his antics and fights, such scenes are confined to the barroom and similar sites, with the garden being kept as a place of romance. While the rural and romantic elements of the gardens are maintained, the class of the focal figures had changed in the New York Vauxhall by the 1840s, and the mockery of the belief that one could perform class becomes apparent. The clear identification of the space as being open to the lower classes but a locale where the performance of genteel behavior is still expected is not presented in any way other than comically transparent, yet the practice continued. Far from being a simple lowbrow space, the gardens were able to retain a sense of social elevation even within the more limited sphere to which they were confined.

The pleasure gardens of America were the focus of class divisions, tensions, and changes. As sites of the performance of class they presented opportunities to indulge the popular belief in social mobility (or elevation) through performance, yet they also confirmed the *status quo* through the very fact that such behaviors were perceived as superior. Although it was possible to perform class to a limited degree, it was not possible for all the middling sorts with social aspirations to be deemed to be part of the elite purely through performance. The elite were ultimately those who defined what that performance was, with the rules becoming more mysterious and specific with time in order to prevent transparency and openness to all. The operations of hegemony were thus very apparent within the gardens.

Although the pleasure gardens initially seemed to embrace the concept of a classless society (and were popularly held to do so in England), they simply did not do this in America, and the operations of class divisions and hierarchies became increasingly pronounced. The tactics of elite self-definition (through retreat, use of codes, and encouragement of imitation) were all deployed within the gardens. This saw them morph from superficially inclusive spaces, to attempts at being exclusive ones, to spaces of the masses with no pretentions to highbrow status, while still reinforcing the superiority of the elite. Many of the gardens became a focal point for class tensions, with conflicts being played out in a very physical and violent manner.

The gardens were spaces in which class concerns were played out through individual performances, but they were also a locus for the performance of other elements of identity; as already discussed, these venues allowed for the exploration of what it meant to be American in terms of a national identity and class. The performance of race and ethnicity was a further aspect of identity seen within the gardens, with the question of how these facets played into the larger national identity being raised. The discussion so far has been largely limited to the discussion of the assumed white (male) American, yet the question of the roles of the African American and Native American were also crucial to the concern of what it meant to be American in the period under discussion here.

4. Performing Race: Native Americans and African Americans Within the Gardens

In 1857, John W. Francis described a performance by Native Americans at Vauxhall, New York, recalling that

> amidst fireworks of dazzling efficacy... [the Osage Indians] yelled the war-whoop and danced the war-dance, while our learned Dr. Mitchell, often present on these occasions, translated their songs for the advancement of Indian literature, and enriched the journals with ethnological science concerning our primitive inhabitants.[1]

In describing this event, Francis was making several assumptions: that the Indians seen on the stage were actual Native Americans of the Osage tribe; that their performance was "authentic" (at least, sufficiently so to be deemed educational); and that the Native American ways of life were relics of the past, or "primitive." These questions of identity, authenticity, and temporal relevance played out within the gardens in the presentation of racial identities and their relation to white American identities. The regulations of the various gardens largely prevented Native Americans and African Americans from being counted among the patrons, and when granted admittance, they were required to perform entertainments onstage or inferiority offstage. Depictions of Native Americans and African Americans within pleasure gardens were constructions that allowed white Americans to define themselves in opposition to them, and these depictions in turn responded to a wider ambiguity about the place these racial groups held in the new nation. In this chapter, I investigate the performance of race both on and off stage within the pleasure gardens and argue that treatment of race in the garden responded to, and contributed to, debates about the role of racial identities within what it meant to be American.

Native Americans were granted access to the pleasure gardens, but only under very particular circumstances and with a view to their consciously performing for white patrons. For example, Vauxhall (New York), Washington Gardens (Boston), and Columbia Gardens (Baltimore) all hosted Native American war dances; Palace Gardens in New York welcomed "Indians from the far West"; and Niblo's Garden was among the many to stage plays with Native American characters, such as Brougham's burlesque *Po-ca-hon-tas*.[2] These various performances are investigated here in terms of how they allowed for and presented Native American identities, and what these proclaimed "authentic performances" contributed to ever-evolving American identities.[3]

African Americans were similarly excluded from pleasure gardens as legitimate patrons.[4] However, they were permitted entry as waiters (in which capacity they played a servile role, as opposed to that of patron), and were represented in the highly artificial form of minstrelsy.[5] Once theatres began to be built in the pleasure gardens and seating could be segregated, African Americans were allowed to be patrons, but only if they sat in designated areas, meaning that in gardens such as Washington Gardens they were allowed a physical presence as patrons, but only if they were willing to perform inferiority.[6] Unlike Native Americans, however, free blacks created pleasure gardens run by and for African Americans, and in New York, there were at least four such gardens: the African Grove (1821), Mead Garden (Manhattan, 1827), Mead Garden (Brooklyn, 1828), and Haytian Retreat (1829). These spaces are explored within this chapter in terms of how they permitted certain forms of typically excluded African American identities to be performed.

In chapter 3, I explored how performances resembling role playing have been seen within the pleasure gardens, focusing on class-inflected dress and conduct. While in this chapter I still acknowledge the performances of white American identities in this manner, I am doing so in relation to highly constructed performances of/by Native Americans and African Americans, including overtly framed performances upon the stage. War dances by Native Americans (genuine and/or impersonations), minstrelsy, and stage types within plays are the main ways in which Native Americans and African Americans were introduced into the principal pleasure gardens, and so their overt performances upon a stage will be considered here in relation to the everyday performance of the patrons.

These staged performances were often billed as being authentic, as in the opening example. Applying this term to some of these performances can be seen to be problematic when the authenticity of the context and, indeed, the performers themselves are brought into question. In the ensuing discussion of performances of/by Native Americans and African Americans, I pay particular attention to what is understood by "real" and "authentic," and the implications for American identities.

NATIVE AMERICANS

Given nineteenth-century associations of Native Americans with untamed wilderness and nature, it is, perhaps, unsurprising that they played a role in the pleasure gardens. The "natural" (albeit artificial, pruned, and constructed) setting of the pleasure garden may have been perceived as a "safe" yet appropriate space within which to encounter Native Americans. When Catlin toured with several Native Americans to England, it was in Vauxhall, London, that they lodged for a while, which he asserted gave the Indians "very great pleasure" as it afforded them "almost a complete resumption of Indian life in the wilderness." While camped at Vauxhall, they "erect[ed] their four wigwams of buffalo hides," and played "various games and amusements, whilst blue smoke was curling out their tops," presenting what Catlin called "one of the most complete and perfect illustrations of an Indian encampment... [where] the men, women, and children [were] living and acting on a similar green turf, as they do on the prairies of the Missouri."[7] For Catlin, the "prairies of the Missouri" and the "green turf" of a city pleasure garden were interchangeable—the latter having the added benefit of being accessible to the city's population and controllable.[8]

Despite Catlin's assertion that the spaces were one and the same, the tamed nature of the straight walkways lined with pruned shrubs and pastoral paintings meant that the gardens were constructed spaces. In using such a space, Catlin was allowing for encounters with these "wild" and "savage" beings, in a safe, tamed manner. The authenticity of these displays was, of course, an illusion, and the choice of space allowed for the mere *idea* of authenticity in a constructed space. However, Native Americans in American pleasure gardens were not typically presented as being observed in their "natural habitat," as appeared to be the case in London.

In the American pleasure gardens, Native Americans were typically admitted—not as equal patrons, but rather as sources of education, anthropological exhibition, or pure entertainment. In all documented instances of Native Americans in the pleasure gardens, there were attempts to present this diverse race of peoples as being singular, fixed, and known, ignoring the multiple tribal and individual differences. Further, the complexity of their temporal and spatial proximity to contemporaneous American geographic realities was glossed over, creating a single, homogenized Native American identity. In this section, I identify a number of events that may stand in for the great number of incidents wherein Native Americans were introduced to the space of the gardens and how their presence was commented on in newspapers and other printed sources after the fact. In doing so, I identify the commonalities between the various events in which Native Americans appeared, and argue that these various performances operated within a narrative of authenticity. This focus on accuracy and legitimacy lent credibility to assertions inherent in the performances that Native Americans were part of American identities only when geographically and temporally distant; they were only to be absorbed into contemporaneous American identities as part of America's heritage and not as a present-day component.

Native Americans have occupied a number of positions in relation to the American national consciousness, being variously excluded and included—being distanced as savages, and embraced as part of a utopian ideal; of being feared and admired due to being at one with the untamed wild; and romanticized and pitied as part of a mythic past. The relationship of Native Americans to "new" Americans was problematic, and this struggle was played out within the gardens. As Philip Deloria argues, Native Americans were central to the formation of American identities, and in order "to understand the various ways Americans have contested and constructed national identities, we must constantly return to the original mysteries of Indianness."[9] The native identity of the country was an important element in defining "Americanness," yet it was not clear what role that identity would play, since, while wanting to embrace aspects of what they symbolized (native identity, affinity with nature), Americans simultaneously sought to wrest land and power from them, relocating them to increasingly distant frontiers. These issues were wrestled with in the American pleasure gardens through the presentation of war dances, rituals, and stage plays.

War dances and other rituals were chief among the Native American performances staged within the gardens and were often billed as "authentic," and Vauxhall and Palace Gardens, New York, and Columbia Gardens, Baltimore, were among the many pleasure gardens to advertise such dances for the paying public. In Vauxhall on 11 August 1804, for example, Delacroix planned a "Fete dedicated to Friendship" in which "Osage Chiefs" would perform "the Indian dances of Joy and Friendship" and the "Osage War Dance."[10] The event was later described in papers as beginning with the arrival at 8 p.m of the "king," who was accompanied by music and dressed in "a laced blue coat, and corresponding under vestments, wore a cocked hat, and had a handsome sword by his side," accompanied by other chiefs in "blue jackets and red capes." Other members of the party were described as "savage" and as almost naked, with "their bodies, arms, and faces" being painted red with streaks of white on their cheeks, having "polished bones, pieces of various metals, beads, and other trinkets" hanging from their ears, and wearing only a feather on their heads.[11]

The degree of specificity in this description suggests a scientific or anthropological attitude toward documenting the event. Paying particular attention to details such as times, colors, materials, and specifics of dress, this commentator presented the event as a piece to be recorded and analyzed for its educational nature. Such treatment was not reserved solely for this event, and similar responses to "authentic" war dances were recorded, including the event described at the opening of this chapter in which Francis recalled how Dr. Mitchell studied and recorded their performances "for the advancement of Indian literature, and enrich[ing] the journals with ethnological science concerning our primitive inhabitants."[12] These accounts obscure the performance aspects of what was presented, suggesting that they were writing anthropological studies designed to better the knowledge of settlers and city-dwellers. These stagings are presented as educational, thus implying they are authentic action, and not (re)constructed performances, despite the fact that they are presented out of context and on a constructed stage.

Similar events could be found in Washington Gardens and Palace Gardens; at Boston, "a company of Oneida Indians" performed the "Grand Indian War Dance" in October 1828, while the Iroquois Indians staged a variety of dances at Palace Gardens, New York, in 1858. In the case of the latter example, "Indians from the Far West" were advertised as being "visitors" to the gardens, yet they were clearly there to perform. Throughout the advertisement, assertions of their authenticity are continually made, providing the name of the tribe ("the great tribe of Iroquois Indians"), the names of dances ("THE WAR DANCE, THE GREEN CORN DANCE, THE BUFFALO DANCE, THE SPY DANCE, [and] THE DEATH DANCE"), and referring to specific individuals by name (such as "the young chief BLACK HAWK grandson of the celebrated old chief of the same name. The young warrior, WHITE EAGLE. The braves Big Thunder, Halt Time, Young Elk, Big Tree, and Mud Turtle").[13]

Despite referring to them as both "guests" and "performers," the author of the advertisement attempts to highlight the authenticity of these individuals and their various dances, through recording specific names and details while overlooking the fact that these rituals were being (re)created out of context.

By taking away the motivation for, context of, and thus meaning of these rituals and ceremonies, the performances were not (and could not be) exactly the same as if performed in context. Indeed, they were "pretended" rituals. In addition, it should also be noted that the bodies of the performers themselves should not be assumed to be authentic. As Rosemarie K. Bank notes in her article "Staging the 'Native'," there have been recorded incidences of "genuine" performances of Native American dances and rituals, being uncovered as fraudulent. In 1836, for example, the National Theatre, Washington, DC, advertised that "TEN CHEROKEE CHIEFS...will this evening appear and perform their real INDIAN WAR DANCE." Just a few days later, a notice was printed reporting John Ross (Chief of the Cherokees) as stating "neither I nor any of my associates of the Cherokee delegation have appeared on the stage" in a letter to the newspaper.[14] It is not made clear if the performers were in fact white actors in makeup and costumes, Indians of a different tribe, or actually Cherokee Indians performing without Ross's knowledge, but the potential for forgery in these performances is clear. It is apparent that even on occasions when the presence of Native Americans is stressed as being authentic, the accuracy of such statements must always be questioned.

Not all Native American performances were billed as "authentic"—indeed some were clearly advertised as being impressions or close renderings of Native American customs. Baltimore's Columbia Gardens, for example, hosted "The American Wigwam" from 1805, which consisted of "The Osage War Dance, and The Chipawaw Eagle Tail Dance."[15] Later that year, it was made very apparent that these were not real Native Americans that were performing, but rather their resident actors simply performing a skit. On 7 September 1805, the "Wigwam Sports" was advertised as being "a striking likeness of the manner and custom of the Savage Dances."[16] On 6 August 1806, the "striking likeness" descriptor was retained, and the advertisement was extended to describe the dance as "historical" and "characteristic."[17] The constructed nature of these performances became increasingly apparent at this Baltimore venue, and the Native Americans were progressively further removed from present-day realities—first by distancing them physically by employing a form of redface performance, then by distancing them temporally by positioning them in an historic context.

The use of "real" Native Americans performing their "manners and customs," would suggest an attempt to present Native Americans as being very much a part of the present day. As opposed to the portrayal of historical tales and dying Indians as seen in the stage plays, having "real" Indians perform their "genuine" rituals would suggest showing the customs of another people in the present day to be the goal. However, through labeling such pieces "historical," and having an anthropologist record their movements and cries with a view to recording them for posterity (as seen in New York), these activities were placed in the past tense. This temporal distance was also enforced by referring to them as "primitive" in many instances, consigning them to the past.

In addition, death, war, and destruction were foregrounded in most of these performances in an effort to make them appear barbaric and primitive. For example, by putting WAR DANCE and DEATH DANCE in capital letters in an advertisement for Palace Gardens, with the statement "and go through the Courting and Marriage ceremonies" being placed beneath in lowercase, the focus was clearly placed upon sensation and savagery, with a lesser interest in other, more domestic, aspects of Indian culture.[18] The primitive and brutal aspects of the manufactured image of Native Americans were emphasized in this manner, sustaining the idea that Indians were inferior and uncivilized, while distracting patrons from the violence employed against them.

In defining what it meant to be American, there was a simultaneous affiliation with and rejection of Native Americans. This contradiction in attitudes toward Native Americans becomes clearer when concerns of proximity (in time and space) are considered: As Wolfgang Hockbruch argues, "whereas contemporary Indians were objects of wrath and contempt, Indians of the past were accepted as geographical ancestors because they proved that the United States had a cultural history of its own"—as figures of the present day they were to be rejected, but as figures from the past they were to be embraced.[19] This disconnect between idea and reality, between past and present, put them in a problematic position in relation to their role in constructing American identities, which was reflected in the activities at the pleasure gardens. There, Native Americans were used to define the American present in opposition to the American past, positioning Native Americans as intrinsic to American heritage, yet simultaneously rejecting them as part of present identities. Referring to Native Americans and their rituals as primitive was just one of the ways in which this distance was obtained.

In presenting Native American performances and positioning them as authentic, management presented patrons with a known Other backed by some form of authority. Despite the fact that there were a great number of markedly different Indian tribes, the desire for a single image further speaks to this need for fixity. As Robert F. Berkhofer asserts, despite "being aware of differences between both individuals and individual tribes," "whites... persist[ed] in using the general designations, which required the lumping together of all Native Americans as a collective entity," creating a cohesive Other against which to define whiteness.[20] As Theresa Gaul argues, such performances allowed for a stable, fixed image of the Native American to be presented, adding to the "stability of the knowledge of their own whiteness."[21] As the identity presented was fixed, Native Americans became known and fixed, thus allowing white patrons to define themselves as known in relation to them. Stage plays allowed for a fixed and temporally distanced version of Native Americans through using the stage "types" that populated dramas of the period. The specific "type" of the Native American has been studied by a number of scholars, including Don B. Wilmeth, Jeffrey H. Richards, Eugene H. Jones, Richard E. Amacher, and Theresa Strouth Gaul, and they have identified that Native Americans have been presented on the stage in a multitude of ways:[22] as brutes to be eradicated through force or through destiny, as noble savages, and as other distinctly positive or negative (and often inherently contradictory) stereotypes.[23] These stage versions presented conceptions of Native Americans which were often apolitical, ignoring the reality of relocation and active attempts at eradication. The plays *Metamora* and *Indian Princess* have garnered particular attention by the above-named scholars, and both of these plays (or versions of them) were performed in the pleasure gardens. Both these playtexts and the Native American characters they depict supported the perception of Native Americans as part of the American past, but not of the American present.

John Augustus Stone's *Metamora* was a popular piece created for Edwin Forrest in 1829 and performed on stages across the country, including that at Niblo's Garden.[24] The character Metamora was an exemplar of the noble savage stage type. Loyal to his tribe and family, honorable, and vengeful, the noble savage was a male type destined to die, portrayed simultaneously as admirable (due to his sense of honor and his nobility) and as uncivilized (due to his vengeful nature, or savagery). Metamora embodied these characteristics throughout the play, and he supported the idea of manifest destiny, wherein the race was seen as being admirable in the past tense, but destined to die out. As Marvin McAllister notes, although the "stage Indian reminded Euro-America of the core values, such as freedom and individuality, on which the nation was allegedly founded... Euro-Americans also crafted stage Indian dramas to justify destroying or relocating Indians as part of their manifest destiny."[25] In doing this, the playwright was consigning Metamora (and by extension, all Native Americans) to the soon-to-be past.

Various versions of the well-known Pocahontas story were also popular in the pleasure gardens.[26] Zoe Detsi-Diamanti identifies that although this story "centered around such broad issues as miscegenation, racial conflict, and colonial expansion...[it] avoided any form of social criticism."[27] Promoting the romantic idea of encountering a virgin land complete with maidens ready to convert and assimilate, this story indulged the idea of a romantic, mythic past; the various tellings allowed white colonizers to be seen as the successors to the original inhabitants of the land, and Native Americans as being "complicitous in ensuring the success of the white race."[28] This traditional tale was performed in August 1858 at Palace Gardens, New York, when *Pocahontas: Saving the Life of Captain Smith* was staged.[29] Depicting this tale of Smith and Pocahontas necessitated a look back in time, again positioning Native Americans as figures from the past rather than the present.

A very different example can be seen in Niblo's Garden in 1858, when John Brougham's *Po-Ca-Hon-Tas; or, The Gentle Savage* was staged.[30] This two-act musical burlesque took the popular Pocahontas story as its focus and highlighted the various errors and contradictions within its various forms. The historical inaccuracy of the traditional tale is commented on, for example, by the hyper-specific assertion that the action is set on "Wednesday, Oct. 12, A.D. 1607, at twenty-six minutes past 4 in the afternoon," and further by the note that scenery designs drew on Mr. Isherwood's "vivid imagination." The benevolent Smith of the traditional tale is portrayed as one who seeks riches and tells the Indian King that "we are come out here your lands to ravage," losing all pretence of fair dealings. The relationship between Smith and Pocahontas is seen not as a love story, but rather as a business transaction, since Smith is prepared "to marry any red queen that in [his] way should fall."[31] The Indian characters are not presented as primitive, but rather as having all the trappings of contemporary New York society, presenting the various characters as attending finishing school, debating taxation, and even visiting their own pleasure garden (Castle Garden).

Yet for all its identification of the problems with the traditional retelling of the Pocahontas story and ridicule of the conventional narrative, *Po-Ca-Hon-Tas* avoids addressing the problem of the Native American in contemporary society. Indeed, at the end of the play, Smith and Pocahontas do not marry; rather, Smith observes that "with her [Pocahontas], in name alone, I'll be united."[32] As Robert S. Tilton observes, this "comic ahistorical ending does away with the need to portray even the possibility of miscegenation," instead, asking the audience to applaud the actors' comic presentation.[33] While this play is concerned with questioning the role of Native Americans in the American past, it avoids the question of what followed and the contemporaneous attitudes, leaving them comic and ahistoric.

Other staged depictions of Native Americans included plays and ballets, such as Vauxhall, New York's, various *ballets d'action* featuring Native American characters. In June 1823, for example, *Indian Heroine; or, the Rival Chiefs* was staged, starring an Indian Princess called Mina, a chief named Miami, and two other unnamed chiefs, who engaged in a series of competitive dances.[34] Without knowing more than the short description provided in the advertisement, one could presume that the three chiefs danced in order to "win" the affections of Mina, Miami presumably being triumphant. In this piece, there seems little room for complexity of character, but plenty of opportunity for display of dances and rituals—the focus of the events discussed above. In addition, performances such as these had a tradition stretching back to court dances, and thus were not based on perceived realities. Rather than responding to the physical reality of Native Americans, such performances were continuing a performance tradition and were thus further removed from any semblance of authenticity.

The simplicity of these pieces and of the Native American characters within them are laughable to present day readers, yet the proprietors went to great lengths to assure patrons of the authenticity of these performances. In the 1858 production of *Pocahontas: Saving the Life of Captain Smith* at Palace Gardens, New York, for example, various parts were performed by the same Indians who earlier in the same program recreated war dances.[35] In this instance, the clearly constructed stage Indian is given added authority by the advertised fact that genuine Native Americans would be playing certain roles. Similarly, the play *Metamora* had a general acceptance of being accurate, due to Edwin Forrest's "extensive researches" for the role when it was first staged.[36] By studying a specific Native American, Forrest presented a supposedly accurate portrayal of all Native Americans, allowing his studies of Push-ma-ta-ha, a Choctaw chief, to suffice for an accurate portrayal of a Wampanoag chief. Such studies allowed him to be seen almost as an anthropologist, presenting the "picture," "personification," "delineation," and "portrait" of Native Americans, and thus an "authentic interpretation of the native."[37] By drawing on the experiences and bodies of genuine Native Americans in this way, this performance assured spectators that what they were witnessing was an accurate and genuine depiction of Native Americans. Although Forrest did not appear in the Niblo's Garden production, the establishment of Metamora as an authoritative and accurate depiction of Native Americans had been firmly established long before 1858. Here another false "authentic" tradition was being followed, as by 1858, the "authenticity" of the performance of this role was to be assessed in relation to Forrest's depiction, rather than any reality.

The manner in which patrons then defined themselves can be seen in the various attitudes elicited in response to these staged performances of plays and war dances. For example, after describing the dance performed at Vauxhall, New York, in 1804, the *Morning Chronicle* records that "the general impression which the scene left on our minds was that of pity for our fellow creatures, ignorant of civilized life, ignorant of themselves as rational and moral beings, ignorant of the end of their creation and their future destiny, and strangers to those principles and sentiments which ennoble our nature and elevate us to a near relation with the Supreme Being."[38] In this description, the focus is on the observers more than on the performers; the interest for this commentator lay in the reactions and beliefs of the audience members. The description specifically invokes pity of their inferiority and notes that the observers of the spectacle felt "gratitude to heaven [that they were not] ignorant... [and] cruel" like the Osage Indians. In presenting them as pitiful and ignorant, this reporting makes it clear that Native Americans are to serve as reminders of white American superiority. Despite claims that such portrayals were educational, Indians were invited into the space not in order to envelop them as equals or part of American civilization, but rather as a foil against which to mark (white) American superiority, as seen in this description.

The importance of Native Americans to American white identities was acknowledged in terms of a past history in many gardens. By watching such performances, white patrons were able to acknowledge the place of Native Americans in their past, perceive them as pitiable and inferior, and reassure themselves that they were superior. Confining their relevance to past identities, the entertainments of the pleasure gardens appeared to exclude Native Americans from contemporary definitions of Americanness. That the Native American was still considered to be part of American heritage, however, could be seen in the prominence of such events in relation to national celebrations. For example, the "American Wigwam" included a "representation of the tomb of Washington," who had died in 1799, replaced in a later program by "the Apotheosis of the illustrious Lieut. Gen G. Washington."[39] Such performances allowed the figure of the Native American to be part of larger structures of the construction of American identities, and, as Jeffrey Richards argues, encouraged audience members to see "American identity as [one] of overwhelming whiteness," which, while it might absorb the heritage of the natives of the land, would not display "any palpable mark of difference."[40]

Two principal tensions appear to be central in depictions of Native Americans in pleasure gardens: authentic versus staged and past versus present. Native Americans played an important role in establishing the "distinctive heritage of the nation" (established in chapter 1 as an essential component of national identity), yet their "primitive" ways were not seen as part of contemporary identities.[41] Native Americans were a real and present component of the populations of the North American continent and thus of the United States, but their usefulness in creating American identities related solely to their role in America's past, not in its present. As such, the establishment of the Native American figures in the pleasure gardens as temporally distant through "vanishing Indian" stage characters or using anthropological tactics to frame their rituals as curiosities supported the creation and assertion of Native American identities as part of American historical identities. The anthropological approach employed in many descriptions of and advertisements for war dance presentations relegated such activities to the past. In order to support the inclusion of Native Americans in the American past and removal from American present identities, authority needed to be assigned to their portrayals of Native Americans as a dying people. Through enlisting Native American performers, labeling pieces such as war dances "historical," and presenting staged roles as being fully researched, proprietors were asserting the accurate and authoritative nature of these constructions. In addition, tying these displays to American leaders and national celebrations assured their position within national identities despite relegating them to the past.

This problem of inclusion or exclusion of an entire race from American identities was not restricted to Native Americans, and the anxiety over what it meant to be American (and how that related to racial "others") grew. As Hochbruck notes, "after the War of 1812," orations on the Fourth of July began to change, as "speakers started to point out that many of the promises and principles of the *Declaration of Independence* were... as yet unfulfilled."[42] The question of slavery and the social position of free blacks led to similar instances of exclusion and restrictive inclusion of African Americans within pleasure gardens.

AFRICAN AMERICANS

Free black populations were "in their economic standing and social aspirations... becoming more distinct and class conscious," as they considered their place in the nation in the early nineteenth century.[43] No longer slaves and thus not "inferior" by default, African Americans began to assert their right to be citizens in a country founded on equality and democracy, but this change was met with much opposition. While it is clear that many African Americans (especially free blacks) saw themselves as part of the nation, the dominant consensus was that one was either African or American (the hyphenated identity was not an option), and many whites were hostile to attempts to change this situation. As African Americans began to assert their right to live as American citizens, with equal access to culture, fashion, and national pride, the reaction from the white population was largely one of ridicule and mockery, which occasionally turned to violence. The adoption of "white" behaviors and customs was met with "humor demeaning blacks, and physical violence against them" by white society.[44] Shane White further observes that African Americans were often perceived as performing an "inappropriate black translation of whites' mores into blacks' own lowly situation."[45] Travel writers noted of Philadephians that "the black women are, indeed... eager to imitate the fashions of the whites," and that "as a whole [Philadelphian African Americans] show an overweening fondness for display and vainglory—fondly imitating the whites in processions and banners."[46] These writings attempted to assert white superiority by mocking attempts of blacks to stake a claim to class and society, and trying to make them appear ridiculous.

While such a backlash was witnessed in many cities, a series of images printed in Philadelphia in the late 1820s provides a good illustration of the kind of reactions seen. The "Life in Philadelphia" series was a popular and widely circulated set of fourteen images printed in Philadelphia between 1828 and 1829, which "satirized the dress and doings of Philadelphians, both white and black," with the middle-class African American figures (the focus of the collection) portrayed as "inept mimics of white high society."[47] Clay's "Life in Philadelphia" series employed biting humor and portrayed the various figures as "slightly exotic, irresponsible, non-threatening beings with a childish fondness for fancy clothes and manners."[48] The activities of these figures range from purchasing stockings to calling on a suitor, and appear to "flow from actual observed situations."[49] The examples seen in figures 4.1 and 4.2 demonstrate the nature of these pieces, poking fun at attempts of African Americans to mimic white fashions, by mocking

Figure 4.1 "Have you any flesh coloured silk stockings…?" E. W. Clay, *Life in Philadelphia*, 1829. Library Company of Philadelphia.

their speech and dress. This mockery was seen when African Americans were perceived as aping other "white" cultural forms, including pleasure gardens.

Advertisements for Vauxhall, Charleston, frequently proclaimed the gardens to be off limits to African Americans, as did Vauxhall, New York, which listed "No admittance for coloured [sic] people" as one of its 16 rules.[50] This policy was seen in most of the pleasure gardens, reflecting a general exclusion of free blacks from cultural activities considered to be "white." However, African Americans could be found in pleasure gardens in specific roles. For example, performances of inferiority granted

Figure 4.2 "How do you like de waltz, Mr. Lorenzo?" E. W. Clay, *Life in Philadelphia*, 1829. Library Company of Philadelphia.

African Americans admission through service roles, such as wait staff. As a result of a fire that resulted in a death, we know that in 1835 Niblo's, New York, employed at least one "colored man."[51] Similarly, Conoit Garden, New York, employed African Americans as wait staff, while Vauxhall, Charleston, offered a concession of public chairs operated by "a careful negro man."[52] As patrons, African Americans were later admitted to some pleasure gardens, but only if they were prepared to perform inferiority by sitting in separate areas for productions, such as in Washington Gardens in Boston, which offered seats for persons of color for 50 cents from 1819.[53] By granting entry under such conditions, whites were able to reaffirm the superiority of whiteness; by forcing African Americans to perform inferiority within the space of the pleasure gardens, the superiority of the white patrons was asserted and assured.

African Americans were also granted a form of admittance through minstrelsy. While not granting them an actual presence, minstrelsy saw whites inserting a physical construction of blackness that was under their control. From the 1830s, minstrelsy began to appear increasingly frequently in the northern pleasure gardens, and while it was often a part of a larger program of a variety of events, occasionally, the minstrel element was the highlight and was billed accordingly. For example, in 1838, T. D. Rice appeared at Vauxhall, New York, where he performed his "celebrated Negro Extravaganza of Jim Crow" and played "Ginger Blue" in a burletta called *Virginia Mummy*.[54] During the 1840s, minstrelsy became increasingly popular. In this manner, patrons were presented with a childlike (and thus inferior and harmless) representation of African Americans, which allowed the status quo to be reaffirmed. Of course, minstrelsy entailed more complex operations than simply the mockery and infantilizing of African Americans by whites, but much like the function of representations of Native Americans, minstrelsy acts allowed an entire race to be presented as containable, knowable, and (most importantly) inferior.

Unlike Native Americans, however, African Americans responded to being excluded from the main pleasure gardens as equal patrons by establishing gardens particularly for their own use. In the 1820s, a variety of pleasure gardens were opened in New York by and for African Americans, allowing them access to this form of cultural self-display as legitimate patrons.[55] New York hosted at least four pleasure gardens open to persons of color, including the African Grove (1821), two by the name of Mead Garden (1827 and 1828), and the Haytian Retreat (1829). William Brown's African Grove was established in the backyard of his residence at 48 Thomas Street for "fellow black stewards."[56] Open for only one month, this site was specifically designed for "the People of Color" and provided "every refreshment peculiar to such places."[57] There is limited information about this site beyond the very brief advertisements placed by Brown and the highly racist and biased commentary provided by Mordecai M. Noah.[58] The first of the Mead Gardens (at 13 Delancy Street) was operated "for the accommodation of genteel and respectable persons of colour [sic]," and was announced on 8 June as having opened on 1 June by Nicholas Pierson.[59] Another venue of the same name was opened the following year at 116 Front Street (at the corner with Jay Street) in Brooklyn on 1 May by Edward Haines.[60] It is not clear if these two sites were connected in any way other than having the same name, and there is no information to be found in newspapers regarding further activities at either site. The Haytian Retreat was located at the corner of Broadway and Prince Street in 1829 on a site owned by Lewis K. Storms.

Such venues were not generally welcomed by white citizens, and they were greeted with a combination of disdain, mockery, and anger. The African Grove, for example, was forced to close after just one month due to complaints of noise,[61] and when the Haytian Retreat opened in New York in 1829, the owner's anger and desire to disassociate himself from its operations were made clear in the announcement he published:

> TO THE PUBLIC. The undersigned in justice to himself deems it his duty to inform the public, that he has no participation whatever in changing the "Military Garden" at the corner of Broadway and Prince Street into a place of resort for colored people, under the name of the "Haytian Retreat." This has been done against my expectation and wholly contrary to my wishes or approbation, by the person who has at present a lease of the Garden. LEWIS K. STORMS.[62]

The fact Mr. Storms thought it necessary to place an advertisement of this nature suggests the urgency he felt regarding distancing himself from such a venture. Although the site was his and he was content with it being used as a pleasure garden (under the name of Military Gardens), he tries to make it very clear here that he does not support the use of the land for an African American garden. The angry and aggressive nature of this announcement betrays a widely held reaction against such venues—they were not welcomed by white society at large.

Pleasure gardens were predominantly presented as exclusively white venues that actively sought to exclude and/or diminish the status of African Americans.[63] By establishing sites allowing entry to African Americans, proprietors were providing a "semiprivate, semipublic" space, which "provided leisure-seeking Afro-New Yorkers with their own privileged escape."[64] Mirroring the claims of other pleasure gardens, the Mead Garden sought "genteel and respectable" people and denied entry to "unprotected females," apparently seeking the same respectable reputation as the more established gardens.[65] Establishing the cultural and moral standing of these venues was clearly important to these proprietors, and they did so by employing the same tactics as other (white) pleasure gardens. From the limited sources we have, it appears that the form of the garden was essentially the same, as were their methods of advertising, entertainments offered, and associations. These gardens were essentially imitations of the main gardens, and the activity of dressing for, attending, and socializing at such gardens fostered a form of whiteface minstrelsy, which served a number of functions, including questioning white superiority, severing race from class-based identities, and allowing African Americans to rehearse American citizenship.

Whiteface minstrelsy is here defined "as extratheatrical, social performances in which people of African descent assume 'white-identified' gestures, dialects, physiognomy, dress, or social entitlement," borrowing from McAllister.[66] This form of performance has been discussed in relation to urban African Americans of the 1820s by Shane White in relation to "dandys and dandizettes," and by McAllister in relation to the African Grove.[67] As both of them observe, acts of whiteface minstrelsy were not empty imitations or parroting, but rather were complex actions deserving of close study. Little is known about the activities at the African American gardens, but we do have more information about the African Grove than the other three, so it this venue that we must draw from. Unfortunately, the only source from which we can recover details of these performances are the writings of one Mordecai Noah.

Mordecai M. Noah (editor of the *National Advocate*, playwright, and politician) visited the African Grove and his clearly biased and patronizing account was printed in his newspaper. He describes how "the little boxes in this garden were filled with black beauties 'making the night hideous'" and remarks that "it was not an uninteresting sight to observe the entrée" of a gentleman who wore a "cravat tight to suffocation, having the double faculty of widening the mouth and giving a remarkable protuberance to the eyes." These "black fashionables," Noah continued, "sauntered up and down the garden in all the pride of liberty and unconscious of want." He described the concert as "vile," and mocks the conversations as imitative and the participants as having little understanding of what they were talking about. The attempt of one patron to touch on topics of international relations and voting practices is reduced to superficial and vague remarks. Noah concludes by noting that the African Americans of the African Grove "run the rounds of fashion; ape their masters and mistresses in every thing; talk of projected matches; rehearse the news of the kitchen…fear no Missouri plot; care for no political rights; happy in being permitted to dress fashionable, walk the streets, visit the African Grove, and talk scandal."[68] Turning their actions into empty parody, Noah infantilizes and mocks the African Americans at the African Grove, much like the "Life in Philadelphia" series did.

Yet some "recovery" can be undertaken. In Noah's description of the evening he attended at the African Grove, he noted that ice cream was eaten; he heard a musical concert and observed as the various patrons wore fashionable clothing, exchanged social pleasantries, and discussed politics. The content of Noah's report suggests that the individuals were participating in a cultural and social form that McAllister describes as "seemingly reserved for Euro Americans."[69] In doing so, he continues, they were questioning the "presumed associations of whiteness with progress and blackness with backwardness, thus contesting absolute claims of white supremacy," and rejecting "the negative connotations associated with blackness and advocated an alternative, more self-possessed African American identity."[70] Far from playing "dress up" and engaging in empty practices of parroting, the activities of African Americans at the pleasure gardens, while directly imitating white venues, were not empty—they were reclaiming and asserting a validity to their identities as American citizens. The reported activities at the gardens also suggest attempts to allow for the performance of class. Due to the existence of slavery (actively or in the past tense), African Americans were associated with slave labor and menial work and thus were perceived as being of a low class (below that of whites undertaking paid manual labor). For many white Americans in the early nineteenth century, it was difficult to conceive of African Americans as being equal or superior to them in terms of class, and the concept of them performing class was ridiculed (as discussed above); yet there were attempts to sever race from class by the activities of African Americans. Although mocking the gesture, the dialogue recorded by Noah overheard on his visit to the gardens included the reference to voting for "Harry." As McAllister observes, Harry was the candidate for the Federalist Party that opposed the Irish immigrants. By identifying themselves with the wealthy candidate who opposed the lower-class immigrant candidate, these African Americans were separating race from class as part of a wider attempt to separate "gentility from whiteness" by setting themselves against the "unrefined [white] Irish."[71] Tactics such as these allowed African Americans to begin to position themselves as having the ability to advance in terms of class.

Such activities can also be seen to be a form of rehearsal for forthcoming performances of citizenry and equality. As McAllister argues, the African Grove could be seen as "a training ground or rehearsal hall for greater political and social participation in public life" in which African Americans had the opportunity "to rehearse dominant social sensibilities and to 'self-create' a liberated Afro-America."[72] This "rehearsal space" allowed blacks to perform as equal American citizens and also presented a place in which to imitate white (assumed inherently superior) culture.

While the African American venues played multiple important roles, they were mostly short-lived, and I have not been able to identify any venue surviving more than one season. Met with hostility, these sites were forced to close due to complaints or perhaps financial instability, meaning they were unable to have any lasting impact on the pleasure gardens more broadly. Thus, in pleasure gardens, African Americans were largely excluded, and despite their attempts to forge their own American identities in their own comparable venues, they were only used in the major gardens to perform inferior identities, allowing white patrons to retain a belief in their superiority.

CONCLUSION

Superficially, both Native Americans and African Americans can be seen to have been excluded from the main pleasure gardens and from constructions of American identities, yet their roles within and without the gardens were more complex. Within the spaces of the pleasure gardens, much control was exerted over how these races were to be constructed. Native Americans were framed as a fixed and stable singular identity of the past, adopted as an element of American heritage (a crucial component of any national identity), while simultaneously positioned as temporally and spatially distant. African Americans were constructed as inferior (through playing servile roles) and as simple persons with great entertainment value through minstrelsy. Through these various forms of minstrelsy (redface, blackface, and whiteface), white American identities were constructed in opposition to inferior others, allowing "primitive" Native Americans and "servile" African Americans to act as foils against which (white, superior) American identity could be performed. As Deloria identifies, "blackness, in a range of cultural guises, has been an essential precondition for American whiteness," and within the gardens, both Native Americans and African Americans provided the required "blackness" against which "whiteness" could be performed.[73]

African Americans used the gardens in another way to reconfigure what American identities were. Rather than accepting their inferior place within the gardens, several instances have been recorded of pleasure gardens being established by and for African Americans. Although there were probably such venues in other cities, New York boasted at least four such sites, and the limited records we have of them reveal that they were used to create and perform alternative American identities in which the hyphenated identity became possible.

The pleasure gardens of America can thus be seen as fascinating windows into identity construction through inclusion and exclusion, and were important venues as the nation came to grips with who and what it was. What, then, caused these venues to disappear from the major cities, and what took their place? In chapter 5, I explore the principal roles of the gardens and then suggest the various forms that stemmed from these gardens.

5. Beyond the Pleasure Garden

So, what happened to the pleasure gardens? I have asserted their importance throughout this book, yet at some point after the 1840s they began to die out. Various scholars have put forth a variety of opinions on the matter, arguing that it was due to their not being "economically viable" as the "value of land climbed," suffering from "the public's preference chang[ing] gradually from active to passive entertainments," or conversely, that that there was a "desire for more participatory and fast-paced forms of recreation."[1] Suggestions of what pleasure gardens literally became have ranged from transforming "from pleasure gardens to parks," to their evolving "into concert saloon theatre," and to their being an "ancestor of the later amusement park."[2] Of course, explanations that focus on single influencing factors or simple trajectories hide a wealth of nuances present within the form and its development. This tendency to observe the form in a vacuum, without relating them to more than one other form of entertainment has led to the legacy of pleasure gardens being obscured. This oversight, which has allowed the complexities of pleasure gardens and their importance in the cultural landscape of America to be largely overlooked, is what I address in this concluding chapter.

To jump to these short, simple answers of what happened to the gardens avoids the more interesting questions: What impact did the gardens have on other forms of popular entertainment? What replaced the gardens in terms of the social space they had created and filled? In this chapter, I ask what happened to pleasure gardens, in the literal sense of what happened to the geographical space they occupied, but then (and principally) in terms of what happened to the cultural and social space they had created and sustained. As I have argued throughout this study, the pleasure gardens of America played many important roles and were spaces in which Americans could address through performance concerns over what it meant to be American. I have explored how various answers to questions of nation, class, and race were performed within these spaces, yet these questions were not definitively answered in 1840 when pleasure gardens began to disappear from the American cultural landscape. Instead, these questions took on new dimensions as America progressed through the nineteenth century and into the twentieth.

So what *did* happen to pleasure gardens? The literal answers to this question are easy—many became theatres, some succumbed to pressures for land development, and a few continued as pleasure gardens.[3] Botanical gardens, public parks, zoos, amusement parks, concert saloons, and roof gardens are all examples of outdoor venues that have variously been claimed to have grown out of the pleasure gardens.[4] There is merit of varying degrees to be assigned to each of these claims: While amusement parks clearly do owe a debt to the pleasure gardens, for example, botanical gardens did not emerge after pleasure gardens, and McArann's Garden in Philadelphia provides an instance of the inverse being true—the botanical garden became the pleasure garden. Pleasure gardens were an invaluable piece of American popular entertainment history and they played an important role in the development of various venues and forms. In this chapter, I first highlight a small number of entertainment venues that can be seen to owe a debt to pleasure gardens, and then examine the trajectory from pleasure garden to amusement park in more detail, questioning the aspects of social context that persisted and/or shaped the form. In doing this, I ensure the gardens the place in the conversation regarding popular entertainments that they have largely been denied to date.

Roof garden theatres have been argued to stem from pleasure gardens by Stephen Burge Johnson, who cites Rudolph Aronson's dissatisfaction with outdoor amusements and his desire to run an elegant concert garden in New York in the early 1880s as an example of the impulse to replace pleasure gardens with roof gardens. In seeking to establish a "small, elegant garden" in which he could offer concerts and various entertainments, Aronson found operating traditional pleasure gardens was not commercially viable due to increasingly high land costs and short seasons limited to the warmer months. Aronson considered "indoor, or convertible, facilities" for his concerts, but, unsatisfied with using a single space for multiple functions, he turned to roof space (on top of theatres). By having his "summer garden above his winter theatre," Aronson allowed one to sustain the other throughout the year—offering outdoor concerts during the summer, and indoor entertainments in the winter and in inclement weather.[5] Spaces such as the Casino Theatre (1882) and Madison Square Garden (1890) offered summer concerts and variety acts from the late nineteenth century and into the twentieth.[6] This use of roof space allowed the theatres to support the gardens (and vice versa), extending the life of the pleasure garden through the use of affordable space, albeit on a much smaller scale.

In this instance, the pleasure garden can be seen to have adapted to the increasing density of the city: As land became increasingly expensive and limited (at least in central locations), spaces for outdoor entertainment surrounded by plants and flowers only made commercial sense if previously unused spaces were used—maximizing the land available by using rooftops. Providing entertainments similar to those offered at pleasure gardens, roof garden theatres coupled hints of a garden landscape with entertainments in the heart of the city, and thus illustrate an example of the concept of pleasure gardens being sustained into the late nineteenth century.

Concert saloons provide another example of an important entertainment venue that grew out of the pleasure gardens. In his book on New York concert saloons, Brooks McNamara defines concert saloons as indoor venues that served refreshments, offered free or low-cost entertainments, and provided music, "flourish[ing] in New York City during, and for twenty years or so after, the Civil War."[7] McNamara asserts that saloons were influenced by pleasure gardens (along with music halls and Parisian concert cafés), citing the fact that "many people who appeared at concert saloons also performed from time to time at pleasure gardens" to support his case.[8]

Katy Mattheson is more direct in her assertion of tangible links between pleasure gardens and concert saloons, arguing that the latter were a "vulgarization of the functions of an establishment like Niblo's Garden," and that pleasure gardens (especially Niblo's) "played a pivotal role in the evolution of variety theatre in America and of the term 'concert saloon.'"[9] Matheson's argument overlooks the importance of English music hall and American taverns in the establishment of concert saloons and uses just one case study (that of Niblo's) to make her claim, but there is further evidence to support her assertion, as Vauxhall, New York, for example, also became a concert saloon. As discussed in the introduction, the site for the final Vauxhall Garden was gradually broken into various smaller parcels of land, and different versions of the garden continued to operate until the 1850s. From the late 1840s, the last remnant of the garden became known as the Vauxhall Saloon (and later, as Vauxhall Variety Theatre). Though few details of this site can be established after 1840, there are a small number of extant playbills that testify to its operations and refer to the site explicitly as a concert saloon. While there are problems with Mattheson's argument, it is apparent that pleasure gardens had important and clear links with the concert saloons that were to emerge, and more importantly, with the variety theatre and later vaudeville so often cited as originating in concert saloons.

"Vaudeville" is difficult to define with any precision, yet its importance within American popular entertainments is well-established. Like variety shows, vaudeville in this period was composed of a number of individual acts, and according to the *OED*, the term was used to "designate variety theatre," in turn defined as "music-hall or theatrical entertainments of a mixed character (songs, dances, impersonations, etc.)."[10] Pleasure gardens were an early venue for vaudeville entertainments—both for the form and the use of the term. As discussed in chapter 3, pleasure gardens engaged an increasingly varied selection of entertainers for a single night, and examples found in many of the gardens attest to this.[11]

In addition, advertisements for activities at the pleasure gardens actually used the term vaudeville. Although an encyclopedia entry on the subject identifies the first use of the term "vaudeville" in America as being in Boston in 1840, Odell's *Annals of the New York Stage* reveals that Niblo was employing the term to describe "unrelated acts on a single bill" in his gardens from at least 1836.[12] It would appear, then, that pleasure gardens were an early venue for vaudeville, employing the term in the commonly understood manner before the 1840s.

These various forms all demonstrate direct descent from pleasure gardens, but of more interest is the performance space created by pleasure gardens. The need to celebrate the anniversary of the nation in order to create and perpetuate a sense of national identity and history persisted beyond the early nineteenth century, as did the fascination with technological innovations and the desire to display such progress. Similarly, although the roles of the city and agrarianism were not fraught with as much tension as they had been in the 1790s and 1800s, the problems of the city (in terms of health, wealth, and morality) were still of concern into the twentieth century. The experimentation with, and enforcement of, class hierarchies perceived in the pleasure gardens in the 1820s, 1830s, and 1840s persisted (albeit in new ways) in the decades after pleasure gardens closed. Additionally, despite monumental steps taken in favor of equality through the nineteenth century and into the twentieth, the white male continued to be the primary figure in American identities, with those of other races/ethnicities being presented as exotic Others.

The need for an outlet such as pleasure gardens continued, but the surrounding social and material circumstances changed, meaning the concept of the pleasure garden had to adapt. The most common answer to the question of what happened to pleasure gardens (that they became amusement parks) provides an avenue along which the development of the gardens can be examined more thoroughly.[13] The standard argument is this: pleasure gardens were privately owned, outdoor entertainment venues catering to the paying public. As interest in the garden elements declined and the focus on pleasure through mechanized exhibits increased, amusement parks emerged—privately owned, outdoor entertainment venues catering to the paying public.[14] However, to reduce this development to such a simple trajectory overlooks the various social and economic factors at play, and the other developments that contributed to this evolution. While I agree that there is a relationship between the two, I suggest there is much to be gained by examining this relationship in more detail. The social and economic changes that led to the development from the pleasure garden to the amusement park, owe a debt to public parks and world's fairs as well.

FAIRS AND PARKS

Before the leap from pleasure gardens to amusement parks can be made, the intervening emergence of public parks and world's fairs should first be examined, as each of these forms engaged directly with the development of pleasure gardens. It is only when these "siblings"—pleasure gardens, public parks, and world's fairs—are viewed in relation to one another that the trajectory of amusement parks (and later, theme parks) can be seen to emerge from the changing attitudes toward urbanization, industrialization, nation, and race discussed here in relation to pleasure gardens.[15]

Despite claims by Garrett to the contrary, the public park system did not signal the end of pleasure gardens, with the function of the latter being replaced by that of the former.[16] Pleasure gardens and parks certainly shared a number of concerns—both, for example, contained elements of self-conscious display (seeing and being seen), both drew on the idea of escaping from the chaos of the city without actually leaving the city, and both provided spaces in which those of lower classes could (and were actively encouraged to) perform as though of a higher class, with a view to being considered more "respectable." Pleasure gardens did have an impact on public parks, and parks were, in turn, to influence the development of world's fairs, but the relationship between the three was not the direct trajectory suggested by Garrett. Rather, a more complex relationship was seen, with aspects of public parks rejecting the form of and associations with pleasure gardens, while also retaining similarities.

When designing Central Park, for example, the Central Park Commission considered pleasure gardens as a model for park development. Roy Rosenzweig and Elizabeth Blackmar identify that planners had to decide when looking at the various submitted proposals what the function of the park was to be—"Pleasure garden? Civic monument? Pastoral Eden?"[17] From a design viewpoint, pleasure gardens had an aesthetic of "popular eclecticism," employing "variety, flexibility, and unpredictability in arrangement and use of space."[18] Rosenzweig and Blackmar note that the Commission determined that the park should not reflect pleasure garden sensibilities, but rather have a "unified artistic and social purpose" and be "insulated from both the novelties of pleasure gardens and the social unpredictability of the streets," and they selected Frederick Law Olmsted and Calvert Vaux's design as best suited to their purposes.[19] In this sense, the artistic vision driving the design of Central Park can be seen to be distanced from pleasure gardens. Heath Schenker argues that the rejection of the pleasure garden as a model for Central Park was also driven by issues of social class, and while pleasure gardens were "associated with working-class leisure" by the mid-century, Central Park was to create "an escape from urban crowds and boisterous revelry," for all residents who desired such escape.[20]

While this may appear to suggest that Central Park (and public parks generally) sought to distance themselves from pleasure gardens,[21] it could also be argued that they were trying to recapture the ideals pleasure gardens still represented to some in the 1850s. Raymond Weinstein suggests that public parks and pleasure gardens both responded to "the burst in urban populations and the desire of reformers to counteract the negative effects of overcrowding,"[22] and Neil Harris labels them both as "wholesome antidotes to urban congestion," operating as "safety valves" and "public health measures," which allowed for the elevation of society from the squalor and poverty that plagued cities.[23] Both public parks and pleasure gardens responded to increasing urbanization and were artificial constructions of the country created within urban environments by providing an escape from city congestion. Counteracting the landscape of the city with that of the country was not merely a case of aesthetics and illusions of clean air, however, but extended to moral reform.

As demonstrated in chapter 2, cities were growing rapidly throughout the nineteenth century, and they were often portrayed as dens of vice, while the country was associated with innocence, honesty, and patriotism. In the mid-nineteenth century, the elite residents of cities became increasingly aware of the impact of city-living on the working-class residents and sought to socially educate and reform the public. Olmsted, in particular, saw public parks as being "instrument[s] of moral reform" and as having a "refining influence upon the most unfortunate and lawless classes of the city."[24] Olmsted's views on the importance of public parks in increasingly dense cities have been well documented, and his designs, underlain by his ideals, led to public parks in cities of over 20 states, including Boston's "Emerald Necklace" and Baltimore's Druid Hill Park.[25] Much like Delacroix's open invitation to all to attend his Vauxhall, Olmsted believed that public parks should be egalitarian venues open to everyone, and believed that social consciousness and respectability could be imparted through the influence of nature. Just as Delacroix reversed this position when he instilled dress codes and increased admission, Olmsted and Vaux were unable to continue this egalitarian approach in Central Park when management switched in 1870 from the elite Board of Commissioners to the Department of Public Parks under Tammany Hall in 1870.[26] Public parks did, however, remain free of admission charges.

Public parks shared their origins with pleasure gardens in that both forms were created to counteract the ills of rapid urbanization, and both attempted to provide democratic spaces for citizens. Additionally, both presented a highly constructed version of a country landscape in the heart of the city. Although there is no direct link to suggest that public parks led to the demise of pleasure gardens, or that public parks filled a void created by the closure of pleasure gardens, it is clear that despite efforts to differentiate their designs from those of pleasure gardens, they actually shared much in common in terms of the social functions they attempted to fulfill. At the same time as the public park system was emerging, another form was developing that shared links with pleasure gardens—world's fairs.

The display of technological innovations played an important role in many of the pleasure gardens, and nowhere was this more apparent than in the exhibits held in New York by the American Institute.[27] Founded in 1828, the American Institute held yearly exhibits that showcased "the finest products of agriculture and manufacturing, the newest types of machinery, the most recent contributions of inventive genius" with the goal of "encouraging and promoting domestic industry in this State and the United States."[28] These fairs were held at Niblo's Garden between 1834 and 1845, with later fairs being held at other pleasure gardens, including Castle Garden (1846–1853) and Palace Gardens (1859).[29]

Using an entertainment venue for the display of new technologies was more than a matter of mere convenience (i.e., pleasure gardens were not the only suitably sized spaces). By using the space of the pleasure gardens, organizers of the fair were part of an ongoing coupling of education with entertainment that was later employed at museums (such as Peale's and Barnum's in Philadelphia and New York, respectively), in the theatres (such as the temperance reform melodramas, *The Drunkard* and *Ten Nights in a Barroom*), and the circus (with its displays of exotic Others and foreign animals). It was relatively common for entertainments of the late nineteenth century to be touted as being not frivolous activities, but rather respectable and educational pastimes, and the use of pleasure gardens for educational exhibitions can be seen as sharing such aims. In the American Institute's annual fairs, the displays of products were a means of celebrating the nation's achievements and delighting visitors with displays both static and mechanic. The "great annual national jubilee" featured steam-powered machines, ploughing matches, and firework displays, among its many offerings.[30] Similar exhibits had been occurring in European countries, such as the d'Avèze exhibition in France, which became an annual event from 1797. As John Findling and Kimberly Pelle argue, part of the goal of this French exhibit was to demonstrate (perhaps to their citizens more than other nations) France's ability to compete with British industries—a similar motivation can be seen to have operated in the fairs held by the American Institute.[31]

Although Findling and Pelle argue that mechanics fairs in the US "seem to have had negligible impact on the individuals who were involved in the planning of the earliest international fairs held in the United States," it cannot be denied that they served many of the same functions.[32] Indeed, the first fair run by the American Institute that lost money was the one of 1892, and both the depressed economy and interest in the forthcoming 1893 world fair were cited as the causes of this deficit.[33] The exhibit of the following year was cancelled due to coinciding with the Chicago fair, which makes the direct links between the Institute's exhibits and the world's fairs even more apparent.[34] World's fairs were not the direct product of the fairs held in pleasure gardens,[35] but the links between the two forms are worth considering nonetheless.

The Institute's fairs were popular for many years, but the world's fairs quickly filled this function as the goal switched from a state-level representation to national and international stages. America's first world's fair came in 1853 with the "Exhibition of the Industry of all Nations" in New York. Inspired by London's Crystal Palace, a large building on the site of what is now Bryant Park, designed by Charles Gildemeister and Georg J. B. Carsten (designer of Copenhagen's Tivoli Park), housed the various exhibits.[36] When the main building burned in 1858, it was hosting the annual fair of the American Institute, again highlighting the links between the two.[37]

The Columbian Exposition of 1893 (or the White City, as the 1893 fair was popularly known) was projected as a unified vision of "harmony, unity, and beauty" which was compared to an "ideal city."[38] Although it could not be seen as "a real alternative to the American city or, especially, to the city of Chicago," it did influence future city planning.[39] After the fair, Daniel Burnham tried to transfer the ideas of symmetry and unity to Chicago, and this had a subsequent impact on city planning elsewhere in America.[40] The goals of presenting alternative urban environments, it can thus be seen, underlay pleasure gardens, public parks, and world's fairs to varying degrees.

John Kasson identifies close ties between the goals of the planners of early public parks and those of the White City, as both "provided an alternative environment that expressed a strong critique of urban conditions and culture," with Central Park providing a "picturesque rural retreat" and the 1893 Exposition, a "heighten[ed]...sense of possibility of what a city might be."[41] Indeed, there were many direct links between the planning of parks, fairs, and cities, as Olmstead was involved with the planning of both Central Park and the Columbian Exposition,[42] and Daniel Burnham was central in the designing of the exposition and in subsequent planning in Chicago.[43] According to James Gilbert, Chicago's elite "envisioned a genteel city. They aimed to impose moral order that would, like a map, guide the resident to the proper places and into the proper attitudes," in an attempt to address the growing concerns they had with the moral, economic, and cultural depravity they saw in the city.[44] Rather than creating a small enclave in which people could be instructed through communion with nature, the creators of this exposition sought to guide the visitors in a more direct way, elevating them by presenting a vision of what the city might be: not creating an escape, but an alternative. As discussed above, rapid urbanization was met with different reactions; the pleasure garden was an early version, in which proprietors provided a pastoral space in the heart of the city to escape the chaos of the city. Public parks shared this goal, but did not have the same financial motives as pleasure gardens. The Columbian Exposition, meanwhile, also tackled the question of what to do about the problems inherent to cities, but rather than providing an escape within the city, it offered an alternative (however unfeasible and temporary that alternative might be) that combined business operations with patriotic and social-reform objectives.[45]

Adjacent to (and technically part of) the White City was the Midway Plaisance—a strip of land connecting Jackson and Washington Parks, housing popular entertainments and "anthropological" exhibits apart from the "formal" White City. World's fairs were expensive endeavors, and previous fairs had almost universally lost money. Initially, the exposition was to house only the exhibits of the main site, but the high number of requests from "amusement vendors, restaurateurs, circus acts, musical troupes, and speculators of all sorts," combined with the economic value of allowing for such stands and the likelihood of them operating on the outskirts of the fair anyway, led to the creation of the Midway Plaisance.[46] This entertainment and exhibit area led to the common feature of the "Midway," which was soon considered indispensible to subsequent fairs. The contents and position of this segment of the exposition reveal much about how the attitudes toward race, gender, and class seen in the operations of pleasure gardens continued and had a tremendous impact on the development of the amusement park.

At all the pre-1893 world's fairs, the focus was squarely on the exhibits, and sanctioned entertainments were limited to displays and demonstrations, such as "machines-in-motion, tethered balloon ascensions, frequent fireworks displays, drills by the U.S. Life Saving Service in Exposition Lake, and torpedo explosions."[47] These official entertainments were very similar to those that had been offered by pleasure gardens in their formative years (especially fireworks and balloons), and the links between technical innovation, education, and entertainment were paramount. Entertainments of a more popular variety frequently emerged on the outskirts of fairs, where showmen would exhibit their freak shows and performances to the thousands of visitors to the fairs for a small fee. It was only in 1893, with Chicago's World's Columbian Exposition, that popular entertainments became an intrinsic part of world's fairs, and it is this particular fair that best exhibits the links between this form, pleasure gardens, and the later amusement parks.

The Midway was home to rides (such as the captive balloon and the now-infamous Ferris wheel), numerous theatres (including the Chinese and Persian theatres), displays (various panoramas and the Eiffel Tower model, for example), restaurants (including the Java Lunch Room, Vienna Restaurant, and the New England Farmer Diner), and a large number of "villages" and "streets" (spanning Cairo, Algeria, Austria, and Lapland). As can be seen from the brief overview given here, the supposedly anthropological exhibits dominated the Midway, yet they all provided entertainment.

Gilbert describes the Midway as being populated with "popular culture and unregulated commercialism," which contrasted starkly with the "planned high culture" of the White City; operating between the focal point of the fair and the city itself, he asserts that the Midway served as a "cushion" between the fair and Chicago, between the white and black cities.[48] An underlying current of class-distinction and hierarchies could be seen in the very fact that these "popular" elements were distinguished from the "high culture" of the heart of the fair by being positioned on the outskirts of the fair. Much like the attitudes witnessed in the changing management practices of pleasure gardens described in chapter 3, the exposition set up a supposedly ideal and democratic space, but built hierarchies of class into its very design; as Russell Lewis asserts, the exposition did not present a democratic, ideal city, but rather revealed "the nation's prejudices and exclusionary practices [that] were incorporated into the planning, building, and running of the exposition."[49]

When most pleasure gardens were in operation, slavery was still a reality in many states, but by the opening of the 1893 Exposition, slavery had been legally abolished. However, African Americans were largely prevented from exhibiting at the fair and were initially excluded from positions of responsibility in the planning. In doing this, organizers of the fair reaffirmed prevailing racist assumptions, but were not allowed to do so quietly. Following protests by the African American community, a Jubilee—or "Colored People's Day," as it was also called—was announced, which was greeted with divided reactions: Ida B. Wells urged African Americans to boycott the fair, while Frederick Douglass saw an opportunity to showcase black accomplishments and condemn white supremacy.[50] As was seen with the establishment of the African Grove pleasure garden, the restricted inclusion of African Americans was met with opposition and then action.

The "ideal city," then, was designed to restrict the roles of African Americans, and in doing so, reasserted their positions in the hierarchy. Also operating within this hierarchy was the position of other ethnic groups, and the Midway itself was where this ranking was most apparent. As Badger notes, American world's fairs perpetuated "Western imperialism, and 'scientific' racism" through presenting ethnic Others, including Native Americans, Chinese, Algerians, and Arabs in a manner that encouraged viewers to perceive them as subhuman.[51] By positioning these "villages" in the Midway, surrounded by panoramas, balloons, ice rinks, and the Ferris wheel, a clear message was being put forward about such exhibits being a form of entertainment and about the view that the subjects were decidedly inferior to the ideal (white male) occupants of the White City.

The exhibition of various ethnic groups had occurred before the world's fairs, but world's fairs welcomed a broader range and created so-called villages, where visitors could watch "specimens" in recreations of their "natural habitat"; according to Rydell, "beginning with the 1893 Chicago World's Columbian Exposition, every American international fair held through World War I included ethnological villages sanctioned by prominent anthropologists."[52] Such displays aimed "not simply to amuse, but to perpetuate an image of underdevelopment," much as was seen in the reporting of the "savage" and primitive beings in Vauxhall (discussed in chapter 4), which reporters and advertisers alike encouraged spectators to pity.[53] Pleasure gardens had been an early place to exhibit Native Americans as "anthropological curiosities" used to assert the superiority of white Americans, and while museums continued to present Others as exhibits, they did so as individual "specimens" and not within so-called villages or enacting rituals. Thus the world's fairs were a primary venue which continued this pseudo-anthropological tradition.

Of equal importance in this trajectory from pleasure gardens to amusement parks via world's fairs are the various entertainments found within the Midway; the "captive balloon," various panoramas, and theatres coupled with the exotic villages nod toward the activities at pleasure gardens, while the Ferris wheel, "Snow and Ice Railway" (a version of the rollercoaster), and "Street in Cairo" hint at the direct contributions this (and other) world's fairs were to give to the amusement park. As Judith Adams observes, it was the World's Columbian Exposition that "gave us the midway; the Ferris wheel... the presentation of exotic cultural environments as exhibits; a clearly sectored landscape design; [and] a celebration of American technology and industry in a highly entertaining mode of presentation"—all features of the then emerging amusement park.[54]

The rise of the amusement park in America was not simply a product of technological innovation.[55] As John Kasson argues, "America in the late 19th century was at a critical juncture where essential values were in conflict," including "the agrarian ideal" and "the concept of a nation" which were being challenged by "industrial capitalism," and "the [continuing] rise of cities."[56] These questions and conflicts were not new to the late nineteenth century, but rather had been present in America through the early part of the century, and the amusement park was a significant entertainment venue of the 1880s onward that addressed these concerns. Much like pleasure gardens and public parks, amusement parks were enclosed areas "segregated from urban environments," which Kasson identifies as being an attempt to "eliminate the unsavory elements of city life."[57] Requiring transportation to visit, early amusement parks were located outside of the city, inviting patrons to escape the evils of day-to-day city life and to take an excursion to a place designed for escape and release. As will be shown, the development of amusement parks in America owes much to pleasure gardens, public parks, and world's fairs.

The first American amusement park is generally agreed to have been Coney Island, Brooklyn.[58] Initially a seaside resort in 1824, Coney Island offered visitors "seclusion and surf" in an area that was not significantly developed.[59] However, as Coney Island's fame grew, and, more importantly, transportation became more efficient, a series of establishments emerged, run by a number of individual entrepreneurs.[60] Operating over the summer months (from May to early September), Coney Island's various parks were marked by several features that were shared by pleasure gardens: a concern with improving the moral quality of both the entertainments and patrons, the enclosure of outdoor areas into defined spaces requiring admission, the introduction of mechanical inventions, and the display of "anthropological" exhibits.[61] The first two of these features stemmed from the rising association of the area with rowdy behavior, which resulted in the enclosure of areas by proprietors and introduction of an admission fee. Much like the requirement to pay to enter pleasure gardens, this allowed managers to have better control over the caliber of their clients. Although the "cleaning up" of Coney Island through the establishment of specific parks, such as Steeplechase (opened in 1897 by George C. Tilyou; see figure 5.1), Luna Park (1903, Frederick Thompson and Elmer Dundy), and Dreamland (1904, William H. Reynolds) is often presented as being the result of the various individuals sharing a philanthropic goal, in Kasson's view, "the creators of these amusement parks were more animated by pecuniary interest than reformist zeal," and it was as a business that these parks operated (much like pleasure gardens).[62]

Another aspect of amusement parks that is shared with pleasure gardens are the acts of seeing and being seen. As noted in the introduction and chapter 2, the performativity inherent in attending pleasure gardens in both England and America was an important aspect of their allure, as individuals could perform being of a higher social class and typically enjoyed observing other patrons. In amusement parks, pleasure was to be found in the mechanical rides, which often saw patrons become the object of spectacle. Figure 5.2 reveals the degree to which patrons of the amusement parks were also part of the spectacle, betraying the fact that seeing and being seen was part of the appeal. In the figure below, for example, a

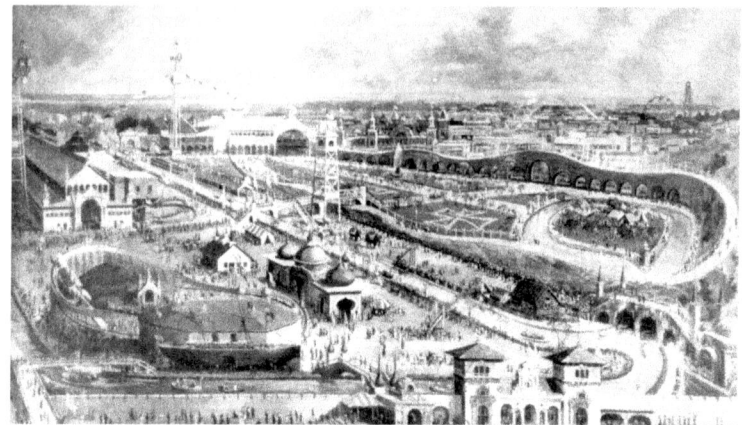

Figure 5.1 Steeplechase Park (1897–1906). Image provided by the Digital Content Library, University of Minnesota.

Figure 5.2 Photograph of the "Human Whirlpool" at Steeplechase Park, ca. 1910. Image provided by the Digital Content Library, University of Minnesota.

large number of spectators can be seen to closely watch the participants—our attention is drawn to the act of watching.

A similar example of the visitor becoming the object of observation can be seen in the "blowholes" at Steeplechase Park, which saw small groups (often couples) being taken by surprise by jets of air that blew garments and accessories. After making their way through the various elements of this attraction, participants would end up in an auditorium where they were able to view the people behind them going through the same experience—the visitor to this attraction would literally be the spectator and spectacle.[63] While the degree of participation and transparency of the acts of observing and being observed were more pronounced in this setting, pleasure gardens, public parks, and amusement parks all share "seeing and being seen" as an essential component.[64]

A further similarity between pleasure gardens and amusement parks can be observed in the introduction of technological innovations. The importance of rides employing new technologies within the amusement parks is well known—what would an amusement park be if we were to ignore such rides as the rollercoaster, carousel, and Ferris wheel? The introduction of technologies into pleasure gardens had already been witnessed with the American Institute exhibits, and early rollercoasters were introduced into the pleasure gardens in France, but the introduction of such mechanical rides into the American was not as simple or straight forward as many have suggested.[65]

The exact origin of the rollercoaster has been explored fairly comprehensively in Robert Cartmell's *The Incredible Scream Machine*, in which he identifies "Russian mountains" as being the first examples of rollercoasters.[66] Dating to the fifteenth century, these early prototypes were initially made of ice, and wheels were added to the cars in 1784. When introduced in Paris from 1804, these rides gained much popularity and appeared in many Parisian pleasure gardens. In America, the first rollercoaster appears to have been devised independent of the French craze. In 1827, Josiah White developed the switchback railway at Maunch Chuck, Pennsylvania, that employed gravity to transport coal and workers from the top to the bottom of the mountain. To return the carts to the top again, mules, then later, steam engines were employed. In 1872, the use of this railway switched to tourism exclusively, and the ride became a popular attraction. It was this basic idea that Richard Knudsen drew upon when he submitted his 1878 patent for his "Inclined-Plane Railway," which first saw fruition in "Thompson's Switchback railway," which Fred Thompson built in 1884 in Luna Park, Coney Island.[67] In this and subsequent years, numerous variations and developments of this basic model could be found in Coney Island, including the iconic Steeplechase created by George Tilyou. The connection between coal mining and the rollercoaster can also be seen in Butte, Montana (see figure 5.3), where one of the latest pleasure gardens I have identified

Figure 5.3 Postcard of Columbia Gardens, Butte, Montana. Author's collection.

employed a similar device drawing on the mechanics required by the town's mining industry.⁶⁸

These links between amusement parks and mining notwithstanding, the role of world's fairs in stimulating the development of the amusement park through technological innovations used for pleasure deserves attention. Tilyou (of Steeplechase) provides a direct link between world's fairs and the rides at amusement parks: After having seen George Washington Gale Ferris's wheel at the Columbian Exposition of 1897, Tilyou attempted to buy the machine once the exhibition closed in order to bring this technology designed for recreation to the masses in Coney Island. After Ferris refused to sell his creation, Tilyou created his own version for Steeplechase Park.⁶⁹ Similarly, Tilyou's dramatic cyclorama "A Trip to the Moon" was opened after he saw a similar display at the 1901 Pan-American Exposition in Buffalo.⁷⁰ Earlier links can be seen in 1877, when, as Harris observes, one of "Coney Island's first major novelties was directly imported, in 1877, from the Philadelphia Centennial"—the Sawyer Observatory.⁷¹ Frederick Thomson (cofounder of Luna Park) further cements these ties to world's fairs, as he was involved with the 1901 Pan-American Exposition in Buffalo, where he encouraged a focus on the entertainments of the fair, culminating in "Midway Day."⁷²

The links between the pleasure gardens, public parks, world's fairs, and amusement parks are numerous: from the desire to create an escape from or alternative to the city, to attempts to introduce social reform; from interests in democratic spaces (even if they could not be fully delivered), to reinforcing social hierarchies that placed white men at the center and delegated women and ethnic Others to peripheral spaces; and from positioning the patron as both spectator and spectacle, to exploring technical innovation as being educational, entertaining, and patriotic. The philosophies behind these various forms, the combination of concerns with business and respectability, and the specific content (balloon ascents, garden landscapes, volcanic eruption recreations, and the Ferris wheel, for example),[73] are shared by these forms, creating a complex trajectory that does not present a simple "A became B" pattern, but rather a variety of forms responding to similar concerns and drives in different ways.

In addition to concert saloons, variety, vaudeville, roof garden theatres, public parks, world's fairs, and amusement parks, traces of elements of the pleasure gardens have been observed by other scholars in modern-day department stores, shopping malls, and museums, among other locations.[74] In these instances, the organization of knowledge, the drive to see and be seen, and increasing commercialization lie at the heart of these assertions. Other connections and distinctions could also be made between travelling fairs and carnivals, and their relationships with amusement parks and theme parks. While the influence of pleasure gardens can indeed be seen in fields beyond those I have focused upon here, I have chosen to restrict my focus to these selected forms and the period before 1920. At the heart of what was occurring in the nineteenth century to which the pleasure gardens responded most forcefully were the issues of urbanization and industrialization. The year 1920 marks the first time that more Americans lived in urban areas than rural, meaning a fundamental shift had occurred with regard to the relationship between the rural/urban tension and American identities.[75] While nonurban American identities continue today, the place of the city in American national identities took on newfound widespread acceptance. Additionally, the continuing development of film (transitioning from Nickelodeons to feature films in the late 1920s) saw an ever-strengthening focus upon technologically produced mass culture through film and television, providing a very different means by which to represent American identities for and by the masses.[76]

CONCLUSION

That the issues, philosophies, and concerns explored in pleasure gardens can be seen in these other forms is hardly surprising given that questions of American identities permeate popular culture. As concerns about what it means to be American have never been resolved in any final way, Americans have found different ways of addressing them, and popular entertainments have continued to provide a venue in which to do so. Pleasure gardens allowed for a space in which patrons could explore (consciously or unconsciously) a variety of issues concerning American identities, but in a manner unlike other contemporaneous forms. Pleasure gardens were simultaneously gardens, entertainment venues, nostalgic retreats, venues for displays of technological advancement, sites of commemoration and celebration, and spaces of inclusion and exclusion. These veritable heterotopias were at once all of these, yet not definable by any one at any given time.

I have argued throughout this study that patrons were able to perform identities, with the concept of "American" being at the heart of these experimental performative acts. The "identities" under discussion have been fluid and multiple, often encompassing apparently contradictory elements, and ranging from the identities of an individual to those shared by groups on local and national levels. Concurrently, the term "performance" has encompassed a multitude of meanings here, including the performance of the everyday, and the overtly staged performances of plays and displays. The "performers" of these acts have included the proprietors and patrons of the gardens as well as actors upon the stage, but the focus has remained upon the performance of the American self both independently of, and in relation to, others.

Pleasure gardens (and later related forms) were populated with people who enjoyed "seeing others and being seen," and these performances were with varying degrees of consciousness.[77] For example, patrons of pleasure gardens could be perceived as performing as though of a class status different from their own (and, indeed, were occasionally actively encouraged to do so), or as performing whiteness in opposition to blackness or Otherness. Especially apparent instances of performance in the pleasure gardens were those by Native Americans (as constructed Others) and African Americans (as waiters and minstrel performers). In several of the forms identified here as being the successors to pleasure gardens, the body of the patron was overtly made the object of the spectator's gaze. The rides and exhibits at Coney Island encouraged such spectacle, with the spectators viewing participants on rides (see figure 5.2), for example. The "blowholes" of Steeplechase Park further emphasize this aspect, with the patron becoming very literally the spectator and spectacle.[78] This element is continued with modern-day rollercoasters through the practice of taking photographs of riders at specific points on the ride, then displaying the photos at a booth for immediate observation, as well as their purchase and subsequent display outside the park.

With regard to performances addressing specific concerns of American identities, the relevance of the rural–urban tension has been shown to have been a particularly important one in the context of the pleasure gardens. Pre-1920, the anxiety over the relationship of American identities to the city and the country was more palpable than in subsequent years. The ills of the cities and the vices cities harbored were persistent topics of discussion, and while some forms of entertainment emerged to educate and warn against such ills, others emerged to counteract their effects and/or to provide an alternative. Pleasure gardens (followed by public parks, and, in a slightly different manner, world's fairs) responded to this anxiety. Pleasure gardens and public parks both presented patrons with a tamed wilderness—a highly constructed version of the Edenic landscape at the heart of early American visions of the nation. In providing such spaces, planners and proprietors created reassurance for city-dwellers in their attempt to counteract the vices of the city. The phrase "rural retreat" was a common name for pleasure gardens, yet many of the post-1800 sites were found in the heart of the city—a retreat without departing from the city. Such venues provided the semblance of escape and catered to a nostalgia that was hard to find at other venues within rapidly expanding cities, allowing city-dwellers to indulge in aspects of and associations with the country, without abandoning their city lives. World's fairs such as the Columbian Exposition drew on elements of this idea by providing an alternative—not an escape or haven within a city, but rather, an alternative model.

Despite (or perhaps because of) the English origin of pleasure gardens, these venues provided Americans with an interesting place in which to experiment with what it meant to be American. Embracing, rejecting, and adapting English and French elements and associations, patrons and proprietors performed a multitude of reactions to the position of these nations in American heritage. As discussed in chapters 1 and 3, aping English cultural forms and activities was accompanied by protests and assertions of independence. Most significant, perhaps, was the fact that these venues became central locations for the affirmation of American national identities through commemorations, celebrations, and exhibitions. Defined by Smith as the "maintenance and continual reinterpretation of the...symbols, memories...and [newly created] traditions" of the nation, national identities were performed within the pleasure gardens through a number of methods, including fireworks.[79] Fireworks (with their strong associations with the French Revolution) were embraced in the gardens as a suitable method in which to acknowledge the anniversary of the nation, which continues to this very day.

Along with the place of the city and the relationship of the nation to other countries, technological developments played a central role in defining American identities. The period under discussion here witnessed many rapid developments in the fields of science and engineering, and the importance of these developments was seen in the way celebrations and events trumpeted such successes and developments, positioning American industriousness on a national stage. Presenting the best aspects of industrialization in a space that excluded the detrimental effects of urbanization was a feature of pleasure gardens (and later, world's fairs and amusement parks); whether it be demonstrations of a velocipede, fireworks, exhibits at the American Institute's fairs, or eruptions of volcanoes, pleasure gardens celebrated technological advances. This display of American industriousness was combined with a vigorous assertion of national worth on an international level with the Exhibition of the Industry of All Nations (New York's world fair of 1853) and subsequent American world's fairs. As Neil Harris asserts, the amusement parks that developed out of fairs and gardens continued in this vein, as they were "linked physically and spiritually, to the industrial and technological changes transforming the lives of millions of people," continuing the importance of technological advancement into the twentieth century.[80]

Class and equality were two other central concerns with regard to defining American identities. In chapter 3, the fallacy that pleasure gardens were a classless space was collapsed along with the idea that the new nation was in any sense "classless" or a place of actual equality. In reality, while there was evidence of people adopting or exploring a new social equality through actively inviting patrons to perform gentility, class structures were inherent in both the operations of pleasure garden and in society at large. Indeed, as the pleasure gardens demonstrated, class tension was tangible, with conflict ultimately erupting in several of the gardens, including those in Philadelphia, New York, and Baltimore. Such tensions remained after the pleasure gardens' demise, but rather than the two-tier highbrow–lowbrow binary described in chapter 3, managers, proprietors, and entertainers found themselves able to profitably address the growing middle without requiring highbrow overtones or overt nods to respectability. As Neil Harris observes, world's fairs and similar forms after the 1930s "no longer had to serve as bridges between high and low; they could, instead, acknowledge the broad middle without apology."[81] The "broad-based, popular culture" of amusement parks and later theme parks were part of a wider shift being seen in the emergence of the middlebrow—the easily accessible, sufficiently respectable, popular forms of entertainment.[82]

The concept of equality was one on which the United States was founded, yet as has been discussed throughout this study, the entertainments presented and practices followed within the pleasure gardens responded to prejudices and inequalities tied to issues of race and ethnicity. Native Americans were depicted within the gardens as anthropological exhibits, yet responses of pity and claims of primitivism permeated advertising and commentary, revealing that such displays served to reinforce white supremacy. While other entertainment venues (such as museums and theatres) presented Native Americans as exhibits, pleasure gardens held events and housed encampments, removed from the humbuggery of Barnum and the fictional veneer of drama. Similar tactics were employed (albeit largely unconsciously) at world's fairs, where Native Americans and a host of ethnic Others were presented as being inherently inferior and primitive, nestled among trivial entertainments and physically exhilarating rides. Pleasure gardens and their related forms provided a space in which Americans could witness framed performances of Others, allowing them to perceive their implied superiority as (largely) white Americans.

While African Americans could open their own pleasure gardens in northern cities in the antebellum era, they too were represented as inferior. Restricting their entry as patrons and mocking their attempts to establish venues such as the African Grove, white proprietors and patrons alike were able to use the pleasure gardens to reassert their white superiority even after slavery was abolished and legal citizenship granted. This was continued through the subsequent related forms, with racism being intrinsic to many of the decisions made regarding the Columbian Exposition, for example, and has continued beyond even this. In pleasure gardens, the resistance to allowing African Americans to bear the title "American" was countered through such activities as the founding of the African Grove, at the Columbian Exposition, through the protests and celebrations surrounding the Colored People's Day.

In all these ways, pleasure gardens have spoken to multiple anxieties about what it meant to be American at a time when the question was being vigorously debated and continuously renegotiated. Through their form as garden, their various locations, the policies of proprietors, patterns of patronage, and the entertainments presented within them, pleasure gardens served many functions within the construction and performance of American national identities. That they became largely obsolete in the late twentieth century should not be taken as evidence of their insignificance—throughout the nineteenth century, the gardens served important roles in national identity formation, and their impact can still be felt in forms of popular entertainment familiar to us all today.

Concert saloons, roof garden theatres, vaudeville, world's fairs, public parks, and amusement parks can all be traced back to pleasure gardens. From presenting anthropological exhibits and variety entertainments, to celebrating technological advances in the context of national achievement and entertainment, pleasure gardens can be seen to have had a significant impact on these later alternative urban environments.

Though American pleasure gardens have been largely neglected to date, and difficult to pin down due to scarce resources, the value of these so-called rural retreats is clear. In addition to their centrality to performances of American identities during a time of fervent national identity negotiation, the American pleasure garden has been seen to have contributed to such fundamental aspects of American culture as fireworks on the Fourth of July, vaudeville, and theme parks. Wide-reaching, both chronologically and geographically, pleasure gardens hold an important position with American popular culture.

Appendix

This list of gardens (accompanied by their dates of operation, location, and known proprietors) is provided for reference; it includes only those gardens mentioned in this volume. For a more complete list of the pleasure gardens across America, see www.americanpleasuregardens.com.

Name	Dates	Location	Known proprietors
African Grove, New York	1821	Thomas and Church Streets	William Brown
Apollo's, New York	1797	*See Ranelagh Garden*	
Bowling Green, New York	ca. 1722–1771		
Castle Garden, New York	1824–1855	Greenwich and Warren Streets	Samuel Francis
Chatham Garden, New York	1815–1826	Chatham Street (now Park Row), Pearl, Augustus, and Duane Streets	Hyppolite Barrière, Abraham Rider, and Jonathan D. Stevenson
Chatsworth Gardens	1794–1805	*See Gray's Gardens*	
Columbia Gardens, Baltimore	1809–1847	Bond Street and Dulany Road.	Margaret Myers, Nicholas W. Easton, Thomas Leaman, and William Curtain
Columbian Garden, New York	1820–1829	SW of Broadway and Prince Streets, diagonally opposite Niblo's	John J. Shaffer, Asa Taylor, Thomas Patrick, Uriah Ryder, John Lamb, and Lewis K. Storms
Colombian Vauxhall, Boston	1798 (never opened)	In "the rural groves at the western end of West Boston Bridge"	
Easton's Garden, Baltimore	1801–1803	*See Columbia Gardens*	
Gray's Ferry, Philadelphia	1789–1792	Ferry over Schuykill river	George and Robert Gray
Gray's Gardens, Baltimore	1794–1805	Green and Saratoga Streets	John Gray, then John J. Mang
Harrowgate, Philadelphia	1789–1791, 1810	4 miles NE of Philadelphia	George Esterly
Haytian Retreat, New York	1829	*See Columbian Garden*	
Ice-House Garden	1796–1798	*See Vauxhall Gardens, Ice House*	
McArann's Garden, Philadelphia	1839–1842	Filbert Street between Schuylkill Fifth and Sixth Streets	John McArann

Mead Garden, New York	1827	13 Delancy Street	Nicholas Pierson
Mead Garden, New York	1828	116 Front Street (corner with Jay Street), Brooklyn	Edward Haines
Military Garden, New York	1824–1828	See Columbian Garden	
New Vauxhall, New York	1797	See Ranelagh Garden (1797–1800)	
Niagara, Charleston, SC	ca. 1842		
Niblo's Garden, New York	1828–1848 (continued as a theatre to 1895)	Northeast corner of Broadway and Prince Streets	William Niblo
Orange Gardens, Charleston, SC	ca. 1760		
Palace Gardens, New York	1858–1862	Sixth Avenue between 14th and 15th Streets	Cornelius Deforest and Tisdale, James Nixon
Ranelagh Garden, New York	1765–1768	Church and Thomas Streets,	John Jones
Ranelagh Garden, New York	1797–1800	5 Pearl Street near the Battery	Peter Thorn and Benjamin Isherwood
Rural Felicity, Baltimore	1804–1808	See Columbia Gardens	
Rural Retreat, Baltimore	1789–1847	See Columbia Gardens	
Seige of York, Baltimore	1804–1808	See Columbia Gardens	
Tivoli, Charleston, SC	ca. 1825		
United States Garden, New York	1785–1811	253 Broadway (between today's Murray and Warren Streets)	Henry Kennedy, Mary Armory and Mr. Miller, John Conoit, Augustus Parise, and Charles Bernard
Vauxhall, Boston	1798 (never opened)	See Columbian Vauxhall	

continued

Name	Dates	Location	Known proprietors
Vauxhall, Boston	1815–1828	*See Washington Gardens*	
Vauxhall, New York	1750	*See Bowling Green*	
Vauxhall Gardens, Charleston, SC	1795–1821	Queen, Broad, and Friend (later Legare) Streets	Joseph Bulit and Antoine Lavalette, Alexander Placide
Vauxhall Gardens, Ice House, New York	1796–1798	East of Broadway, Pine and Cedar Streets	Joseph Delacroix
Vauxhall Garden, New York	1798–1805	Between Grand, Broome, Crosby, and Lafayette Streets	Joseph Delacroix
Vauxhall Garden, New York	1805–1855	Between Bowery, Astor Place, Broadway, and 4th Street	Joseph Delacroix, Timothy Madden (Delacroix's son-in-law), Joseph Hunt, Thomas Taplin Cooke, Henry Jones and Frederick(?) Bancker/Samuel Rockenburg, Bradford Jones, and P. T. Barnum
Vauxhall Garden, Philadelphia	1813–1825	Broad Street between Walnut and Chestnut Streets	
Vauxhall Harrowgate, Philadelphia	1789–1791, 1810	*See Harrowgate*	
Vauxhall Rural Felicity, New York	1793–1811	*See United States Garden*	
Washington Gardens, Boston	1814–1828	Common Street	John H. Schaffer and James Hewitt

Notes

INTRODUCTION

1. Pleasure gardens frequently offered exhibits of curiosities and waxworks (amongst other items), with the gardens providing a temporary site for circuses in several cities, including Charleston. For a discussion of the development of an American identity through museums, see Joel J. Orosz, *Curators and Culture: The Museum Movement in America, 1740–1870* (Tuscaloosa: University of Alabama Press, 1990). For a discussion of the role of the circus within the development of class-based cultural identities in Philadelphia, see, for example, Heather S. Nathans, *Early American Theatre From the Revolution to Thomas Jefferson: Into the Hands of the People* (New York: Cambridge University Press, 2003), chap. 4.
2. These dates reflect the dates of operation of the significant pleasure gardens in America.
3. The *OED* cites the first use of this term as being in 1961. *OED*, s.v. "pleasure," 6b.
4. Thomas M. Garrett, "A History of Pleasure Gardens in New York City, 1700–1865" (PhD diss., New York University, 1978), 4.
5. James Granville Southworth, *Vauxhall Gardens: A Chapter in the Social History of England* (New York: Columbia University Press, 1941).
6. This history is compiled from the chronology in appendix 3 of David Coke and Alan Borg, *Vauxhall Gardens: A History* (New Haven: Yale University Press, 2012).
7. See Jonathan Conlin, ed. *The Pleasure Garden, from Vauxhall to Coney Island* (Philadelphia: University of Pennsylvania Press, 2013); and Coke and Borg, *Vauxhall Gardens*, for examples of recent full-length books on the subject of British pleasure gardens. Other chapter-length studies of the past two decades hailing from a broad array of disciplines include David Coke, "Roubiliac's Handel for Vauxhall Gardens: A Sculpture in Context," *Sculpture Journal* 16, no. 2 (Autumn 2007): 5–22; Peter De Bolla, "Vauxhall Gardens: The Visibility of Visuality," in *The Education of the Eye: Painting, Landscape, and Architecture in Eighteenth-Century Britain* (Stanford: Stanford University Press, 2003), chap. 2; David H. Solkin, "Vauxhall Gardens," in *Painting for Money: The Visual Arts and the Public Sphere in Eighteenth-Century England* (New Haven: Yale University Press, 1993), chap. 4; Paul F. Rice,

"Music Nationalism and the Vauxhall Gardens," *Lumen* 19 (2000): 69–88; John Dixon Hunt, "Theatres, Gardens, and Garden Theatres," in *Gardens and Picturesque: Studies in the History of Landscape Architecture* (Cambridge: Massachusetts Institute of Technology, 1992), chap. 2; and Gregory Gerald Nosan, "Pavilions, Power, and Patriotism: Garden Architecture at Vauxhall," in *Bourgeois and Aristocratic Cultural Encounters in Garden Art, 1550–1850*, ed. Michel Conan (Washington, DC: Dumbarton Oaks Research Library and Collection, 2002), 101–21.

8. Wolfgang Cillessen, "Exoticism and Commerce: Vauxhalls in Pre-revolutionary France" (paper presented at "Vauxhall Revisited: Pleasure Gardens and Their Publics, 1660–1880," Tate Britain, London, 15–16 July 2008); Shirine Hamadeh, *The City's Pleasures: Istanbul in the Eighteenth Century* (Seattle: University of Washington Press, 2008), chap. 4; Garrett, "A History of Pleasure Gardens," 46–8; Ian Dougherty, *Vauxhall Gardens: Dunedin's Notorious Victorian Pleasure Gardens* (Dunedin, New Zealand: Saddle Hill Press, 2007).

9. Garrett, "A History of Pleasure Gardens"; Harold Donaldson Eberlein and Cortlandt Van Dyke Hubbard, "The American 'Vauxhall' of The Federal Era," *Pennsylvania Magazine of History and Biography* 57 (1944); Barbara Wells Sarudy, *Gardens and Gardening in the Chesapeake, 1700–1805* (Baltimore: Johns Hopkins University Press, 1998), chap. 9; Stephen M. Vallilo and Maryann Chach, eds. "Pleasure Gardens," special issue, *Performing Arts Resources* 21 (1998).

10. See, for example, Bolla, *The Education of the Eye*, chap. 2.

11. This image was painted almost 100 years after the closure of the gardens, meaning the reconstruction is unlikely to be accurate. Indeed, it is possible that the arches depicted in this image are reflective of the arches in the London site.

12. Erving Goffman, *Behavior in Public Places: Notes on the Social Organization of Gatherings* (New York: Free Press, 1966), chap. 13.

13. Nosan, "Pavilions, Power, and Patriotism," 101–21.

14. *OED*, s.v. "performance," 4a and 4c.

15. Francis Hodge, *Yankee Theatre: The Image of America on the Stage: 1825–1850* (Austin: University of Texas Press, 1964); Rosemarie K. Bank, *Theatre Culture in America, 1825–1860* (New York: Cambridge University Press, 1997); Nathans, *Early American Theatre*; Jeffrey H. Richards, *Drama, Theatre and Identity in the American New Republic* (Cambridge: Cambridge University Press, 2005). Also see: Jason Shaffer, *Performing Patriotism: National Identity in the Colonial and Revolutionary American Theater* (Philadelphia: University of Pennsylvania Press, 2007); and S. E. Wilmer, *Theatre, Society and the Nation: Staging American Identities* (Cambridge: Cambridge University Press, 2002).

16. Len Travers, *Celebrating the Fourth: Independence Day and the Rites of Nationalism in the Early Republic* (Amherst: University of Massachusetts

Press, 1997); David Waldstreicher, *In the Midst of Perpetual Fetes: The Making of American Nationalism, 1776–1820* (Chapel Hill: University of North Carolina Press, 1997); Simon P. Newman, *Parades and the Politics of the Street: Festive Culture in the Early American Republic* (Philadelphia: University of Pennsylvania Press, 1997).

17. For a discussion of how to approach Early American history when confronted with absences, see Odai Johnson, *Absence and Memory in Colonial American Theatre: Fiorelli's Plaster* (New York: Palgrave Macmillan, 2006), introduction to part I.
18. Malini Johar Schueller and Edward Watts, eds., *Messy Beginnings: Postcoloniality and Early American Studies* (New Brunswick, NJ: Rutgers University Press, 2003), 15.
19. Michel Foucault, "Of Other Spaces," in *The Visual Culture Reader*, ed. Nicholas Mirzoeff, trans. Jay Miskowiec (New York, Routledge, 1998), 239.
20. Ibid., 243.
21. Ibid., 241.
22. Waldstreicher, *In the Midst of Perpetual Fetes*, 17.
23. See Lake Douglas, "Pleasure Gardens in Nineteenth-Century New Orleans: 'Useful for all Classes of Society,'" in *The Pleasure Garden, from Vauxhall to Coney Island*, ed. Jonathan Conlin, 150–176 for a discussion of the various gardens in New Orleans.
24. D. T. Valentine, *The Manual of the Corporation of the City of New York* (New York: McSpedon and Baker, 1856), 472; Edwin G. Burrows and Mike Wallace, *Gotham: A History of New York City to 1898* (New York: Oxford University Press, 1999), 176.
25. *New-York Mercury*, 11 February 1765; *New-York Gazette*, 25 July 1768; *New-York Chronicle*, 22–29 June 1769, 63; *New-York Chronicle*, 14–21 September 1769, 165. See figure 2.2 for a map of this location.
26. *Daily Advertiser*, 27 June 1793; *Minerva*, 23 May 1797.
27. See chap. 2 for a more detailed discussion of this location.
28. O. H. Holley, *A Description of the City of New York: With a Brief Account of the Cities, Towns, Villages, and Places of Resort Within Thirty Miles. Designed as a Guide for Citizens and Strangers, to All Places of Attraction in the City and its Vicinity* (New York: J. Disturnell, 1847), 53.
29. D. T. Valentine places the opening in 1803, Burrows and Wallace in 1804, and Stokes in 1805. Newspapers of 1805 confirm the opening as being official in 1805. D. T. Valentine, *The Manual of the Corporation of the City of New York* (New York: Edmund Jones, 1866), 586; Burrows and Wallace, *Gotham*, 448; I. N. Phelps Stokes, *The Iconography of Manhattan Island, 1498–1909*, vol. 5 (New York: Robert H. Dodd, 1926), 1436; *New York Gazette*, 20 April 1805.
30. The details of this site have been gathered from the New York newspapers *Commercial Advertiser*, *American Citizen*, *New York Morning Herald*, and *Evening Post*, 1808–1830.

31. For example, Delacroix's Fourth of July program announcements had previously been very grand and enthusiastic; by contrast, his advertisement on 3 July has a much more despondent tone, pleading with would-be patrons to visit his garden on the fourth despite the high probability of rain in order to prevent the site falling into "a state of decay and ruin." *Evening Post*, 3 July 1809.
32. P. T. Barnum, *The Life of P. T. Barnum Written by Himself* (New York: Tubbs, Nesmith and Teall, 1854; Urbana: University of Illinois Press, 2000), 210. See Garrett for a more detailed discussion of the various managers of the site in the final years. Garrett, "A History of Pleasure Gardens," 366–409.
33. Burrows and Wallace, *Gotham*, 585.
34. W. Harrison Bayles, *Old Taverns of New York* (New York: Frank Allaben Genealogical Company, 1915), 455.
35. Details of this site have been gathered from the *Spectator*, 1834–1838.
36. Antonio Blitz, *Fifty Years in the Magic Circle: Being an Account of the Author's Professional Life; His Wonderful Tricks and Feats; With Laughable Incidents and Adventures as a Magician, Necromancer, and Ventriloquist* (San Francisco: A. L. Bancroft, 1871), 122.
37. *New York Herald*, 13 May 1848.
38. *Weekly Herald*, 16 June 1849.
39. *New York Times*, 24 March 1895.
40. Garrett, "A History of Pleasure Gardens," i. Garrett's number of 48 has been supplemented by other sites I have uncovered. Also see www.americanpleasuregardens.org.
41. Others include Lombardy Gardens, Lebanon Gardens, Tivoli Gardens, and the Labyrinth Gardens. See Eberlein and Hubbard, "The American 'Vauxhall,'" 167, and Geraldine A. Duclow, "Philadelphia's Early Pleasure Gardens," *Performing Arts Resources* 21 (1998): 1–17.
42. A description of the gardens can be found in William Parker Cutler and Julia Perkins Cutler, eds., *Life Journals and Correspondence of Rev. Manasseh Cutler, L.L.D.* (Cincinnati: Robert Clarke, 1888), 1: 276; David John Jeremy, ed., *Henry Wansey and his American Journal: 1794* (Philadelphia: American Philosophical Society, 1970), 112; and *Dunlap's American Daily Advertiser*, 22 February 1792.
43. In compiling the details of Gray's Ferry presented here, I have consulted the *Pennsylvania Packet* and *Pennsylvania Mercury*.
44. *Pennsylvania Mercury*, 3 July 1790. The various appeals to patriotism and the links with the rural aspects will be discussed in greater detail in subsequent chapters.
45. *General Advertiser*, 6 July 1791. The details and implications of this riot will be more fully discussed in chapter 3.
46. Duclow, "Philadelphia's Pleasure Gardens," 5; newspapers consulted for a description of the gardens and the activities therein were compiled from *Independent Gazetteer*, *Pennsylvania Packet*, and *Federal Gazette*.

47. Thomas J. Scharf and Thompson Westcott, *History of Philadelphia, 1609–1884* (Philadelphia: L. H. Everts, 1884), 2:943.
48. Duclow, "Philadelphia's Pleasure Gardens," 5–6; Alan S. Downer, ed., *The Memoir of John Durang: American Actor, 1785–1816* (Pittsburgh: University of Pittsburgh Press, 1966), 33.
49. F. H. Shelton, "Springs and Spas of Old-Time Philadelphians," *Pennsylvania Magazine of History and Biography* 47 (1923): 216.
50. Joseph Jackson, *Encyclopedia of Philadelphia*, vol. 4 (Harrisburg: National Historical Association, 1933), 1154; *Poulson's Daily Advertiser*, 28 September 1813.
51. Joseph Jackson, "Vauxhall Garden," *Pennsylvania Magazine of History and Biography* 57 (1933): 290.
52. In compiling the history of this site, *Poulson's American Daily Advertiser* has been consulted throughout.
53. See Gerald Kahan, *George Alexander Stevens and the Lecture on Heads* (Athens: University of Georgia Press, 1984) for more on this piece.
54. Jackson, "Vauxhall Garden," 293; Jackson, *Encyclopedia of Philadelphia*, 1155. James Hewitt was a "music publisher, composer, performer, seller, importer, teacher, and orchestra leader," best known for his leading of the Park Theatre orchestra, New York. See John W. Wagner, "James Hewitt, 1770–1827," *Musical Quarterly* 58, no. 2 (April 1972): 259.
55. Duclow, "Philadelphia's Pleasure Gardens," 9–10. A detailed description of the gardens and Pavilion Theatre can be found in *Franklin Gazette*, 2 July 1819. Also see Scharf and Westcott, *History of Philadelphia*, 958.
56. Historical Society of Pennsylvania, Soc. Misc. Coll., box 4a, folder 8; Scharf and Westcott, *History of Philadelphia*, 598; Eberlein and Hubbard, "The American 'Vauxhall,'" 168. This riot will be discussed more fully in chapter 3.
57. Duclow, "Philadelphia's Pleasure Gardens," 13–14; Jackson, *Encyclopedia of Philadelphia*, 1156; and *National Gazette*, 7 July 1827.
58. Blitz, *Fifty Years in the Magic Circle*, 171; Thomas Meehan, "An Early Philadelphia Nursery," *The Gardener's Monthly and Horticulturist* 29, no. 347 (November 1887): 346.
59. *Philadelphia Inquirer*, 11 June 1839. Schuylkill Fifth and Sixth Streets became known as 18th and 17th Streets, respectively, in 1853 (as they are still known today). See Jefferson M. Moak, *Philadelphia Street Name Changes* (Philadelphia: Chestnut Hill Almanac Genealogical Series, 1996).
60. *Public Ledger*, 1 and 5 June 1840.
61. *North American*, 21 July 1841 and 12 April 1842; *Philadelphia Inquirer*, 10 April 1843.
62. The scarcity of pleasure gardens in this city has been explained as being due to the fact the Bostonians had access to Boston Common, but, as will be discussed in chapter 3, the common did not, in fact, replace the function of the pleasure garden.

63. William W. Clapp, *Record of the Boston Stage* (1853, reprint; New York: Greenwood Press, 1969), 21; and Nathans, *Early American Theatre*, 73, 220.
64. *Columbian Centinel*, 10 February 1798.
65. In compiling the history of the Washington Gardens, *The Repertory*, *Boston Daily Advertiser*, and *Columbian Centinel* have been consulted.
66. William S. Rossiter, ed., *Days and Ways in Old Boston* (Boston: R. H. Stearns, 1915), 121–23.
67. See Sarudy, *Gardens and Gardening in the Chesapeake*, chap. 9, for a cursory discussion of the variety of outdoor entertainment venues in Baltimore and neighboring areas during this time frame.
68. *Federal Gazette*, 30 January 1800; Mary Ellen Hayward and Frank R. Shivers, eds., *The Architecture of Baltimore: An Illustrated History*. (Baltimore: Johns Hopkins University Press, 2004), 12. See figure 2.1 for a map of this location.
69. See the *Federal Gazette*, 1800–1809.
70. *American and Commercial Daily Advertiser*, 21 February 1812 and 17 March 1814; William Fry, *The Baltimore Directory for 1810, Containing the Names, Occupations and Residences of the Inhabitants, Alphabetically Arranged* (Baltimore: G. Dobbin and Murphy, 1810); *Fry's Baltimore Directory for the year 1812: Containing the Names, Occupations, Residences, &c. of the Inhabitants, Within the City and Precincts, Alphabetically Arranged* (Baltimore: B. W. Sower, 1812).
71. See the *Maryland Journal* and *American and Commercial Daily Advertiser*.
72. See figure 2.1 for a map of this location.
73. James Robinson, *The Baltimore Directory for 1804, Containing the Names, Trades & Residences of the Inhabitants of the City & Precincts* (Baltimore: Warner and Hanna, 1804).
74. Downer, *The Memoir of John Durang*, 118, 127.
75. *Baltimore Gazette and Daily Advertiser*, 27 May 1833 and 10 October 1833.
76. Other venues include Orange Gardens (ca. 1760), Tivoli (ca. 1825), and Niagara (ca. 1842). I am indebted to Nicholas Butler (author of *Votaries of Apollo*) for bringing the first of these short-lived two gardens to my attention. A small number of newspaper advertisements alerted me to the existence of the Niagara Gardens.
77. South Carolina Historical Society, Pinckney Family Documents, 1097.02.02 (1795), [1].
78. See the *City Gazette* and *Charleston Courier* for details of this site.
79. Stanley W. Hoole, *The Antebellum Charleston Theatre* (Tuscaloosa: University of Alabama Press, 1946).
80. Baron de Montlezun, "A Frenchman Visits Charleston, 1817," ed. Lucius Gaston Moffat and Joseph Médard Carrière, *South Carolina Historical and Genealogical Magazine* 49, no. 3 (1948): 147.
81. Eberlein and Hubbard, "The American 'Vauxhall,'" 174.
82. Hobsbawm identifies the fact that nations often impose national identity retroactively and that revolutionary nations often define themselves in opposition

to other nations. See Eric J. Hobsbawm, *Nations and Nationalism Since 1780* (New York: Cambridge University Press, 1990), chap. 1.
83. Eberlein and Hubbard, "The American 'Vauxhall,'" 154, 157; Garrett, "A History of Pleasure Gardens," 604; Duclow, "Philadelphia's Pleasure Gardens," 2.
84. *Pennsylvania Packet*, 28 May 1789.

1 PERFORMING NATION: THE PLEASURE GARDEN AS A SPACE FOR DEFINING AMERICA

1. "Ode to Vauxhall Garden," *City Gazette* (Charleston), 3 July 1799. Emphasis in original.
2. Thomas M. Garrett, "A History of Pleasure Gardens in New York City, 1700–1865" (PhD diss., New York University, 1978), 604.
3. For a discussion of the position of the American nation within established scholarship on nation and nationalism, see Susan-Mary Grant, "When was the First New Nation?: Locating America in a National Context," in *When is the Nation?: Towards an Understanding of Theories of Nationalism*, ed. Atsuko Ichijo and Gordana Uzelac (London: Routledge, 2005), 157–76.
4. Anthony D. Smith, *Chosen Peoples: Sacred Sources of National Identity* (Oxford: Oxford University Press, 2003), 24.
5. Ibid., 24–5.
6. Hobsbawm identifies the fact that nations often impose national identity retroactively and that revolutionary nations often define themselves in opposition to other nations. See Eric J. Hobsbawm, *Nations and Nationalism Since 1780* (New York: Cambridge University Press, 1990), chap. 1.
7. Harold Donaldson Eberlein and Cortlandt Van Dyke Hubbard, "The American 'Vauxhall' of The Federal Era," *Pennsylvania Magazine of History and Biography* 57 (1944): 154, 157; Garrett, "A History of Pleasure Gardens in New York City," 604; Geraldine Duclow, "Philadelphia's Pleasure Gardens," *Performing Arts Resources* 21 (1998): 2.
8. These ideas are further problematized by the fact that identity is constructed in these terms as a single, monolithic entity.
9. David Gerstner, "Nineteenth-Century Formulations of Masculinity and Realism: The Body of Edwin Forrest," chap. 1 in *Manly Arts: Masculinity and Nation in Early American Cinema* (Durham: Duke University Press, 2006); Kim C. Sturgess, *Shakespeare and the American Nation* (Cambridge: Cambridge University Press, 2004).
10. Jeffrey H. Richards, *Drama, Theatre and Identity in the American New Republic* (Cambridge: Cambridge University Press, 2005), part II.
11. Jared Brown, *The Theatre in America during the Revolution* (Cambridge: Cambridge University Press, 1995), 170.
12. Royall Tyler, *The Contrast: A Comedy in Five Acts* (1787; Boston: Houghton Mifflin, 1920), 20.

13. Michael Warner, "What's Colonial About Colonial America?" in *Possible Pasts: Becoming Colonial in Early America*, ed. Robert Blair St. George (Ithaca: Cornell University Press, 2000), 62; Malini Johar Schueller and Edward Watts, eds, *Messy Beginnings: Postcoloniality and Early American Studies* (New Brunswick, NJ: Rutgers University Press, 2003), 2–3 and 11.
14. *Pennsylvania Gazette*, 1 July 1754 and 30 June 1768.
15. *City Gazette*, 28 June 1794; *Philadelphia Gazette*, 3 May 1799.
16. *The Poor Lodger* was based on the novel *Evelina* by Frances Burney, which is well known among Vauxhall scholars for its depictions of activities within Vauxhall, London.
17. *The Mail*, 18 October 1791; *Pennsylvania Gazette*, 30 June 1768.
18. Garrett, "A History of Pleasure Gardens in New York City," 55.
19. *Columbian Centinel*, 10 and 24 February 1798.
20. *New York Gazette*, 8 June 1797.
21. David John Jeremy, ed., *Henry Wansey and His American Journal: 1794* (Philadelphia: American Philosophical Society, 1970), 95, 112.
22. Baron de Montlezun, "A Frenchman Visits Charleston, 1817," ed. Lucius Gaston Moffat and Joseph Médard Carrière, *South Carolina Historical and Genealogical Magazine* 49, no. 3 (1948): 147.
23. Garrett, "A History of Pleasure Gardens in New York City," 281. It should be noted that the accuracy of this image should be questioned, as it was titled "Sperry's Garden" in other editions, which was the name of the nursery operating on this site prior to Vauxhall's opening.
24. William Parker Cutler and Julia Perkins Cutler, eds., *Life Journals and Correspondence of Rev. Manasseh Cutler, L.L.D.* (Cincinnati: Robert Clarke, 1888), 1:278. *Henry Wansey and his American Journal* also notes a few details of the gardens in 1794, but offers much less detail.
25. Cutler and Cutler, *Life Journals and Correspondence of Rev. Manasseh Cutler*, 1:275–77.
26. *New York Daily Advertiser*, 2 July 1804; *New York Gazette*, 20 April 1805; *New York Evening Post*, 11 June 1838.
27. *Columbian*, 11 June 1811.
28. *Freeman's Journal* (Philadelphia), 15 June 1785.
29. See the famous literary visit to Vauxhall depicted in *Evelina*, for example. Fanny Burney, *Evelina; or, The History of a Young Lady's Entrance into the World* (London: Harrison, 1861), 217.
30. *National Advocate*, 9 May 1817.
31. *Gazette of the United States*, 9 May 1789 to 13 May 1789, issue 9, 34. Emphasis in original.
32. *Spectator* (New York), 23 September 1833.
33. *Poulson's American Daily Advertiser*, 3 June 1819.
34. The drama of the period provides us with excellent displays of the assumption that European culture was considered to be more refined, with the plays *Fashion* (by Anna Cora Mowatt, 1845) and *The Contrast* (by Royall Tyler,

1787) openly mocking the general acceptance of the superiority of French and English culture.
35. *New-York Packet*, 18 August 1785; *New-York Mercury*, 9 November 1767.
36. *Pennsylvania Packet*, 19 June 1790.
37. Warner, "What's Colonial about Colonial America?" in *Possible Pasts*, ed. St George, 62; Schueller and Watts, *Messy Beginnings*, 2–3 and 11.
38. Ruth M. Elson, *Guardians of Tradition: American Schoolbooks of the Nineteenth Century* (Lincoln: University of Nebraska Press, 1964), 103.
39. Ian Dougherty, *Vauxhall Gardens: Dunedin's Notorious Victorian Pleasure Gardens* (Dunedin, NZ: Saddle Hill, 2007).
40. Garrett, "A History of Pleasure Gardens in New York City," 10.
41. Alan S. Downer, ed., *The Memoir of John Durang: American Actor, 1785–1816* (Pittsburgh: University of Pittsburgh Press, 1966), 33.
42. *Pennsylvania Packet*, 4 July 1789.
43. *Evening Post*, 22 May 1821.
44. See for example Stanley Elkins and Eric McKitrick, *The Age of Federalism* (New York: Oxford University Press, 1993).
45. *Federal Intelligencer*, 13 July 1795.
46. *Federal Gazette*, 3 July 1790.
47. The XYZ Affair refers to a series of events in 1798 and the resulting scandal when three French agents made a series of demands for continuing negotiations, including money, loans, a bribe (on behalf of Talleyrand), and a formal apology by President Adams.
48. *The Diary or Loudon's Register*, 17 July 1797.
49. *Gazette of the United States*, 26 May 1797.
50. *City Gazette*, 22 October 1795 and 2 May 1796.
51. *City Gazette*, 8 July 1799 and 9 August 1800.
52. Anne C. Loveland, *Emblem of Liberty: The Image of Lafayette in the American Mind* (Baton Rouge: Louisiana State University Press, 1971).
53. *Boston Commercial Gazette*, 23 August 1824; A. Levasseur, *Lafayette in America in 1824 and 1825; or, Journal of a Voyage to the United States* (Philadelphia: Carey and Lea, 1829), 1:97–98.
54. *Daily Advertiser*, 22 June 1805. For a more detailed discussion of this, see Caroline Winterer, *The Culture of Classicism: Ancient Greece and Rome in American Intellectual Life, 1780–1910* (Baltimore: Johns Hopkins University Press, 2004).
55. *Federal Gazette*, 25 July 1791; *Morning Chronicle*, 24 April 1804; *Weekly Herald*, 10 July 1852 and 26 August 1854.
56. P. T. Barnum, *The Life of P. T. Barnum Written by Himself* (New York: Tubbs, Nesmith, and Teall, 1854; Urbana: University of Illinois Press, 2000), 210; Garrett, "A History of Pleasure Gardens in New York City," 385.
57. Information for this site has been gathered from appendix 3 of David Coke and Alan Borg, *Vauxhall Gardens: A History* (New Haven: Yale University Press, 2011).

58. Smith, *Chosen Peoples*, 25.
59. Ibid., 24–5.
60. *Pennsylvania Packet*, 28 May 1789.
61. *Pennsylvania Packet*, 19 June 1790.
62. *Columbian Centinel*, 7 July 1819. Emphasis in original.
63. These fairs were held here each year until 1845 when they moved to Castle Garden (another New York pleasure garden) from 1846 to 1853. The fair was also held at New York's Crystal Palace from 1853 to 1858, and then Palace Garden in 1859. These events (and the venues) will be discussed at greater length in chapter 5. Ethan Robey, "The Utility of Art: Mechanics' Institute Fairs in New York City, 1828–1876" (PhD diss., Columbia University, 2000), 628–35.
64. James Tallmadge, *Address, Delivered at the Close of the Sixteenth Annual Fair of the American Institute, New-York, October, 1843* (New York: James Van Norden, 1843), 19.
65. See, for example, *Spectator*, 9 September 1839.
66. *The Mail*, 12 July 1792.
67. *The Spectator*, 22 June 1835.
68. *The Sun*, 10 September 1846.
69. *Commercial Advertiser*, 7 July 1817; *Boston Gazette*, 2 July 1818.
70. *Morning Chronicle*, 22 July 1805; *Evening Post*, 12 August 1815.
71. *North American*, 2 July 1808; *City Gazette*, 10 August 1809; *New-England Palladium*, 23 February 1819.
72. *Commercial Advertiser*, 12 June 1817; *Boston Gazette*, 7 July 1817.
73. Loveland, *Emblem of Liberty*, 7.
74. *Columbian*, 30 June 1820.
75. Michael R. Lynn, "Sparks for Sale: The Culture and Commerce of Fireworks in Early Modern France," *Eighteenth-Century Life* 30, no. 2 (Spring 2006): 75.
76. Other sites were used as well, with an example being found in Boston in 1820, when a fireworks display was given from Boston Common (which was adjacent to the gardens); a concert was given that night from within the gardens. *Boston Daily Advertiser*, 4 July 1820.
77. *New-York Daily Advertiser*, 6 July 1818; *Mercantile Advertiser*, 6 July 1820.
78. *Evening Post* (New York), 1 July 1808.
79. *Commercial Advertiser*, 1 July 1817.
80. *Daily Advertiser* (New York), 28 June 1798.
81. David Waldstreicher, *In the Midst of Perpetual Fetes: The Making of American Nationalism, 1776–1820* (Chapel Hill: University of North Carolina Press, 1997); Simon P. Newman, *Parades and the Politics of the Street: Festive Culture in the Early American Republic* (Philadelphia: University of Pennsylvania Press, 1997); Len Travers, *Celebrating the Fourth: Independence Day and the Rites of Nationalism in the Early Republic* (Amherst: University of Massachusetts Press, 1997).

82. Newman, *Parades and the Politics of the Street*, xiii; Waldstreicher, *In the Midst of Perpetual Fetes*, 173.
83. Travers, *Celebrating the Fourth*, 4, 6.
84. *City Gazette* (Charleston), 6 July 1801. This is further discussed by Travers, *Celebrating the Fourth*, chap.4.
85. Smith, *Chosen People*, 24–5.

2 PERFORMING PLACE: THE RURAL/URBAN TENSION

1. The White House, Office of the Press Secretary, "Remarks by the President in State of Union Address," 25 January 2011, http://www.whitehouse.gov/the-press-office/2011/01/25/remarks-president-state-union-address.
2. Leo Marx, *The Machine in the Garden: Technology and the Pastoral Ideal in America* (New York: Oxford University Press, 1964); Mark Caldwell, "Defining American Urbanity: Royal Tyler, William Dunlap, and the Postrevolutionary Theater in New York," *Early American Studies* 8, no. 1 (Fall 2009): 309–332.
3. Thomas Bender, *Toward an Urban Vision: Ideas and Institutions in Nineteenth Century America* (Baltimore: Johns Hopkins University Press, 1975), 4.
4. Marx, *Machine in the Garden*, 3.
5. Richard Hofstadter, *The Age of Reform: From Bryan to F.D.R.* (New York: Alfred A. Knopf, 1956), 23.
6. Ibid., 28–9.
7. Albert Henry Smyth, "Introduction," *The Writings of Benjamin Franklin* (New York: Haskell House, 1970), 148; Merrill D. Peterson, ed., *Thomas Jefferson: Writings* (New York: Library of America, 1984), 301.
8. Richard Hofstadter, *The Age of Reform*, 24.
9. Marx, *Machine in the Garden*, 5.
10. Tamara Thornton, *Cultivating Gentlemen: The Meaning of Country Life among the Boston Elite, 1785–1860* (New Haven: Yale University Press, 1989).
11. Hofstadter, *The Age of Reform*, 28, 24.
12. The United States presents problems in terms of identifying nationalism in the eighteenth and nineteenth centuries, due to the lack of traditional markers (such as language, culture, and history). However, as many scholars have argued, a national consciousness developed and was sustained through print, festival, commemoration, and celebration. See, for example, David Waldstreicher, *In the Midst of Perpetual Fetes: The Making of American Nationalism, 1776–1820* (Chapel Hill: University of North Carolina Press, 1997); Len Travers, *Celebrating the Fourth: Independence Day and the Rites of Nationalism in the Early Republic* (Amherst: University of Massachusetts Press, 1997); and Benedict Anderson, *Imagined Communities: Reflections on the Origin and Spread of Nationalism*, rev. ed. (New York: Verso, 1991).

13. The figure of 12 acres comes from the advertisement for the sale of the grounds in 1792, *Dunlap's American Daily Advertiser*, 22 February 1792. A description of the gardens can be found in William Parker Cutler and Julia Perkins Cutler, eds., *Life Journals and Correspondence of Rev. Manasseh Cutler, L.L.D.* (Cincinnati: Robert Clarke, 1888), 1:276, and David John Jeremy, ed., *Henry Wansey and His American Journal: 1794* (Philadelphia: American Philosophical Society, 1970), 112.
14. *Independent Gazetteer*, 15 May 1790; *Pennsylvania Packet*, 14 July 1789; *Federal Gazette*, 4 June 1791 and 20 August 1791; Geraldine Duclow, "Philadelphia's Pleasure Gardens," *Performing Arts Resources* 21 (1998): 5–6; Alan S. Downer, ed., *The Memoir of John Durang: American Actor, 1785–1816* (Pittsburgh: University of Pittsburgh Press, 1966), 33.
15. Hofstadter, *The Age of Reform*, 24.
16. The reasons for the closures of the individual gardens and the demise of the form as a whole are complex and multiple and will be discussed further in chapter 5.
17. *Columbian Centinel*, 10 February 1798 and 24 February 1798. See also *Federal Gazette*, 28 February 1798.
18. *Federal Gazette*, 8 March 1798.
19. Diaries, 1821–1824, New York Historical Society (New York, 10 May 1822).
20. See, for example, *Spectator*, 10 September 1830 and 19 July 1831.
21. *Spectator*, 16 July 1838 and 23 August 1838; Antonio Blitz, *Fifty Years in the Magic Circle: Being an Account of the Author's Professional Life; His Wonderful Tricks and Feats; With Laughable Incidents and Adventures as a Magician, Necromancer, and Ventriloquist* (San Francisco: A. L. Bancroft, 1871), 122.
22. *Spectator*, 30 June 1841; *Weekly Herald*, 24 July 1841; *OED*, s.v. "Rus in urbe."
23. *Weekly Herald*, 24 July 1841.
24. The night-blooming Cereus was noted as were various flowers and shrubs in several advertisements of 1831. *Spectator*, 19 July and 13 September 1831. The Horticultural Society used Niblo's for a ball in 1830 and an exhibition in 1839, for example. *Spectator*, 10 September 1830 and 5 September 1839.
25. Thomas M. Garrett, "A History of Pleasure Gardens in New York City, 1700–1865" (PhD diss., New York University, 1978), 537.
26. *Federal Gazette* (Baltimore), 30 January 1800; *Maryland Journal*, 7 July 1789; *North American* (Philadelphia), 11 June 1841. "Vauxhall Rural Felicity" was not one of the Vauxhalls run by Delacroix. This business operated on Great George Street for a short period of time. *Daily Advertiser*, 27 June 1793.
27. *Public Ledger*, 30 August 1841; *North American*, 11 June 1841; and *National Gazette*, 21 July 1841.
28. *Federal Gazette* (Philadelphia), 3 July 1790.
29. *Pennsylvania Packet*, 19 May 1789.
30. *National Advocate*, 15 June 1820 and 27 May 1819; *City Gazette* (Charleston, South Carolina), 4 July 1799.

31. *American and Commercial and Daily Advertiser* (Baltimore), 1 July 1805.
32. *National Advocate* (New York), 27 May 1819.
33. *Pennsylvania Packet*, 28 May 1789. The author of this piece is referring to the idea that people of all classes could socialize in pleasure gardens, which until recently was a commonly made assertion of the English sites as well. As Hannah Greig has asserted, this was not, in fact, a reality. Nor, I argue, was it true of the American gardens, where class concerns increasingly dictated who could and could not be admitted to the gardens. Hannah Greig, "'All Together and All Distinct': Public Sociability and Social Exclusivity in London's Pleasure Gardens, ca. 1740–1800," *Journal of British Studies* 51, no. 1 (January 2012): 50–75.
34. Bender, *Toward an Urban Vision*, 13.
35. *Federal Gazette* (Baltimore), 6 June 1800.
36. *American Citizen* (New York), 3 July 1840; *Boston Gazette*, 4 July 1814.
37. Malcolm C. Watkins, "Artificial Lighting in America: 1830–1860," in *Annual Report of the Board of Regents of the Smithsonian Institution Showing the Operations, Expenditures, and Condition of the Institution for the Year Ended June 30, 1951* (Washington, DC: Government Printing Office, 1952), 393.
38. *Boston Gazette*, 7 July 1817.
39. *Federal Gazette* (Philadelphia), 25 July 1791; *The Mail* (Philadelphia), 23 August 1792.
40. *OED*, s.v. "panorama," 1a, and "panoramic," 2.
41. *Evening Post* (New York), 22 August 1815.
42. Such displays were most common on Fourth of July celebrations, which were typically well-attended nights.
43. *Evening Post*, 22 August 1815; *Boston Gazette*, 2 July 1818.
44. Simon Werrett, *Fireworks: Pyrotechnic Arts and Sciences in European History* (Chicago: University of Chicago Press, 2010), 243.
45. Ibid., 133.
46. Ibid.
47. *American Citizen*, 9 June 1806; *New York Gazette and General Advertiser*, 4 August 1804.
48. *New York Gazette*, 24 July 1800.
49. *North American* (Philadelphia), 9 June 1840.
50. *Public Ledger* (Philadelphia), 5 June 1840; *Columbian* (New York), 8 July 1817; *Evening Post* (New York), 17 September 1821; *Boston Gazette*, 2 July 1818.
51. *Baltimore Gazette and Daily Advertiser*, 8 October 1833.
52. *Poulson's American Daily Advertiser* (Philadelphia), 15 May 1819; *New York Herald*, 9 July 1847; *National Advocate* (New York), 9 May 1817.
53. *Mercantile Advertiser* (New York), 21 July 1819; *Columbian Centinel* (Boston), 2 August 1817; *New-York Daily Advertiser*, 1 October 1817; *Franklin Gazette* (Philadelphia), 4 September 1819; *Mercantile Advertiser*, 30 June 1800.
54. *New-York Daily Advertiser*, 1 October 1817.

55. See the conclusion for a more extensive discussion of the evolution of pleasure gardens and displays of increasingly sophisticated technologies.
56. John W. Frick, "'Fireworks, Bonfires, Balloons and More': New York's Palace Garden," *Performing Arts Resources* 21 (1998): 20.

3 PERFORMING CLASS: THE CHALLENGE TO AND REAFFIRMATION OF CLASS DIVISIONS AND HIERARCHIES

1. *Pennsylvania Packet*, 28 May 1789.
2. James N. Barker, *An Oration Delivered at Philadelphia Vauxhall Gardens, on the Forty-First Anniversary of American Independence* (Philadelphia: John Binns, 1817), 9.
3. For a refutation of this popular claim, see Hannah Greig, "'All Together and All Distinct': Public Sociability and Social Exclusivity in London's Pleasure Gardens, ca. 1740–1800," *Journal of British Studies* 51, no. 1 (January 2012): 50–75.
4. James Flint, *Letters From America, Containing Observations on the Climate and Agriculture of the Western States, the Manners of the People, the Prospects of Emigrants, &c., &c.*, ed. Reuben Gold Thwaites (Cleveland: Arthur H. Clark, 1904), 292.
5. Thomas M. Garrett, "A History of Pleasure Gardens in New York City, 1700–1865" (PhD diss., New York University, 1978), 614.
6. Joyce Appleby, "The Social Consequences of the American Revolutionary Ideals in the Early Republic," in *The Middling Sorts: Explorations in the History of the American Middle Class*, ed. Burton J. Bledstein and Robert D. Johnston (New York: Routledge, 2001), 39.
7. Richard Bushman, *The Refinement of America: Persons, Houses, Cities* (New York: Vintage, 1993), xiii.
8. Sean Wilentz, *The Rise of American Democracy: Jefferson to Lincoln* (New York: W. W. Norton, 2005), 20.
9. This assertion is made after surveying newspaper advertisements for the pleasure gardens in the cities discussed herein. The admission fees varied with time and location, and the fact that there was more than one currency in circulation makes simple comparisons between relative costs of entry problematic. In addition to the British shilling and newly created American dollar, the Spanish dollar was also in common circulation at the end of the eighteenth century. The relative worth of these various currencies is an inexact science, with exchange rates fluctuating widely over short periods of time, and having different relative values in different cities. For a more detailed discussion of the problems associated with currency conversions during this time period, see Lawrence H. Officer, *Between the Dollar-Sterling Gold Points: Exchange Rates, Parity, and Market Behavior* (Cambridge: Cambridge University Press,

1996). Precise details of income are difficult to establish, but a report of 1885 for Massachusetts identifies typical wages for various trades from 1752 to 1860, with 1820 being used as the point of comparison for discussion here on the basis of wage information availability and the fact that most of the gardens were in operation with a 50 cent admission charge at that time. Carroll D. Wright, *Comparative Wages, Prices, and Cost of Living, From the Sixteenth Annual Report of the Massachusetts Bureau of Statistics of Labor, for 1885* (Boston: Wright and Potter, 1889).
10. *Boston Daily Advertiser*, April–August 1820.
11. *Boston Daily Advertiser*, 29 April 1820. It was not until the late nineteenth century that Boston developed an elite entertainment culture, with the Boston Museum of Fine Arts being founded in 1870 and the Boston Symphony Orchestra as late as 1881, for example. See Paul DiMaggio, "Cultural Entrepreneurship in Nineteenth-Century Boston: The Creation of an Organizational Base for High Culture in America," in *Cultural Theory and Popular Culture: A Reader*, ed. Paul Storey (Athens: University of Georgia Press, 1998), 454–75.
12. In the South, class divisions were even more pronounced, yet a similar audience was targeted. As Nicholas Butler notes, "there was a clear sense of social stratification in South Carolina," and of class "inflation" coupled with social ambition that allowed for numerous balls and series of concerts to be sustained. Nicholas Michael Butler, *Votaries of Apollo: The St. Cecilia Society and the Patronage of Concert Music in Charleston, South Carolina, 1766–1820* (Columbia: University of South Carolina Press, 2007), 8–9.
13. It should be noted here that the 50 cents admission was for activities in the gardens and not for the performances in the newly opened theatre found within Washington Gardens. Access to the theatre will be discussed later.
14. Lawrence W. Levine, *Highbrow/Lowbrow: The Emergence of Cultural Hierarchy in America* (Cambridge: Cambridge University Press, 1988), 177.
15. *Franklin Gazette*, 2 July 1819.
16. *Baltimore Daily Intelligencer*, 28 May 1794; *Spectator*, 2 July 1835.
17. *Pennsylvania Packet*, 5 September 1789; *Federal Gazette*, 30 January 1800.
18. *North American*, 11 June 1841; *Maryland Journal*, 7 July 1789.
19. *Pennsylvania Packet*, 28 May 1789.
20. *Boston Daily Advertiser*, 17 August 1815; *New York Herald*, 17 June 1845.
21. *Pennsylvania Packet*, 19 June 1790.
22. *Baltimore Gazette and Daily Advertiser*, 8 October 1833.
23. *City Gazette*, 18 July 1804; *Boston Gazette*, 17 July 1815; *Boston Intelligencer*, 15 May 1819.
24. *Commercial Advertiser*, 10 August 1801.
25. *Spectator*, 9 September 1839.
26. Even in the "Temple of Love" event described above, women were targeted, but tickets were sold to men so they could accompany the women.
27. Garrett, "A History of Pleasure Gardens in New York City," 608.

28. *American and Commercial Daily Advertiser*, 19 September 1801, and 10 July 1802; *Boston Gazette*, 31 August 1815; *Public Ledger*, 3 August 1839; *Baltimore Patriot*, 31 July 1831.
29. *New York Herald*, 30 July 1847; *Mercantile Advertiser*, 30 June 1800; *City Gazette*, 13 June 1807.
30. *Boston Intelligencer*, 29 August 1818; *City Gazette*, 7 April 1809.
31. Bruce A. McConachie, *Melodramatic Formations: American Theatre and Society, 1820–1870* (Iowa City: University of Iowa Press, 1992), 157.
32. Ibid., 158.
33. *Daily Advertiser*, 2 May 1803; David John Jeremy, ed., *Henry Wansey and His American Journal: 1794* (Philadelphia: American Philosophical Society, 1970), 95.
34. *Daily Advertiser*, 14 April 1800.
35. Of course, requiring certain standards of dress even on free days, meant that the extreme lower classes would have been unable to attend even on such days, as they would not necessarily have had access to appropriate attire.
36. Levine, *Highbrow/Lowbrow*, 177.
37. Ibid.
38. Gardens with theatres included Washington Gardens, Columbian Gardens, Niblo's Garden, Vauxhall, New York, and Vauxhall, Charleston.
39. Edwin G. Burrows and Mike Wallace, *Gotham: A History of New York City to 1898* (New York: Oxford University Press, 1999), 585.
40. *Daily Advertiser*, 2 May 1803.
41. Ibid.
42. Burrows and Wallace, *Gotham*, 585, 642.
43. Paul Gilje, *The Road to Mobocracy: Popular Disorder in New York City, 1763–1834* (Chapel Hill: University of North Carolina Press, 1987), 252.
44. Levine, *Highbrow/Lowbrow*, 177.
45. Bruce A. McConachie, "New York Operagoing, 1825–50: Creating an Elite Social Ritual," *American Music* 6, no. 2 (Summer 1988): 189, 181.
46. L. Maria Child, *Letters From New York: Second Series* (Boston: J. H. Francis, 1845), 171.
47. Asa Greene, *Glance at New York: Embracing the City Government, Theatres, Hotels, Churches, Mobs, Monopolies, Learned Professions, Newspapers, Rogues, Dandies, Fires and Firemen, Water and Other Liquids, &c. &c.* (New York: A. Green, 1837), 216–17.
48. Child, *Letters From New York*, 171.
49. *Federal Gazette*, 10 September 1796; *Daily Advertiser*, 4 July 1799; *Boston Daily Advertiser*, 1 August 1814; *Baltimore Gazette and Daily Advertiser*, 18 February 1832.
50. *City Gazette*, 7 April 1809.
51. *New-York American*, 4 May 1826.
52. *Federal Gazette*, 10 September 1796.
53. *General Advertiser*, 6 July 1791.

54. Joseph Jackson, "Vauxhall Garden," *Pennsylvania Magazine of History and Biography* 57 (1933): 294.
55. Ibid., 295; Alan S. Downer, ed., *The Memoir of John Durang: American Actor, 1785–1816* (Pittsburgh: University of Pittsburgh Press, 1966), 141.
56. Gilje, *The Road to Mobocracy*, 246.
57. *American and Commercial Daily Advertiser*, 13 July 1805.
58. *Public Ledger*, 5 June 1840.
59. *New York Herald*, 17 August 1845.
60. Harold Donaldson Eberlein and Cortlandt Van Dyke Hubbard, "The American 'Vauxhall' of The Federal Era," *Pennsylvania Magazine of History and Biography* 57 (1944): 166; Garrett, "A History of Pleasure Gardens in New York City," 611.
61. Cornelius Matthews, *The Career of Puffer Hopkins* (1842; New York: Garrett Press, 1970), 214–15.
62. Ibid., 217–8, 223.
63. Benjamin Baker, "A Glance at New York (1848)," in *On Stage America!*, ed. Walter J. Meserve (New York: Feedback Theatrebooks and Prospero Press, 1996); Francis A. Durivage, "Love in the Bowery," in *Stray Subjects, Arrested and Bound Over* (Philadelphia: Carey and Hart, 1848), 103–5. Additional literary records of pleasure gardens are found in the various short poems published in newspapers.
64. Tyler Anbinder, *Five Points: The 19th-Century New York City Neighborhood That Invented Tap Dance, Stole Elections, and became the World's Most Notorious Slum* (New York: Free Press, 2001), 180–81.
65. Baker, "A Glance at New York," 195.
66. Durivage, "Love in the Bowery," 103.

4 PERFORMING RACE: NATIVE AMERICANS AND AFRICAN AMERICANS WITHIN THE GARDENS

1. John W. Francis, *Old New York; or, Reminiscences of the Past Sixty Years* (1857; New York: Benjamin Blom, 1971), 20. It is not clear exactly when the performance he witnessed took place; Francis refers to it having been in "earlier days" and from his description of the gardens' size, it was possibly as early as the 1800s—perhaps even the same performance recorded in Vauxhall in 1804 discussed below.
2. *Morning Chronicle* (New York), 11 August 1804; *New York Herald*, 29 August 1858; *American and Commercial Daily Advertiser*, 27 July 1805; William S. Rossiter, ed., *Days and Ways in Old Boston* (Boston: R. H. Stearns, 1915), 123; *New York Herald*, 29 August 1858, 7; *New York Herald*, 22 July 1858, 7.
3. Similar events within the theatre have been noted, and the "authenticity" of war dances has been questioned in such articles as Rosemarie K. Bank,

"Staging the 'Native': Making History in American Theatre Culture, 1828–1838," *Theatre Journal* 45, no. 4 (December 1993): 461–86.
4. See *City Gazette* (Charleston), 29 July 1799, for example.
5. See *Spectator*, 21 September 1835, for evidence of African Americans being employed at Niblo's Garden.
6. See *The Repertory*, 17 July 1819, for an example of an advertisement detailing admission prices for various seating areas, including the "seats...for persons of color."
7. George Catlin, *Catlin's Notes: Eight Years' Travels and Residence in Europe, North American Indian Collection* (London: Burgess, Stringer, 1848), 2: 117–18.
8. A similar instance of assuming the gardens to be an appropriate space for Native Americans within the city can be seen in an error in historiography that led Geraldine Duclow to trust Joseph Jackson's erroneous assertion that John H. Jewitt recounted his experiences of being held captive by Native Americans in Vauxhall, Philadelphia. Geraldine Duclow, "Philadelphia's Early Pleasure Gardens," *Performing Arts Resources* 21 (1998): 10; Joseph Jackson, "Vauxhall Gardens," *Pennsylvania Magazine of History and Biography* 57, no. 4 (1933): 293.
9. Philip J. Deloria, *Playing Indian* (New Haven: Yale University Press, 1998), 4.
10. *Morning Chronicle*, 11 August 1804.
11. *Daily Advertiser*, 15 August 1804.
12. Francis, *Old New York*, 20.
13. *New York Herald*, 29 August 1858, 7. Caps in original.
14. *The Globe*, 11 and 15 February 1836, quoted in Bank, "Staging the 'Native,'" 483.
15. *American and Commercial Daily Advertiser*, 27 July 1805.
16. Ibid., 7 September 1805.
17. Ibid., 6 August 1806.
18. *New York Herald*, 29 August 1858, 7.
19. Wolfgang Hochbruck, "'I Ask for Justice': Native American Fourth of July Orations," in *The Fourth of July: Political Oratory and Literary Reactions 1776–1876*, ed. Paul Goetsch and Gerd Hurm (Tübingen: Narr, 1992), 155.
20. Robert F. Berkhofer Jr., *The White Man's Indian: Images of the American Indian from Columbus to the Present* (New York: Vintage Books, 1979), 23.
21. Theresa Strouth Gaul, "'The Genuine Indian who was Brought upon Stage': Edwin Forrest's Metamora and White Audiences," *Arizona Quarterly* 56, no. 1 (Spring 2000): 9.
22. Don B. Wilmeth, "Noble or Ruthless Savage? The America Indian on Stage and in the Drama," *Journal of American Drama and Theatre* 1, no. 1 (Spring 1989): 39–78; Jeffrey H. Richards, *Drama, Theatre and Identity in the American New Republic* (Cambridge: Cambridge University Press, 2005); Eugene H. Jones, *Native Americans as Shown on the Stage, 1753–1916* (Metuchen, NJ: Scarecrow Press, 1988); Richard E. Amacher, "Behind the

Curtain with the Management of Indian Plays, 1825–1860," *Theatre Survey* 7 (1966): 101–14; and Gaul, "The Genuine Indian who was Brought Upon Stage."
23. See Sally A. Jones, "The First but Not the Last of the 'Vanishing Indians': Edwin Forrest and Mythic Re-creations of the Native Population," in *Dressing in Feathers: The Construction of the Indian in American Popular Culture*, ed. S. Elizabeth Bird (Colorado: Westview Press, 1996), 13–27; Vivien Green Fryd, "Imagining the Indians in the United States Capitol during the Early Republic," in *Native Americans and the Early Republic*, ed. Frederick E. Hoxie, Ronald Hoffman, and Peter J. Albert (Charlottesville: University Press of Virginia, 1999), 297–330; and Bank, "Staging the 'Native.'"
24. See, for example, *New York Times*, 1 December 1862.
25. Marvin Edward McAllister, *White People Do Not Know How to Behave at Entertainments Designed for Ladies & Gentlemen of Colour: William Brown's African & American Theater* (Chapel Hill: University of North Carolina Press, 2003), 88.
26. See Robert S. Tilton, *Pocahontas: The Evolution of an American Narrative* (New York: Cambridge University Press, 1994), for a more detailed discussion of the circulation of this story.
27. Zoe Detsi-Diamanti, "Burlesquing 'Otherness' in Nineteenth-Century American Theatre: The Image of the Indian in John Brougham's *Met-a-mora; or, The Last of the Pollywogs* (1847) and *Po-Ca-Hon-Tas; or, the Gentle Savage* (1855)," *American Studies* 48, no. 3 (Fall 2007): 112.
28. Tilton, *Pocahontas*, 51.
29. *New York Herald*, 29 August 1858, 7. Although the exact text of this production is unclear, it seems unlikely to have been Brougham's burlesque (discussed below), but rather a more serious/traditional retelling, along the lines of James Nelson Barker's *Indian Princess; Or, La Belle Sauvage* (1808).
30. *New York Herald*, 22 July 1858, 7.
31. John Brougham, *Po-Ca-Hon-Tas; or, the Gentle Savage*, in *Dramas from the American Theatre, 1762–1909*, ed. Richard Moody (Cleveland: World Publishing Company, 1966), 406, 404, 408, 409.
32. Ibid., 421.
33. Tilton, *Pocahontas*, 76.
34. *New York American*, 16 June 1823, cited in McAllister, *White People Do Not Know*, 94.
35. *New York Herald*, 29 August 1858, 7.
36. David Gerstner, "Nineteenth-Century Formulations of Masculinity and Realism: The Body of Edwin Forrest," in *Manly Arts: Masculinity and Nation in Early American Cinema* (Durham: Duke University Press, 2006), 16.
37. Ibid; Gaul, "The Genuine Indian Who Was Brought Upon Stage," 10.
38. *Morning Chronicle*, 11 August 1804.
39. *American and Commercial Daily Advertiser*, 27 July and 7 September 1805.
40. Richards, *Drama, Theatre, and Identity*, 187.

41. Anthony D. Smith, *Chosen Peoples: Sacred Sources of National Identity* (Oxford: Oxford University Press, 2003), 24.
42. Hochbruck, "I Ask for Justice," 156.
43. Gary B. Nash, *Forging Freedom: The Formation of Philadelphia's Black Community, 1720–1840* (Cambridge: Harvard University Press, 1991), 223.
44. Shane White, *Stylin': African American Expressive Culture from its Beginnings to the Zoot Suit* (Ithaca: Cornell University Press, 1998), 106.
45. Ibid., 92.
46. [William Newnham Blane], *An Excursion through the United States and Canada during the Years 1822–23 by an English Gentleman* (London: Baldwin, Craddock, and Joy, 1824), 25; John F. Watson, *Annals of Philadelphia, Being a Collection of Memoirs, Anecdotes, & Incidents of the City and its Inhabitants from the Days of the Pilgrim Founders* (Philadelphia: E. L. Carey and A. Hart, 1830), 479.
47. Nancy Reynolds Davison, "E. W. Clay: American Political Caricaturist of the Jacksonian Era" (PhD diss., University of Michigan, 1980), 85. Other series were issued in New York and London.
48. Ibid., 94.
49. Email communication from Shane White to Phil Lapsansky (Curator of African American History at the Library Company of Philadelphia), 27 January 1999. In "Life in Philadelphia" file, Library Company of Philadelphia.
50. See *City Gazette* (Charleston), 29 July 1799; *New-York American*, 4 May 1826.
51. A "colored man" who was a waiter (Charles) died in a fire of 1835. *Spectator*, 21 September 1835.
52. W. Harrison Bayles, *Old Taverns of New York* (New York: Frank Allaben Genealogical Company, 1915), 453; *City Gazette*, 21 July 1801.
53. *The Repertory*, 17 July 1819. Boxes were available for whites at 75 cents.
54. *Evening Post*, 23 August 1838.
55. While I have been able to identify four short-lived pleasure gardens for African Americans in New York, I have not been able to do so for the other cities under discussion. This does not mean that there were not any such venues in the various cities, just that the documentation is difficult to locate. For a discussion of the gardens in New Orleans, see Lake Douglas, "Pleasure Gardens in Nineteenth-Century New Orleans: 'Useful for All Classes of Society,'" in *The Pleasure Garden, from Vauxhall to Coney Island*, edited by Jonathan Conlin (Philadelphia: University of Pennsylvania Press, 2013).
56. McAllister, *White People Do Not Know*, 29. Brown provides the street address in his advertisement, *New-York Gazette*, 13 June 1821.
57. *New-York Gazette*, 13 June 1821. Brown went on to open the African Theatre the following year—a theatre famous for the "Shakespeare riots" and for seeing African American actors, Ira Aldridge and James Hewlett, on the stage.
58. Mordecai Noah's commentary appeared in the *National Advocate*, and his lengthy description of the gardens (dominated by his opinion of how

ridiculous the sight was to him) was reprinted in various newspapers across the country.
59. *Freedom's Journal*, 8 June 1827. The same advertisement was placed each week until 14 September 1827, suggesting the venue was in operation throughout the season.
60. *Freedom's Journal*, 2 May 1828. The same advertisement was placed each week until 11 September 1828, suggesting the venue was in operation throughout the season.
61. McAllister, *White People Do Not Know*, 37.
62. *New York Evening Post*, 16 July 1829.
63. The class status associated with the gardens may not have matched the reality of the patrons, but the association prevailed, as discussed in the previous chapter.
64. McAllister, *White People Do Not Know*, 29. Presumably white people were able to attend if they wished, as Noah was able to enter the African Grove.
65. *Freedom's Journal*, 8 June 1827.
66. McAllister, *White People Do Not Know*, 15.
67. White, *Stylin'*, chap. 4, and McAllister, *White People Do Not Know*, chap. 1.
68. *National Advocate*, 3 August 1821.
69. McAllister, *White People Do Not Know*, 20.
70. Ibid., 18, 22.
71. Ibid., 32.
72. Ibid., 34, 35.
73. Deloria, *Playing Indian*, 5.

5 BEYOND THE PLEASURE GARDEN

1. Stephen Burge Johnson, *The Roof Gardens of Broadway Theatres, 1883–1942* (Ann Arbor: UMI Research Press, 1985), 2; Thomas M. Garrett, "A History of Pleasure Gardens in New York City, 1700–1865" (PhD diss., New York University, 1978), 636; Raymond M. Weinstein, "Disneyland and Coney Island: Reflections of the Evolution of the Modern Amusement Park," *Journal of Popular Culture* 66, no. 1 (Summer 1992): 136.
2. Katy Matheson, "Niblo's Garden and its 'Concert Saloon,' 1828–1846," *Performing Arts Resources* 21 (1998): 93, 54; Brooks McNamara, *The New York Concert Saloon: The Devil's Own Nights* (New York: Cambridge University Press, 2002), 9.
3. Niblo's and Palace Garden, New York, became theatres, as did Vauxhall, Charleston and Washington Gardens, Boston. As late as 1940, a pleasure garden was in operation in Butte, Montana. Opening in 1899, this garden attempted to recreate the feel of a mid-nineteenth-century pleasure garden, evoking a sense of nostalgia for the form, even as it operated as a new business. Harry C. Freeman, *A Brief History of Butte, Montana: The World's*

Greatest Mining Camp (Chicago: Henry O'Shepard, 1900), 48–51. See also figure 5.3.
4. See, for example, Warwick Wroth, *Cremorne and the Later London Gardens* (London: Elliot Stock, 1907); Heath Schenker, "Pleasure Gardens, Theme Parks, and the Picturesque," in *Theme Park Landscapes: Antecedents and Variations*, ed. Terence Young and Robert Riley (Washington, DC: Dumbarton Oaks Research Library and Collection, 2002); Matheson, "Niblo's Garden and its 'Concert Saloon'"; and Johnson, *The Roof Gardens of Broadway Theatres*.
5. Johnson, *The Roof Gardens of Broadway Theatres*, 2–5.
6. Ibid., 7.
7. McNamara, *The New York Concert Saloon*, 1.
8. Ibid., 8.
9. Matheson, "Niblo's Garden and its 'Concert Saloon,'" 99.
10. *OED* s.v. "vaudeville," 2 and "variety," 9b.
11. See, for example, the programs printed for the Columbia Gardens, Baltimore, in the *American and Commercial Daily Advertiser* in 1805 and 1806; the variety recorded for McArann's Garden, Philadelphia, *Public Ledger*, 5 June 1840; and for Vauxhall, New York, in the *New York Herald*, 17 August 1845.
12. Frank Cullen, *Vaudeville Old and New: An Encyclopedia of Variety Performers in America*, vol. 1 (New York: Routledge, 2007), xv; George C. Odell, *Annals of the New York Stage* (1927; New York: AMS Press, 1970), 4:160, 180. See also Foster Rhea Dulles, *America Learns to Play: A History of Popular Recreation, 1607–1940* (New York: D. Appleton-Century, 1940).
13. See, for example, Schenker, "Pleasure Gardens, Theme Parks, and the Picturesque"; and Josephine Kane, "Edwardian Amusement Parks: The Pleasure Garden Reborn?" in Jonathan Conlin, ed. *The Pleasure Garden, from Vauxhall to Coney Island* (Philadelphia: University of Pennsylvania Press, 2013).
14. Other arguments seeing a link between the two forms have focused on the growing eclecticism: "By the early nineteenth century the pleasure garden had the look and feel of a fairground." Johnson, *The Roof Gardens of Broadway Theatres*, 2.
15. Neil Harris describes pleasure gardens, amusement parts, and theme parks as "siblings" in "Expository Expositions: Preparing for the Theme Parks," in *Designing Disney's Theme Parks: The Architecture of Reassurance*, ed. Karal Ann Marling (New York: Flammarion, 1997), 20.
16. Garrett, "A History of Pleasure Gardens in New York City," 616–20.
17. Roy Rosenzweig and Elizabeth Blackmar, *The Park and the People: A History of Central Park* (Ithaca: Cornell University Press, 1992), 103.
18. Ibid., 104.
19. Ibid., 110.
20. Schenker, "Pleasure Gardens, Theme Parks, and the Picturesque," 69–70, 82, 86.

21. While Central Park should not be allowed to stand in for all public parks, this example presents an interesting case study in that planners had actively to choose between specific proposals from various parties, rather than contracting a landscape architect (a new job title at that time) to undertake the commission. However, many public parks (designed by Olmsted or not) adhered to the same principles and were responding to similar drives.
22. Weinstein, "Disneyland and Coney Island," 133.
23. Harris, "Expository Expositions," 20.
24. George L. Scheper, "The Reformist Vision of Frederick Law Olmsted and the Poetics of Park Design," *New England Quarterly* 62, no. 3 (September 1989): 373; Frederick Law Olmstead, *Civilizing American Cities: Writings on City Landscapes*, ed. S. B. Sutton (New York: Da Capo Press, 1997), 96.
25. "National Association for Olmsted Parks," accessed 5 February 2011, http://www.olmsted.org/ht/d/sp/i/1162/pid/1162.
26. John F. Kasson, *Amusing the Million: Coney Island at the Turn of the Century* (New York: Hill and Wang, 1978), 18–20.
27. Other examples of inventions being displayed in pleasure gardens can be seen with the various balloon ascensions (at Vauxhall, New York, Columbia Gardens [Baltimore], and Washington Gardens [Boston], for example), the demonstration of the velocipede at Vauxhall (Philadelphia), and the various developments in firework technologies. This (along with its relationship to national pride) has been discussed in more depth in chapter 2.
28. Edwin Forrest Murdock, "The American Institute," in *A Century of Industrial Progress*, ed. Frederic William Wile (New York: Doubleday, Doran, 1928), v–vi.
29. Ethan Robey, "The Utility of Art: Mechanics' Institute Fairs in New York City, 1828–1876" (PhD diss., Columbia University, 2000), 628–35.
30. "American Institute of the City of New-York. Sixteenth Annual Fair," SY1843, no. 15, New York Historical Society.
31. John E. Findling and Kimberly D. Pelle, eds., Preface to *Encyclopedia of World's Fairs and Expositions* (Jefferson, NC: McFarland, 2008), 6.
32. Ibid., 7.
33. New York Historical Society, "Guide to the Records of the American Institute of the City of New York for the Encouragement of Science and Invention 1808–1983 (Bulk 1828–1940)," finding aid, accessed 5 January 2011, http://dlib.nyu.edu/findingaids/html/nyhs/americaninst2.html.
34. Ibid.
35. Indeed, Findling and Pelle have a valid point when they observe that the world's fairs hosted in France and England played a large role in the decisions made by the US fair organizers.
36. John R. Davis, "New York 1853," in Findling and Pelle, eds., *Encyclopedia of World's Fairs and Expositions*, 18.
37. The American Institute's annual fair was held in the (New York) Crystal Palace every year between 1853 and 1858. Robey, "The Utility of Art," 633.

38. Russell Lewis, Preface to Neil Harris, Wim de Wit, James Gilbert, and Robert W. Rydell, *Grand Illusions: Chicago's World's Fair of 1893* (Chicago: Chicago Historical Society, 1993), xi–xii.
39. Wim de Wit, "Building an Illusion: The Design of the World's Columbian Exposition" in *Grand Illusions*, 71.
40. Ibid., 72.
41. Kasson, *Amusing the Million*, 18–19. While Kasson uses Central Park as his chief example, he allows his argument to encompass all nineteenth-century public parks, using Central Park as the specific example only due to its ubiquity. The problem of allowing Central Park to stand in for all public parks is also seen in discussions of world's fairs, where the White City is frequently permitted to stand in for the idea of American world's fairs.
42. R. Reid Badger, "Chicago 1893," in Findling and Pelle, eds., *Encyclopedia of World's Fairs and Expositions*, 123.
43. Wim de Wit, "Building an Illusion" in *Grand Illusions*, 72.
44. James Gilbert, *Perfect Cities: Chicago's Utopias of 1893* (Chicago: University of Chicago Press, 1991), 36.
45. It should be noted, however, that although American world's typically fairs aimed to make a profit, this was not always the case. The Columbian Exposition did, however, make a small profit. Badger, "Chicago 1893," 123.
46. Ibid., 119.
47. Miki Pfeffer, "New Orleans 1884–1885," in Findling and Pelle, eds., *Encyclopedia of World's Fairs and Expositions*, 83.
48. Gilbert, *Perfect Cities*, 83, 111.
49. Lewis, preface, *Grand Illusions*, xii.
50. Ibid., 144–50.
51. Badger, "Chicago 1893," 123.
52. Robert W. Rydell, *World of Fairs: The Century-of-Progress Expositions* (Chicago: University of Chicago Press, 1993), 21.
53. Rydell, "A Cultural Frankenstein?" in *Grand Illusions*, 164.
54. Judith A. Adams, *The American Amusement Park Industry: A History of Technology and Thrills* (Boston: Twayne, 1991), xiii. I do, however, question her claim that world's fairs "gave us... the presentation of exotic cultural environments as exhibits."
55. In using the term "amusement park," I wish to distinguish it from the more recent term "theme park." Although there is a general consensus that amusement parks and theme parks are different, the definitions vary significantly. Margaret J. King argues that "amusement parks use the immediate physical gratification of the thrill ride," while a theme park "is a total-immersion art form built to capture a coherent mind experience, one that owes more to physics." Weinstein argues that amusement parks can be defined by their "lower admission costs and shorter lines... classic mechanic rides... and provide local residents the opportunity for one-day excursions," with theme parks offering the opposite in all cases. Yet much of this definition consigns amusement

parks to the past (making the definition easy to interpret as meaning that "amusement parks are older than theme parks"). Stephen Mills differentiates between the two by identifying theme parks as defined, contained spaces requiring an admission fee, while amusement parks are open to all, in a space undefined or free to enter (but with rides requiring a fee); yet Coney Island's various amusement parks were defined spaces requiring a fee to enter. In using the terms "amusement park" and "theme park," I acknowledge the main difference being the degree of commercialism and corporate sponsorship associated with the latter. Although the concept of "theme" for theme parks is central, many amusement parks have (and have had) themes that unite the various rides and displays. The overt corporate sponsorship of such modern parks such as Disneyland, Universal Studios, and Island of Adventure is what allows them to be identified as "theme parks," as I understand it—the "theme" is not the unity of concept or idea, but rather its association with the sponsor. Margaret J. King, "Theme and Amusement Parks," in *Encyclopedia of Recreation and Leisure in America*, ed. Gary S. Cross (Detroit: Thomson Gale, 2004), 2:364; Raymond Weinstein, "Amusement Parks," in *Encyclopedia of Urban America: The Cities and the Suburbs*, ed. Neil Larry Shumsky (Santa Barbara: ABC-CLIO, 1998), 1:25; Stephen F. Mills, *The American Landscape* (Edinburgh: Keele University Press, 1997), 101–2.

56. Kasson, *Amusing the Million*, 23–4.
57. Ibid., 27–8.
58. See, for example, Weinstein, "Amusement Parks," 23.
59. Weinstein, "Disneyland and Coney Island," 135.
60. Regular service to Coney Island was offered by steamship from 1847 (the journey taking about two hours) and via a plank road from 1850. By the end of the 1870s, nine steamboats and five rail lines covered the distance in half an hour. Woody Register, "Coney Island," in *Encyclopedia of Recreation and Leisure in America*, ed. Gary S. Cross, vol. 1 (Detroit: Thomson Gale, 2004), 239–40.
61. Kasson, *Amusing the Million*, 37.
62. Ibid., 34.
63. Adams, *The American Amusement Park Industry*, 45.
64. In present-day theme parks, it is common for riders to have their photograph taken while on a rollercoaster, further continuing this focus on the patron as spectacle.
65. See Schenker, "Pleasure Gardens, Theme Parks, and the Picturesque"; and Kane, "Edwardian Amusement Parks: The Pleasure Garden Reborn?"
66. Robert Cartmell, *The Incredible Scream Machine: A History of the Rollercoaster* (Bowling Green: Bowling Green State University Popular Press, 1987), 1–47.
67. Adams, *The American Amusement Park Industry*, 43.
68. Freeman, *A Brief History of Butte, Montana*, 48–51. See figure 5.3 for an illustration of the gardens, ca. 1940.

69. Kasson, *Amusing the Million*, 57.
70. Ibid., 61.
71. Harris, "Expository Expositions," 21.
72. Register, *The Kid of Coney Island*, 80.
73. The volcanic eruption reenactment most commonly seen in pleasure gardens was the eruption of Mount Etna, while Luna Park hosted that of Vesuvius. Adams, *The American Amusement Park Industry*, 49.
74. Register, *The Kid of Coney Island*, 17; Neil Harris, "Museums, Merchandising, and Popular Taste: The Struggle for Influence," in *Material Culture and the Study of American* Life, ed. Ian M. G. Quimby (New York: W. W. Norton, 1975), 140–74.
75. Bureau of the Census, *Fourteenth Census of the United States Taken in the Year 1920*, vol. 1 (Washington, DC: Government Printing Office, 1921), 57.
76. See Michael Kammen, *American Culture, American Tastes: Social Change and the 20th Century* (New York: Alfred Knopf, 1999), chap. 1, for further discussion of popular culture, mass culture, and the change seen in the early twentieth century.
77. Harris, "Expository Expositions," 20.
78. Adams, *The American Amusement Park Industry*, 45.
79. Anthony D. Smith, *Chosen Peoples: Sacred Sources of National Identity* (Oxford: Oxford University Press, 2003), 24–5.
80. Harris, "Expository Expositions," 21.
81. Ibid., 26.
82. Schenker, "Pleasure Gardens, Theme Parks, and the Picturesque," 89.

Selected Bibliography

Adams, Judith A. *The American Amusement Park Industry: A History of Technology and Thrills.* Boston: Twayne, 1991.
Amacher, Richard E. "Behind the Curtain with the Management of Indian Plays, 1825–1860." *Theatre Survey* 7, no. 2 (1966): 101–14.
Anbinder, Tyler. *Five Points: The 19th-Century New York City Neighborhood That Invented Tap Dance, Stole Elections, and Became the World's Most Notorious Slum.* New York: Free Press, 2001.
Anderson, Benedict. *Imagined Communities: Reflections on the Origin and Spread of Nationalism.* 1983. Rev. ed. New York: Verso, 1991.
Appleby, Joyce. "The Social Consequences of the American Revolutionary Ideals in the Early Republic." In *The Middling Sorts: Explorations in the History of the American Middle Class,* edited by Burton J. Bledstein and Robert D. Johnston, 31–49. New York: Routledge, 2001.
Baker, Benjamin. "A Glance at New York (1848)." In *On Stage America! A Selection of Distinctly American Plays,* edited by Walter J. Meserve, 162–96. New York: Feedback Theatrebooks and Prospero Press, 1996.
Bank, Rosemary K. "Staging the 'Native': Making History in American Theatre Culture, 1828–1838." *Theatre Journal* 45, no. 4 (December 1993): 461–86.
———. *Theatre Culture in America, 1825–1860.* New York: Cambridge University Press, 1997.
Barker, James N. *An Oration Delivered at Philadelphia Vauxhall Gardens, on the Forty-First Anniversary of American Independence.* Philadelphia: John Binns, 1817.
Barnum, P. T. *The Life of P. T. Barnum Written by Himself.* Introduction by Terence Whalen. New York: Tubbs, Nesmith, and Teall, 1854; Urbana: University of Illinois Press, 2000.
Barringer, Tim. "The Course of Empires: Landscape and Identity in America and Britain, 1820–1880." In Andrew Wilton and Tim Barringer, *The American Sublime: Landscape Painting in the United States, 1820–1880,* 39–65. Princeton: Princeton University Press, 2002.
Bayles, W. Harrison. *Old Taverns of New York.* New York: Frank Allaben Genealogical Company, 1915.
Bender, Thomas. *Towards an Urban Vision: Ideas and Institutions in Nineteenth Century America.* Baltimore: Johns Hopkins University Press, 1975.

Berkhofer, Robert F. *The White Man's Indian: Images of the American Indian from Columbus to the Present*. New York: Vintage Books, 1979.

Blair, John Purdy Jr. "Productions at Niblo's Garden Theatre, 1849–1862." PhD diss., University of Georgia, 1982.

[Blane, William Newnham]. *An Excursion through the United States and Canada during the Years 1822–23 by an English Gentleman*. London: Baldwin, Craddock, and Joy, 1824.

Blitz, Antonio. *Fifty Years in the Magic Circle: Being an Account of the Author's Professional Life; His Wonderful Tricks and Feats; With Laughable Incidents and Adventures as a Magician, Necromancer, and Ventriloquist*. San Francisco: A. L. Bancroft, 1871.

Bloom, Arthur W. "Science and Sensation, Entertainment and Enlightenment: John Mix and the Columbian Museum and Gardens." *Performing Arts Resources* 21 (1998): 33–49.

Blumin, Stuart M. *The Emergence of the Middle Class: Social Experience in the American City, 1760–1900*. New York: Cambridge University Press, 1989.

Brewer, John. *The Pleasures of the Imagination: English Culture in the Eighteenth Century*. New York: Farrar Straus Giroux, 1997.

Brougham, John. "Po-Ca-Hon-Tas; or, the Gentle Savage." In *Dramas from the American Theatre, 1762–1909*, edited by Richard Moody, 403–21. Cleveland: World Publishing Company, 1966.

Brown, Jared. *The Theatre in America during the Revolution*. Cambridge: Cambridge University Press, 1995.

Buckley, Peter George. "To the Opera House: Culture and Society in New York City, 1820–1860." PhD diss., State University of New York at Stony Brook, 1984.

Burney, Fanny. *Evelina; or, the History of a Young Lady's Entrance into the World*. London: Harrison, 1861.

Burrows, Edwin G., and Mike Wallace. *Gotham: A History of New York City to 1898*. New York: Oxford University Press, 1999.

Bushman, Richard. *The Refinement of America: Persons, Houses, Cities*. New York: Vintage, 1993.

Butler, Nicholas Michael. *Votaries of Apollo: The St. Cecilia Society and the Patronage of Concert Music in Charleston, South Carolina, 1766–1820*. Columbia: University of South Carolina Press, 2007.

Caldwell, Mark. "Defining American Urbanity: Royall Tyler, William Dunlap, and the Postrevolutionary Theater in New York." *Early American Studies* 8, no. 1 (Fall 2009): 309–32.

Cartmell, Robert. *The Incredible Scream Machine: A History of the Rollercoaster*. Bowling Green: Bowling Green State University Popular Press, 1987.

Catlin, George. *Catlin's Notes: Eight Years' Travels and Residence in Europe, North American Indian Collection*. 2 vols. London: Burgess, Stringer, 1848.

Child, L. Maria. *Letters From New York. Second Series*. Boston: J. H. Francis, 1845.

Cillessen, Wolfgang. "Exoticism and Commerce: Vauxhalls in Pre-Revolutionary France." Paper presented at "Vauxhall Revisited: Pleasure Gardens and Their Publics, 1660–1880," Tate Britain, London, July 15–16, 2008.
Clapp, William W. *Record of the Boston Stage*. 1853. Reprint, New York: Greenwood Press, 1969.
Coke, David. "Roubiliac's Handel for Vauxhall Gardens: A Sculpture in Context." *Sculpture Journal* 16, no. 2 (Autumn 2007): 5–22.
———. "Vauxhall Gardens." www.vauxhallgardens.com.
Coke, David, and Alan Borg. *Vauxhall Gardens: A History*. New Haven: Yale University Press, 2012.
Conlin, Jonathan, ed. *The Pleasure Garden, from Vauxhall to Coney Island*. Philadelphia: University of Pennsylvania Press, 2013.
Cross, Gary S. *Encyclopedia of Recreation and Leisure in America*. 2 vols. Detroit: Thomson Gale, 2004.
Cullen, Frank. *Vaudeville Old and New: An Encyclopedia of Variety Performers in America*. 2 vols. New York: Routledge, 2007.
Cutler, William Parker, and Julia Perkins Cutler, eds. *Life Journals and Correspondence of Rev. Manasseh Cutler, L.L.D.* 3 vols. Cincinnati: Robert Clarke, 1888.
Davison, Nancy Reynolds. "E. W. Clay: American Political Caricaturist of the Jacksonian Era." PhD diss., University of Michigan, 1980.
Day, Susan Stockbridge. "Productions at Niblo's Garden Theatre, 1862–1868, during the Management of William Wheatley." PhD diss., University of Oregon, 1972.
De Bolla, Peter. *The Education of the Eye: Painting, Landscape, and Architecture in Eighteenth-Century Britain*. Stanford: Stanford University Press, 2003.
Deloria, Philip J. *Playing Indian*. New Haven: Yale University Press, 1998.
Detsi-Diamanti, Zoe. "Burlesquing 'Otherness' in Nineteenth-Century American Theatre: The Image of the Indian in John Brougham's *Met-a-mora; or, the Last of the Pollywogs* (1847) and *Po-Ca-Hon-Tas; or, the Gentle Savage* (1855)." *American Studies* 48, no. 3 (Fall 2007): 101–23.
DiMaggio, Paul. "Cultural Entrepreneurship in Nineteenth-Century Boston: The Creation of an Organizational Base for High Culture in America." In *Cultural Theory and Popular Culture: A Reader*, edited by Paul Storey, 454–75. Athens: University of Georgia Press, 1998.
Dougherty, Ian. *Vauxhall Gardens: Dunedin's Notorious Victorian Pleasure Gardens*. Dunedin, New Zealand: Saddle Hill Press, 2007.
Downer, Alan S., ed. *The Memoir of John Durang: American Actor, 1785–1816*. Pittsburgh: University of Pittsburgh Press, 1966.
DuBois, W. E. B. *The Philadelphia Negro: A Social Study*. 1899; Philadelphia: University of Pennsylvania Press, 1996.
Duclow, Geraldine A. "Philadelphia's Early Pleasure Gardens." *Performing Arts Resources* 21 (1998): 1–17.

Dulles, Foster Rhea. *America Learns to Play: A History of Popular Recreation, 1607–1940.* New York: D. Appleton-Century, 1940.
Durang, Charles. *History of the Philadelphia Stage between the Years 1749 and 1855.* Philadelphia, 1868.
Durivage, Francis A., and George P. Burnham. *Stray Subjects, Arrested and Bound Over. Being Fugitive Offspring of the "Old 'un" and the "Young 'un," that have been "Lying Round Loose," and are now "Tied up" for Fast Keeping.* Philadelphia: Carey and Hart, 1848.
Eagles, Robin. *Francophilia in English Society, 1748–1815.* New York: St. Martin's Press, 2000.
Eberlein, Harold Donaldson, and Cortlandt Van Dyke Hubbard. "The American 'Vauxhall' of the Federal Era." *Pennsylvania Magazine of History and Biography* 57 (1944): 150–74.
Elam, Harry, J. Jr., and David Krasner, eds. *African American Performance and Theater History: A Critical Reader.* Oxford: Oxford University Press, 2001.
Elkins, Stanley, and Eric McKitrick. *The Age of Federalism.* New York: Oxford University Press, 1993.
Elson, Ruth M. *Guardians of Tradition: American Schoolbooks of the Nineteenth Century.* Lincoln: University of Nebraska Press, 1964.
Findling, John E., and Kimberly D. Pelle. *Encyclopedia of World's Fairs and Expositions.* Jefferson, NC: McFarland, 2008.
Flint, James. *Letters From America, Containing Observations on the Climate and Agriculture of the Western States, the Manners of the People, the Prospects of Emigrants, &c., &c.* Edited by Reuben Gold Thwaites. Cleveland: Arthur H. Clark, 1904.
Foucault, Michel. "Of Other Spaces." Translated by Jay Miskowiec. In *The Visual Culture Reader*, edited by Nicholas Mirzoeff, 237–44. New York, Routledge, 1998.
Francis, John, W. *Old New York; or, Reminiscences of the Past Sixty Years.* 1857; New York: Benjamin Blom, 1971.
Franklin, Benjamin. *The Writings of Benjamin Franklin.* Edited by Albert Henry Smyth. New York: Haskell House, 1970.
Freeman, Harry C. *A Brief History of Butte, Montana: The World's Greatest Mining Camp.* Chicago: Henry O'Shepard, 1900.
Frick, John W. "'Fireworks, Bonfires, Balloons and More': New York's Palace Garden." *Performing Arts Resources* 21 (1998): 19–32.
Garrett, Thomas M. "A History of Pleasure Gardens in New York City, 1700–1865." PhD diss., New York University, 1978.
Gaul, Theresa Strouth. "'The Genuine Indian Who Was Brought Upon Stage': Edwin Forrest's Metamora and White Audiences." *Arizona Quarterly* 56, no. 1 (Spring 2000): 1–27.
Gerstner, David. "Nineteenth-Century Formulations of Masculinity and Realism: The Body of Edwin Forrest." In *Manly Arts: Masculinity and Nation in Early American Cinema*, chap. 1. Durham: Duke University Press, 2006.

Gilbert, Douglas. *American Vaudeville: Its Life and Times*. New York: McGraw-Hill, 1940.
Gilbert, James. *Perfect Cities: Chicago's Utopias of 1893*. Chicago: University of Chicago Press, 1991.
Gilje, Paul. *The Road to Mobocracy: Popular Disorder in New York City, 1763–1834*. Chapel Hill: University of North Carolina Press, 1987.
Gilmor, Robert. "Recollections of Baltimore." *Maryland Historical Magazine* 7 (September 1912): 233–42.
Goffman, Erving. *Behavior in Public Places: Notes on the Social Organization of Gatherings*. New York: Free Press, 1966.
Grant, Susan-Mary. "When was the First New Nation? Locating America in a National Context." In *When is the Nation? Towards an Understanding of Theories of Nationalism*, edited by Atsuko Ichijo and Gordana Uzelac, 157–76. London: Routledge, 2005.
Green, Rayna. "The Tribe Called Wannabee: Playing Indian in America and Europe." *Folklore* 99, no. 1 (1988): 30–55.
Greene, Asa. *Glance at New York: Embracing The City Government, Theatres, Hotels, Churches, Mobs, Monopolies, Learned Professions, Newspapers, Rogues, Dandies, Fires and Firemen, Water and Other Liquids, &c. &c.* New York: A. Green, 1837.
Greig, Hannah. "'All Together and All Distinct': Public Sociability and Social Exclusivity in London's Pleasure Gardens, ca. 1740–1800." *Journal of British Studies* 51, no. 1 (January 2012): 50–75.
Hamadeh, Shirine. *The City's Pleasures: Istanbul in the Eighteenth Century*. Seattle: University of Washington Press, 2008.
Harris, Neil. "Museums, Merchandising, and Popular Taste: The Struggle for Influence." In *Material Culture and the Study of American Life*, edited by Ian M. G. Quimby, 140–74. New York: W. W. Norton, 1975.
———. "Expository Expositions: Preparing for the Theme Parks." In *Designing Disney's Theme Parks: The Architecture of Reassurance*, edited by Karal Ann Marling, 19–28. New York: Flammarion, 1997.
Harris, Neil, Wim de Wit, James Gilbert, and Robert W. Rydell, *Grand Illusions: Chicago's World's Fair of 1893*. An exhibition catalogue. Chicago: Chicago Historical Society, 1993.
Hayward, Mary Ellen, and Frank R. Shivers, eds. *The Architecture of Baltimore: An Illustrated History*. Baltimore: Johns Hopkins University Press, 2004.
Headley, Joel Tyler. *The Great Riots of New York: 1712–1873*. Introduction by Thomas Rose and James Rodgers. New York: E. B. Treat, 1873; Indianapolis: Boos-Merrill, 1970.
Henderson, Mary C. *The City and the Theatre: The History of New York Playhouses. A 250-year Journey from Bowling Green to Times Square*. New York: Backstage Books, 2004.
Hershberg, Theodore. "Free Blacks in Antebellum Philadelphia." In *The Peoples of Philadelphia: A History of Ethnic Groups and Lower-class Life, 1790–1940*,

edited by Allen F. Davis and Mark H. Haller, 111–33. Philadelphia: Temple University Press, 1973.

Hirschfeld, C. C. L. *Theory of Garden Art*. Translated by Linda B. Parshall. 1779–1785; Philadelphia: University of Pennsylvania Press, 2001.

Hobsbawm, E. J. *Nations and Nationalism Since 1780: Programme, Myth, Reality*. New York: Cambridge University Press, 1990.

Hochbruck, Wolfgang. "'I Ask for Justice': Native American Fourth of July Orations." In *The Fourth of July: Political Oratory and Literary Reactions 1776–1876*, edited by Paul Goetsch and Gerd Hurm, 155–65. Tübingen: Narr, 1992.

Hodge, Francis. *Yankee Theatre: The Image of America on the Stage: 1825–1850*. Austin: University of Texas Press, 1964.

Hofstadter, Richard. *The Age of Reform: From Bryan to F.D.R.* New York: Alfred A. Knopf, 1956.

Holley, O. H. *A Description of the City of New York: With a Brief Account of the Cities, Towns, Villages, and Places of Resort within Thirty Miles. Designed as a Guide for Citizens and Strangers, to all Places of Attraction in the City and its Vicinity*. New York: J. Disturnell, 1847.

Hoole, W. Stanley. *The Ante-Bellum Charleston Theatre*. Tuscaloosa: University of Alabama Press, 1946.

Hoxie, Frederick E. Ronald Hoffman, and Peter J. Albert, eds. *Native Americans and the Early Republic*. Charlottesville: University Press of Virginia, 1999.

Hunt, John Dixon. *Gardens and the Picturesque: Studies in the History of Landscape Architecture*. Cambridge: Massachusetts Institute of Technology Press, 1992.

———. *The Genius of Place*. New York: Harper Row, 1975.

Jackson, Joseph. *Encyclopedia of Philadelphia*. 4 vols. Harrisburg: National Historical Association, 1931–1933.

———. "Vauxhall Gardens." *Pennsylvania Magazine of History and Biography* 57, no. 4 (1933): 289–98.

Jefferson, Thomas. *Thomas Jefferson: Writings*. Edited by Merrill D. Peterson. New York: Library of America, 1984.

Jeremy, David John, ed. *Henry Wansey and His American Journal: 1794*. Philadelphia: American Philosophical Society, 1970.

Johnson, Odai. *Absence and Memory in Colonial American Theatre: Fiorelli's Plaster*. New York: Palgrave Macmillan, 2006.

Johnson, Stephen Burge. *The Roof Gardens of Broadway Theatres, 1883–1942*. Ann Arbor: UMI Research Press, 1985.

Jones, Eugene H. *Native Americans as Shown on the Stage, 1753–1916*. Metuchen, NJ: Scarecrow Press, 1988.

Jones, Sally A. "The First but Not the Last of the 'Vanishing Indians': Edwin Forrest and Mythic Re-creations of the Native Population." In *Dressing in Feathers: The Construction of the Indian in American Popular Culture*, edited by S. Elizabeth Bird, 13–27. Colorado: Westview Press, 1996.

Kahan, Gerald. *George Alexander Stevens and the Lecture on Heads.* Athens: University of Georgia Press, 1984.
Kammen, Michael. *American Culture, American Tastes: Social Change and the 20th Century.* New York: Alfred Knopf, 1999.
Kasson, John F. *Amusing the Million: Coney Island at the Turn of the Century.* New York: Hill and Wang, 1978.
Kornwolf, James D. "The Picturesque in the American Garden and Landscape Before 1800." *Eighteenth Century Life* 8, no. 2 (January 1983): 93–106.
Levasseur, A. *Lafayette in America in 1824 and 1825; or, Journal of a Voyage to the United States.* 2 vols. Philadelphia: Carey and Lea, 1829.
Levine, Lawrence W. *Highbrow/Lowbrow: The Emergence of Cultural Hierarchy in America.* Cambridge: Cambridge University Press, 1988.
Lott, Eric. *Love and Theft: Blackface Minstrelsy and the American Working Class.* New York: Oxford University Press, 1993.
Loveland, Anne C. *Emblem of Liberty: The Image of Lafayette in the American Mind.* Baton Rouge: Louisiana State University Press, 1971.
Lynn, Michael R. "Sparks for Sale: The Culture and Commerce of Fireworks in Early Modern France." *Eighteenth-Century Life* 30, no. 2 (Spring 2006): 74–97.
Marx, Leo. *The Machine in the Garden: Technology and the Pastoral Ideal in America.* New York: Oxford University Press, 1967.
Matheson, Katy, "Niblo's Garden and Its 'Concert Saloon,' 1828–1846." *Performing Arts Resources* 21 (1998): 53–105.
Matthews, Cornelius. *The Career of Puffer Hopkins.* 1842; New York Garrett Press, 1970.
McAllister, Marvin Edward. *White People Do Not Know How to Behave at Entertainments Designed for Ladies & Gentlemen of Colour: William Brown's African & American Theater.* Chapel Hill: University of North Carolina Press, 2003.
McConachie, Bruce A. "New York Operagoing, 1825–50: Creating an Elite Social Ritual." *American Music* 6, no. 2 (Summer 1988): 181–92.
———. *Melodramatic Formations: American Theatre and Society, 1820–1870.* Iowa City: University of Iowa Press, 1992.
McNamara, Brooks. *The New York Concert Saloon: The Devil's Own Nights.* New York: Cambridge University Press, 2002.
Meehan, Thomas. "An Early Philadelphia Nursery." *The Gardener's Monthly and Horticulturist* 29, no. 347 (November 1887): 346–47.
Melish, John. *Travels Through the United States of America, in the Years 1806 & 1807 and 1809, 1810, & 1811, Including an Account of Passages Betwixt America & Britain, Ireland, and Canada.* Philadelphia, 1815.
Mills, Stephen F. *The American Landscape.* Edinburgh: Keele University Press, 1997.
Mitchill, Samuel L. *The Picture of New York; or the Traveller's Guide, Through the Commercial Metropolis of the United States.* New York: I. Riley, 1807.

Moak, Jefferson M. *Philadelphia Street Name Changes*. Philadelphia: Chestnut Hill Almanac Genealogical Series, 1996.

Montlezun, Baron de. "A Frenchman Visits Charleston, 1817." Edited by Lucius Gaston Moffat and Joseph Médard Carrière. *South Carolina Historical and Genealogical Magazine* 49, no. 3 (1948): 131–54.

Morgan, Helen M., ed. *A Season in New York, 1801: Letters of Harriet and Maria Trumbull*. Pittsburgh: University of Pittsburgh Press, 1969.

Nash, Gary B. *Forging Freedom: The Formation of Philadelphia's Black Community, 1720–1840*. Cambridge: Harvard University Press, 1991.

Nathans, Heather S. *Early American Theatre from the Revolution to Thomas Jefferson: Into the Hands of the People*. New York: Cambridge University Press, 2003.

Newman, Simon Peter. *Parades and the Politics of the Street: Festive Culture in the Early American Republic*. Philadelphia: University of Pennsylvania Press, 1997.

Nosan, Gregory Gerald. "Pavilions, Power, and Patriotism: Garden Architecture at Vauxhall." In *Bourgeois and Aristocratic Cultural Encounters in Garden Art, 1550–1850*, edited by Michel Conan, 101–21. Washington, DC: Dumbarton Oaks Research Library and Collection, 2002.

Odell, George C. *Annals of the New York Stage*. 15 vols. 1927; New York: AMS Press, 1970.

Officer, Lawrence H. *Between the Dollar-Sterling Gold Points: Exchange Rates, Parity, and Market Behavior*. Cambridge: Cambridge University Press, 1996.

Ogborn, Miles. "The Pleasure Garden." In *Spaces of Modernity: London's Geographies, 1680–1780*, chap. 4. New York: Guilford Press, 1998.

Olmstead, Frederick Law. *Civilizing American Cities: Writings on City Landscapes*. Edited by S. B. Sutton. New York: Da Capo Press, 1997.

Orosz, Joel J. *Curators and Culture: The Museum Movement in America, 1740–1870*. Tuscaloosa: University of Alabama Press, 1990.

Peiss, Kathy. *Cheap Amusements: Working Women and Leisure in Turn-of-the-Century New York*. Philadelphia: Temple University Press, 1986.

Porter, Susan L. *With an Air Debonair: Musical Theatre in America, 1785–1815*. Washington, DC: Smithsonian Institution Press, 1991.

Priest, William. *Travels in the United States of America; Commencing in the Year 1793 and Ending in 1797 With the Author's Journals of His Two Voyages across the Atlantic*. London, 1802.

Register, Woody. *The Kid of Coney Island: Fred Thompson and the Rise of American Amusements*. New York: Oxford University Press, 2001.

Rice, Paul F. "Music Nationalism and the Vauxhall Gardens." *Lumen* 19 (2000): 69–88.

Richards, Jeffrey H. *Drama, Theatre and Identity in the American New Republic*. Cambridge: Cambridge University Press, 2005.

Robey, Ethan. "The Utility of Art: Mechanics' Institute Fairs in New York City, 1828–1876." PhD diss., Columbia University, 2000.

Rosenzweig, Roy, and Elizabeth Blackmar. *The Park and the People: A History of Central Park*. Ithaca: Cornell University Press, 1992.

Rossiter, William S., ed. *Days and Ways in Old Boston*. Boston: R. H. Stearns, 1915.
Rydell, Robert W. *World of Fairs: The Century-of-Progress Expositions*. Chicago: University of Chicago Press, 1993.
St. George, Robert Blair, ed. *Possible Pasts: Becoming Colonial in Early America*. Ithaca: Cornell University Press, 2000.
Sands, Mollie. *Invitation to Ranelagh 1742–1803*. London: John Westhouse, 1946.
———. *The Eighteenth Century Pleasure Gardens of Marylebone, 1737–1777*. London: Society for Theatre Research, 1987.
Sarudy, Barbara Wells. *Gardens and Gardening in the Chesapeake, 1700–1805*. Baltimore: Johns Hopkins University Press, 1998.
Scharf, J. Thomas, and Thompson Westcott. *History of Philadelphia, 1609–1884*. 3 vols. Philadelphia: L. H. Everts, 1884.
Schenker, Heath. "Pleasure Gardens, Theme Parks, and the Picturesque." In *Theme Park Landscapes: Antecedents and Variations*, edited by Terence Young and Robert Riley, 69–89. Washington, DC: Dumbarton Oaks Research Library and Collection, 2002.
Scheper, George L. "The Reformist Vision of Frederick Law Olmsted and the Poetics of Park Design." *New England Quarterly* 62, no. 3 (September 1989): 369–402.
Schueller, Malini Johar, and Edward Watts, eds. *Messy Beginnings: Postcoloniality and Early American Studies*. New Brunswick, NJ: Rutgers University Press, 2003.
Scott, Moses Y. "The Balloon, 1819." In *The Book of New York Verse*, edited by Hamilton Fish Armstrong, 114–16. New York: G. P. Putnam's Sons, 1917.
Scott, W. S. *Green Retreats: The Story of Vauxhall Gardens, 1661–1859*. London: Odhams Press, 1955.
Shaffer, Jason. *Performing Patriotism: National Identity in the Colonial and Revolutionary American Theater*. Philadelphia: University of Pennsylvania Press, 2007.
Shelton, F. H. "Springs and Spas of Old-Time Philadelphians." *Pennsylvania Magazine of History and Biography* 47 (1923): 196–237.
Shumsky, Neil L., ed. *Encyclopedia of Urban America: The Cities and the Suburbs*. 2 vols. Santa Barbara: ABC-CLIO, 1998.
Smith, Anthony D. *Chosen Peoples: Sacred Sources of National Identity*. Oxford: Oxford University Press, 2003.
Smith, Billy G. *The "Lower Sort": Philadelphia's Laboring People, 1750–1800*. Ithaca: Cornell University Press, 1990.
Solkin, David H. *Painting for Money: The Visual Arts and the Public Sphere in Eighteenth-Century England*. New Haven: Yale University Press, 1993.
Sonneck, O. G. *Early Concert Life in America (1731–1800)*. New York: Musurgia, 1949.
Southworth, James Granville. *Vauxhall Gardens: A Chapter in the Social History of England*. New York: Columbia University Press, 1941.

Stokes, I. N. Phelps. *The Iconography of Manhattan Island, 1498–1909.* 6 vols. New York: Robert H. Dodd, 1915–28.
Sturgess, Kim C. *Shakespeare and the American Nation.* Cambridge: Cambridge University Press, 2004.
Tallmadge, James. *Address, Delivered at the close of the Sixteenth Annual Fair of the American Institute, New-York, October, 1843.* New York: James Van Norden, 1843.
Thornton, Tamara. *Cultivating Gentlemen: The Meaning of Country Life among the Boston Elite, 1785–1860.* New Haven: Yale University Press, 1989.
Tilton, Robert S. *Pocahontas: The Evolution of an American Narrative.* New York: Cambridge University Press, 1994.
Tocqueville, Alexis de. *Democracy in America.* Edited by Henry Steele Commager. Translated by Henry Reeve. New York: Oxford University Press, 1947.
Toll, Robert C. *Blacking Up: The Minstrel Show in Nineteenth-Century America.* New York: Oxford University Press, 1974.
Travers, Len. *Celebrating the Fourth: Independence Day and the Rites of Nationalism in the Early Republic.* Amherst: University of Massachusetts Press, 1997.
Turner, Victor. *The Anthropology of Performance.* New York: Performing Arts Journal Publications, 1987.
Tyler, Royall. *The Contrast: A Comedy in Five Acts.* Boston: Houghton Mifflin, 1920.
Valentine, D. T. *The Manual of the Corporation of the City of New York.* New York: McSpedon and Baker, 1856.
———. *The Manual of the Corporation of the City of New York.* New York: Edmund Jones, 1866.
Vallillo, Stephen M., and Maryann Chach, eds. "Pleasure Gardens." Special issue, *Performing Arts Resources* 21 (1998).
Wagner, John W. "James Hewitt, 1770–1827." *Musical Quarterly* 58, no. 2 (April 1972): 259–76.
Waldstreicher, David. *In the Midst of Perpetual Fetes: The Making of American Nationalism, 1776–1820.* Chapel Hill: Published for the Omohundro Institute of Early American History and Culture, Williamsburg, Virginia, by the University of North Carolina Press, 1997.
Watkin, David. *The English Vision: The Picturesque in Architecture, Landscape and Garden Design.* New York: Harper & Row, 1982.
Watkins, Malcolm C. "Artificial Lighting in America: 1830–1860." In *Annual Report of the Board of Regents of the Smithsonian Institution Showing the Operations, Expenditures, and Condition of the Institution for the Year Ended June 30, 1951.* Washington, DC: Government Printing Office, 1952.
Watson, John F. *Annals of Philadelphia, Being a Collection of Memoirs, Anecdotes, & Incidents of the City and its Inhabitants from the days of the Pilgrim Founders.* Philadelphia: E. L. Carey and A. Hart, 1830.
Weinstein, Raymond M. "Disneyland and Coney Island: Reflections of the Evolution of the Modern Amusement Park." *Journal of Popular Culture* 66, no. 1 (Summer 1992): 131–64.

Werner, M. R. *Barnum*. New York: Harcourt, Brace, 1923.
Werrett, Simon. *Fireworks: Pyrotechnic Arts and Sciences in European History*. Chicago: University of Chicago Press, 2010.
White, Shane. *Stylin': African American Expressive Culture from its Beginnings to the Zoot Suit*. Ithaca: Cornell University Press, 1998.
Wile, Frederic William, ed. *A Century of Industrial Progress*. New York: Doubleday, Doran, 1928.
Wilentz, Sean. "Artisan Republican Festivals and the Rise of Class Conflict in New York City, 1788–1837." In *Working-Class America: Essays on Labor, Community, and American Society*, edited by Michael H. Frisch and Daniel J. Walkowitz, 36–77. Urbana: University of Illinois Press, 1983.
———. *The Rise of American Democracy: Jefferson to Lincoln*. New York: W. W. Norton, 2005.
Williams, Raymond. *The Country and the City*. New York: Oxford University Press, 1973.
Williamson, Tom. *Polite Landscapes: Gardens and Society in Eighteenth-Century England*. Baltimore: Johns Hopkins Press, 1995.
Willis, Eola. *The Charleston Stage in the XVIII Century*. Columbia: State Company, 1924.
Wilmer, S. E. *Theatre, Society and the Nation: Staging American Identities*. Cambridge: Cambridge University Press, 2002.
Wilmeth, Don B. "Noble or Ruthless Savage? The America Indian on Stage and in the Drama." *Journal of American Drama and Theatre* 1, no. 1 (Spring 1989): 39–78.
Wilmeth, Don B., and Christopher Bigsby, eds. *The Cambridge History of American Theatre*. Vol 1, *Beginnings to 1870*. Cambridge: Cambridge University Press, 1998.
Winterer, Caroline. *The Culture of Classicism: Ancient Greece and Rome in American Intellectual Life, 1780–1910*. Baltimore: Johns Hopkins University Press, 2004.
Woodbridge, Kenneth. *Princely Gardens: The Origins and Development of the French Formal Style*. New York: Rizzoli, 1986.
Wright, Carroll D. *Comparative Wages, Prices, and Cost of Living, From the Sixteenth Annual Report of the Massachusetts Bureau of Statistics of Labor, for 1885*. Boston: Wright and Potter, 1889.
Wroth, Warwick, and Edgar Wroth. *The London Pleasure Gardens of the Eighteenth Century*. 1896; Hamden, CT: Archon Books, 1979.
Wroth, Warwick. *Cremorne and the Later London Gardens*. London: Elliot Stock, 1907.
Zellers, Parker R. "The Cradle of Variety: The Concert Saloon." *Educational Theatre Journal* 20, no. 4 (December 1968): 578–85.

Index

Note: Page numbers in **boldface** indicates the main text and those with 'n' indicates notes.

acrobatics, 9, 10, 12, 13, 15, 16, 48, 82
 see also circus and Durang and Ravels
African American gardens, 102n
 see also African Grove, Mead Garden, and Haytian Retreat
African Americans and world's fairs, 119, 129
African Grove, New York, 88, 102, 103, **104–6**, 119, 129
A Glance at New York, see Baker, Benjamin
agrarianism, **44–7**, **54–6**, 112, 127
American Institute, 36, 62, **115–17**, 123, 128
amusement parks, 62, 109–10, 113, 118, 120n, **120–5**, 128, 130n
 see also Coney Island *and* theme parks
Anderson, Benedict, *Imagined Communities*, 7, 8
anthropological exhibits, 89, 91, 98, 118–20, 129
artifice, 12, 28, 48–9, 54, 89, 114
 compare with authenticity
art, transparencies, 12, 15, 16, 39, 40, 57–8, 68
Astor Place Opera House, 10, 77
authenticity, 3, 87–93, 96–7, 98
 compare with artifice

Baker, Benjamin, *A Glance at New York*, 83–4
balloons, *see* hot air balloons
Barker, J. B., 14
Barker, James Nelson, 37, 65–7
 Indian Princess, 94
Barnum, Phineas Taylor, 10, 116, 129
battles, 37–8, 58–9, 81
Blitz, Antonio, 10, 53
borders and boundaries, 71–3, 79–81, 120
Bowery b'hoys, 83–4
Bowling Green Garden, New York, 9
Bulet, Joseph, 16, 32

The Career of Puffer Hopkins, see Matthews, Cornelius
Castle Garden, New York, 33, 54, 95, 115
Catlin, George, 89
Central Park, 114–15, 117
Charleston Theatre, 17, 32
Chatham Garden, New York, 54, 55
Chatsworth Gardens, Baltimore, *see* Gray's Gardens
circus, 1n, 16, 32, 73, 116, 118
 see also acrobats
Colombian Vauxhall, Boston (1798; never opened), **14**, 49
colonialism, 25, 30, 95

Index

Columbia Gardens, Baltimore, **15–16**, 37, 50, 53, 55, 58, 60, 61, 69, 70, 71, 79, 81, 88, 90, 92
Columbia Gardens, Butte, Montana, 110n, 123–4
Columbian Exposition, 116–20, 127, 129
Columbian Garden, New York, *see* Haytian Retreat
commemoration, 23, 35–7, 126–7
concert saloons, 110, 111–12, 130
Coney Island, 121–4, 126
Conoit's Garden, 101

Delacroix, Joseph, 9, 26, 29, 32, 38–9, 51, 70, 73, 75–7, 81, 90, 115
democracy, 46, 66–7, 115, 119, 125
Dunlap, John, 12
Durang, Christopher, 16
Durang, John, 12, 16, 31, 48
Durivage, Francis, 83–4

Easton's Garden, Baltimore, *see* Columbia Gardens, Baltimore
Esterly, George, 12, 31, 75

fashion, 3, 69, 75n, 77, 78, 81, 99, 104–5
Federal Theatre, Boston, 14
fireworks, 1, 2, 9, 10, 13, 15, 16, 17, 28–9, 32, 33, 36, 38–9, 40, **59–60**, 70, 81, 87, 116, 118, 127, 130
food, 11, 15, 41, 83–4, 105
Foucault, Michel, 7
  see also heterotopia
Fourth of July, 1, 8, 11–12, 18, 23, 32, 35, **38–40**, 47, 56–7, 65, 80, 130
framing of performance, 3–4, 55, 89
Franklin, Benjamin, 44–5
French nationalism, 31–5
  see also Lafayette, Marquis de (Gilbert du Motier)
French pleasure gardens, 2, 32, 123
French proprietors, *see* Bulet, Joseph,

Delacroix, Joseph, and Lavalette, Antoine

garden design, 11, 26–8, 48–9, 114
garden theory, 4–5
gas lighting, 57
gentility, 66–9, 71, 73, 75–7, 81, 105, 128
Goffman, Erving, 4–5
Gray, George and Robert, 11, 32, 54
Gray, John, 15
Gray's Ferry, Philadelphia, **11–12**, 28, 30, 32, 48, 55–6, 69, 80
Gray's Gardens, Baltimore, **15**, 31, 38, 49, 50, 56, 69, 79

Hamilton, Alexander, 44
Harrowgate, Philadelphia, **12**, 26, 48, 55, 57, 69, 73, 75, 82
Haytian Retreat, 88, 102–3
heterotopia, 1, **7–8**, 23, 34, 44, 126
Hewitt, James, 13, 15
Highbrow/Lowbrow, *see* Levine, Lawrence
Horry, Harriot, 16, 70
hot air balloons, 2, 9, 13, 15, 31, 33, 61, 71, 80, 118, 119–20, 125

Ice-House Garden, New York, *see* Vauxhall Gardens, Ice House
Illuminations, 12, 13, 14, 15, 29, 32, 53, 57, 81
Imagined Communities, *see* Anderson, Benedict
Indian Princess, *see* Barker, James Nelson
innocence, 45–6, 47–9, 54–5, 56–62, 114

Jalland's Garden, Baltimore, 32
Jefferson, Thomas, 44, 45

labor, xiii, 101–2, 105
Lafayette, Marquis de (Gilbert du Motier), 33, 38

Index

Lafayette Place, 9
Lavalette, Antoine, 16, 32
Leaman, Thomas, 16
Levine, Lawrence, 75, 78
"Life in Philadelphia", **99–101**, 104
Love in the Bowery, see Durivage, Francis

Madden, Timothy, 9
Magner, Charles, 12–13
Mang, John J., 15, 57
Marx, Leo, 44, 45
Marylebone Garden, London, 2
Matthews, Cornelius, 82–3
McArann, John, 13
McArann's Garden, Philadelphia, 13, 54, 60, 69, 71, 72, 81, 110
Mead Garden, Brooklyn, New York, 88, 102
Mead Garden, New York, 88, 102–3
Metamora, see Stone, John Augustus
midway, 118–20, 124
Military Garden, New York, *see* Columbian Garden, New York
minstrelsy, 20, 35, 81, 102
  whiteface, 104, 106
Monroe, James, 38, 39
Montlezun, Baron de, 17
morality, 16, 25, 30, 36, 44–5, 47, 61–2, 69–70, 97, 103, 112, 114–15, 117, 121
  see also respectability
Music, 10, 11, 12, 13, 16, 17, 23, 25, 29, 32, 36, 40, 48, 53, 59, 60, 68, 81–2, 95, 105, 111, 112, 118
  see also opera
Myers, Margaret, 15–16, 70

national identities
  American and French, 31–4, 127
  American and UK, 22–3, 24–31, 58, 127
  definition, 22
  national consciousness, 6, 40–1

Native Americans
  and patriotism, 97
  and worlds fairs, 120
  in England, 89
  noble savage, 94
  war dances, 87–8, 90–3, 96–8
New Vauxhall, New York, *see* Ranelagh Garden, New York (1797–1800)
New York Horticultural Society, 47, 53
Niagara, Charleston, South Carolina, 16n
Niblo, William, 10, 53, 70, 77, 112
Niblo's Garden, New York, **10**, 29, 37, 53, 69, 70, 71, 77, 78, 81, 88, 101, 111, 115
Noah, Mordecai, 102, 104–5
nostalgia, 45–8, 55, 57–8, 110n, 126–7

opera, 10, 77, 78, 82
Orange Gardens, Charleston, South Carolina, 16n

Palace Gardens, New York, 63, 88, 90, 91, 115
parachutes, 61, 80
patriotism, 4, 35–7, 40–1, 45–6, 47, 54–6, 58, 60, 62, 97, 125
  symbols of, 40
Pavilion Theatre, Vauxhall Gardens, Philadelphia, 13, 80
performance
  definition, 3, 5–6, 88, 126
  of the self, 3, 34, 36–7, 54, 66, 73, 76, 83–4, 121–3, 125, 126
Placide, Alexandre, 17, 32, 79
pleasure garden
  cost, **68**, 73, 76, 80, 81, 121
  definition, 2
  locations, 47–54, 78
  names, 26, 53–4
  origins, 2–3, 127
Pocahontas, 20, 95–6

Po-Ca-Hon-Tas, 20, 88, 95–6
popular entertainments, 82
 see also circus, vaudeville, acrobats, minstrelsy
Powell, Snelling, 14
public parks, 4, 113, 115, 130
 see also Central Park

Ranelagh Garden, New York (1765–1768), 52
Ranelagh Garden, New York (1797–1800), 9
Ranelagh, London, 2, 26
Ravels (family), 10, 13, 53
 see also acrobatics
respectability, 69–71, 102–3, 128
 families, 71, 79
 prostitution, 70, 71
 women, 69, 70, 103
Rice, T. D., 102
riots, 12, 13, 61, 65, 78, 79–**81**
rollercoasters, 120, 123, 123n
roof gardens, 110–11, 130
rules and regulations, 3–5, 7, 66, 69, 75, 76–8, 79–84, 100
Rural Felicity, Baltimore, *see* Columbia Gardens, Baltimore
Rural Retreat, Baltimore, *see* Columbia Gardens, Baltimore
rural-urban tension, *see* agrarianism

Seige of York, Baltimore, *see* Columbia Gardens, Baltimore
self-performance, *see* performance of the self
spas, 11, 17, 112
Steeplechase Park, 122–4, 126
Stone, John Augustus, *Metamora*, 94–5, 96–7

technology, 9, 13, 16, 36, 56–62, 115, 123–4, 126, 128
theatre, 6, 9, 10, 24, 25–6, 57, 71, 77, 92, 110, 116, 118
 in the gardens, 3, 9, 10, 12, 13, 53, 76, 78, 80, 88
theme parks, 113, 130, 120n
 see also amusement parks
Tivoli, Charleston, South Carolina, 16n
Tivoli Park, Copenhagen, 116
transportation, 11, 49, 120–1
Tyers, Jonathan, 2
Tyler, Royall, 24–5, 30n, 44

United States Garden, New York, 9, 53
urbanization, 43–4, 45, 51–4, 62–3, 114–15, 117, 127

vaudeville, 1, 13, 20, 29, 112, 130
Vauxhall as generic term, 31
Vauxhall, Boston (1798; never opened), *see* Columbian Vauxhall, Boston
Vauxhall, Boston (1815–1828), *see* Washington Gardens, Boston
Vauxhall Garden, New York (1798–1805), **9**, 51, 79, 81
Vauxhall Garden, New York (1805–1855), **9**, 27, 39, 51, 54, 61, 70, 71, 73, 75, 76–7, 81, 82–4, 88, 90, 102, 111
Vauxhall Garden, Philadelphia, 4, 12–13, 54, 61, 65, 72, 80
Vauxhall Gardens, Charleston, South Carolina, 16–17, 26, 54, 55, 70, 71, 100
Vauxhall Gardens, Ice House, New York, **9**, 51, 81
Vauxhall Harrowgate, Philadelphia, *see* Harrowgate, Philadelphia
Vauxhall, London, 2, 26, 27, 66, 89
 popularity, 25–6
 similarities with American sites, 26–9
Vauxhall, New York (1750), *see* Bowling Green, New York

Vauxhall Rural Felicity, New York, *see* United States Garden, New York
velocipede, 13, 61, 128
volcanoes, 13, 39, 60, 81, 125, 128

war, *see* battles
war dances, *see* Native Americans: war dances

Washington Gardens, Boston, **14–15**, 26, 33, 38, 57, 61, 68, 71, 72–3, 74, 76, 79, 88, 91, 101
Washington, George, 37, 97–8
White City, *see* Columbian Exposition
women, *see* respectability
world's fairs, 62, 115, 116–24, 126, 130
see also Columbian Exposition

GPSR Compliance
The European Union's (EU) General Product Safety Regulation (GPSR) is a set of rules that requires consumer products to be safe and our obligations to ensure this.

If you have any concerns about our products, you can contact us on

ProductSafety@springernature.com

In case Publisher is established outside the EU, the EU authorized representative is:

Springer Nature Customer Service Center GmbH
Europaplatz 3
69115 Heidelberg, Germany